Comments on **Diabetes at your fingertips**

From the reviews:

"What sets this book apart from others is the fact that it answers questions that most books dealing with diabetes cannot. It also surprises the reader with questions one perhaps would not even have thought of.

Overall this is a most interesting and useful book suitable for people with diabetes, their families, health professionals and anyone interested in diabetes. It is a book that once bought will be used over and over again, and works out to be good value at £9.95." [1991 price]
Balance

"**Diabetes at your fingertips** is an extensively revised and updated version of the **Diabetes Reference Book** first published in 1985. The original was an excellent book but this is even better."
Professor Robert Tattersall,
Diabetes in the news

"**Diabetes at your fingertips** is a guide, in lively question and answer form, to coping with diabetes. It is quite possible to lead a full life providing the sufferer understands and can control the disease."
Woman's Journal

"Has positive information to help both young and old lead active lives with the minimum of restrictions."
Good Housekeeping

"I would recommend it to people living with diabetes, but also to professionals in the diabetes field."
Professional Nurse

"The book is well presented, with good, clear illustrations and is reasonably priced. I highly recommend it for newly diagnosed diabetics and their families and as a source of reference for nurses dealing with diabetics."
Nursing Standard

"Woe betide any clinicians or nurses whose patients have read this invaluable source of down-to-earth information when they have not."
The Lancet

Comments from readers:

". . . in style and substance, this is an excellent book. Both diabetics and non-diabetics will find it very useful. I recommend every diabetic to own a copy of this interesting book."

Mrs T Menon, London

"An excellent book. It is comprehensive, informative, and easy to read and understand."

Don Kendrick, Seaton, Devon

"**Diabetes at your fingertips** is a marvellous book — just what the layman needs."

Mrs P Pilley, Hornchurch

"I like the form it takes (questions and answers); it makes it much easier to find the specific areas when a problem does arise. Also it makes easier reading for picking up and putting down without having to wade through chapter after chapter of heavy medical jargon which for the lay person can be very difficult to take in and understand."

Mrs Pam Munford, Lincoln

"I have read the book myself from cover to cover and found it to be most informative, up-to-date and presented in a format which is easy to assimilate by the majority of diabetics who will undoubtedly relate some question to a particular experience of their own — and find the answer."

Philip Whitmore, Macclesfield

"I think the book is excellent value since it answers all the basic questions of diabetes and has answers to questions I have not seen written down before. (In fact the whole family is interested in reading it.)"

D Ball, Nottingham

"My family have found the information in your book of great value ... it has been a godsend in many ways ... we hope that it will help many more in the same situation."

Mrs P. Greasley and family, Stoke-on-Trent

". . . it will be a very useful reference book for patients and health professionals alike."

Mrs Penny Rodie, Dietitian, BUPA Roding Hospital, Ilford

Diabetes at your fingertips

THE COMPREHENSIVE DIABETES REFERENCE BOOK FOR THE 1990s

Peter Sönksen MD, FRCP
Professor of Endocrinology, United Medical and Dental Schools of Guy's and St Thomas' Hospitals, St Thomas' Campus, London

Charles Fox BM, FRCP
Consultant Physician with Special Interest in Diabetes, Northampton General Hospital

Sue Judd RGN
Specialist Nurse in Diabetes, St Thomas' Hospital, London

Forewords by: Sir Harry Secombe, CBE, President, British Diabetic Association; and Professor Harry Keen MD, FRCP Chairman of the Executive Council, British Diabetic Association

CLASS PUBLISHING · London

Printing History
First published 1985
Reprinted 1987
Second Edition, revised and expanded 1991
Reprinted with revisions 1991
Reprinted with revisions 1992

The authors and publishers welcome feedback from users of the book.
Please contact the publishers.

Class Publishing, PO Box 1498, London W6 7RS, UK.
Tel: (071) 371 2119, Fax: (071) 371 2119, International (+4471)

British Library Cataloguing in Publication Data
Sönksen, Peter
  Diabetes at your fingertips
  The comprehensive diabetes reference book for the 1990s
  2nd ed
  1 Man. Diabetes
  1 Title II. Fox, Charles III. Judd, Sue
IV. Sönksen, Peter Diabetes reference book
  616.462

ISBN 1-872362-02-8 pbk

Designed by Wendy Bann

Production by Landmark Production Consultants Ltd, Princes
Risborough

Typesetting by Quorum Technical Services, Cheltenham

Colour Separation by Fotographics Ltd, Hong Kong

Printed and bound in Great Britain by Butler and Tanner Ltd, Frome

Contents

APPENDICES

Preface

The Diabetes Reference Book first appeared in 1985 and it is clearly time for a new edition. A number of new developments give rise to many new questions and answers.

We have called the new edition *Diabetes at your fingertips* to make the point that this book provides quick straightforward answers to the questions asked by people with diabetes, and those who live with them and care for them.

We are not sure what ducks are doing in a book about diabetes but we like them and hope you do too.

Foreword

by Sir HARRY SECOMBE, CBE

President, British Diabetic Association

Everyone knows the importance of education in our lives, but if you have diabetes, then learning certainly becomes a way of life.

As someone with diabetes, I realise the more I know about the condition and the way it affects me, the healthier I stay.

So I have no hesitation in commending this book, compiled by people whose active involvement with diabetes is an example to everyone.

Foreword

by Professor HARRY KEEN, MD, FRCP

Chairman, British Diabetic Association, Professor Emeritus, United Medical
and Dental Schools of Guy's and St Thomas' Hospitals, Guy's Hospital
Campus, London

The message of the second edition of this diabetes 'enquire
within' is that although many of the problems are still with
us, medical science moves forward. Most of the questions stay
the same but many of the answers have changed. The outlook
for people with diabetes improves year by year. We can see
real progress in the mangement of the diabetic state itself and
in the treatment, control and prevention of its fearful
complications, blindness, kidney failure, artery obstruction and
nerve damage. These advances are clearly brought to the reader
of **Diabetes at your fingertips.**

One thing remains unchanged, the absolute necessity for
people with diabetes to learn and understand as much as they
can about their disease. With diabetes, ignorance is often
damaging and can sometimes be lethal. Understanding diabetes
is, in itself, not enough; something must be done with that
understanding – by doctors, nurses, dietitians and the whole
team gathered to fight the diabetes. But most of all by the
patient. He or she, young or not so young, makes a vital
contribution to diabetes care. Without that contribution the
work and efforts of the others are incomplete. **Diabetes at
your fingertips** will help diabetic patients to take their proper
place in the front rank of the fight for better health.

Acknowledgements

We are grateful to the following people who helped in the production of *Diabetes at your fingertips* or the original *Diabetes Reference Book*.

Jenny Dyer, past editor of *Balance*.

Peter Swift for advice about babies and their parents.

Clara Lowy for contributing to the chapter on pregnancy.

Pat McDowell, Maureen Brewin and Sara Moore, diabetes specialist nurses.

Gill Jowett for revising the section on feet.

Jill Metcalfe for the section on diet.

Michelle Smith who drew the ducks.

Suzanne Redmond, head of Diabetes Care at the British Diabetic Association, for valuable comments on the new edition.

Sir Harry Secombe and Professor Harry Keen for writing the forewords.

Anna Fox for dreaming up the new title.

Richard Warner, our publisher, for his enthusiastic support.

Lis Lawrence who worked late into the night in order to organise and produce the manuscript by the deadline.

Sheila Nicholass for her encouragement.

We thank the companies who kindly provided illustrations.

Bayer Diagnostics, Bayer PLC

Becton Dickinson UK Ltd.

Boehringer Mannheim UK.

MediSense Britain Ltd.

Novo Nordisk UK.

Finally we thank long-suffering patients at St Thomas' Hospital and Northampton General Hospital. They have asked many of the questions and have worked out solutions to most of the problems. We are simply passing on their experience to others.

In fact much of this book has been written by diabetics – for diabetics.

Peter Sönksen
Charles Fox
Sue Judd

Introduction

What this book is not	**What this book is**
1 A medical text book.	1 Questions of importance for anyone interested in diabetes
2 A dictionary of diabetic terms.	2 Answers of clarity and simplicity
3 A history of diabetes and its treatment.	3 Descriptions of biochemical changes.
4 A collection of case histories.	4 Facts about the problems diabetics face.
5 A battle plan for defeating diabetes.	5 Help in coming to terms with diabetes.

6 A list of miracle cures.	6 Descriptions of modern methods that make living with diabetes easier.
7 A formula for coping with a diabetic child.	7 Practical advice learnt from many parents of diabetic children.
8 A forecast of a cure for diabetes	8 Surveys of current diabetes research and an informed guess about the future.

When diabetes suddenly hits you or a close relative, many unpleasant things come to mind ... injections, strict diets, urine tests, blindness. In fact most diabetics do not need injections, their diet is normal and wholesome, urine tests have gone out of fashion and eye disease can now be successfully treated. However, a diabetic does have to learn to control his diabetes and he can only do this by understanding the condition. The diabetic gets much advice and help from nurses, doctors, dietitians and others, but it is his own decision how well he controls his condition. It is often said that a diabetic is his own doctor.

A lot of effort is being put into the education of diabetics and this book is part of that effort. There is a great deal of information for all of us to learn.

Diabetes is a complex disorder, and parts of this book reflect its complexity. Although some aspects of diabetes are hard to understand, most diabetics manage to lead full lives by incorporating their condition into their normal work and activities. If you have just discovered that you or a close relative have diabetes, you will probably feel shocked and worried. This is not the time to try to learn about the most difficult aspects of the subject. But even at this early stage you, your partner, (and your parents if you are a child) need to know certain basic facts. Once the initial shock reaction is over and your own experience with diabetes increases, you will be ready to learn about the frills. Remember that *no one* involved in this subject (including doctors and nurses) ever stops learning more about it.

Throughout this book we have used the word diabetic to describe a person with diabetes. Some people feel that the word 'diabetic' should be used only as a description, as in 'diabetic clinic', and not as shorthand for a person with this condition. We do not ourselves feel the word diabetic is insulting in any way, and hope that our readers are not offended by it. It would be very cumbersome to write 'a person with diabetes' every time we meant 'diabetic'. Indeed, before making this decision we carried out a survey amongst the diabetic patients attending the clinic at St Thomas' Hospital; we found that the overwhelming majority were in favour of using this term, and no preferable alternative was suggested.

In the text we have used the words glucose and sugar interchangeably when we refer to specific measurements of blood or urine glucose. In questions and answers on diet the word sugar normally refers to cane or beet sugar technically known as sucrose (a compound of glucose and fructose).

In assigning gender in answers we have used 'he' instead of 'he or she' except when 'she' follows from the question. Babies have not been assigned gender but have impersonally been referred to as 'it'.

How to use this book

This book is a series of questions and answers, and it is not designed to be read from cover to cover. Some of the sections do stand on their own, in particular those describing the nature of diabetes in Chapter 1, Chapter 3 on diabetic control and Chapter 8 on long-term complications. A colour plate section on techniques for injection, using a Novopen, and blood glucose monitoring is included in the centre of the book.

If you are a newly diagnosed diabetic, you may not be ready to come to grips with Chapter 9 on research but you may want to find out what is known about the causes of diabetes (p. 11). If you have just started insulin injections you should read the following sections at an early stage:

Hypos (p. 55).
Other illnesses (p. 120).
Insulin (p. 42).
Control and monitoring (p. 78).
Blood glucose (p. 79).
Driving (p. 125).
Emergencies (p. 227).

More experienced diabetics will want to test us out in our answers in Chapter 4 on life with diabetes to see if our answers coincide with their experience. Parents of diabetic children will want to read Chapter 7 on the young diabetic.

There is bound to be some repetition in a book of this sort, but we think it is better to deal with similar topics under separate headings rather than ask the reader to shuttle from one end of the book to the other. We hope that at least we are consistent in our answers.

Feedback is the most important feature of good diabetes care. This relies on the diabetic being honest with the doctor or nurse and vice versa. Not everyone will agree with the answers we give, but the book can only be improved if you let us know when you disagree and have found our advice to be unhelpful. We would also like to know if there are important questions we have not covered. Please write to us c/o Class Publishing, PO Box 1498, London W6 7RS, UK.

1
Diabetes

Introduction

This chapter opens with a description of how a diabetic might feel before his condition has been diagnosed and treated. Once treatment has been started the diabetic should feel perfectly well. We also make the point that older people may have diabetes and yet feel quite well in themselves. In this case the condition will be discovered only if they have a routine blood or urine test for sugar, and diabetes may therefore exist for many years without being discovered. Unfortunately, undetected diabetes may, over a long period, lead to complications affecting eyes, nerves and blood vessels.

So there are two main types of diabetic:

a younger people who feel unwell for a few weeks or months and may become very ill if they do not receive insulin;

b older people who may have had diabetes for many years before it was discovered and who do not feel particularly unwell. In these people it is often discovered by chance and commonly responds well to diet or tablets, although sometimes insulin is needed.

There are other rare types of diabetes mentioned in this chapter.

We also answer the very important questions about the central problem in diabetes, namely an increase in the amount of glucose (sugar) in the blood. We describe why this happens and why it may be dangerous.

Symptoms

1 Why does a young diabetic feel thirsty when the condition is first discovered?

The first signs of diabetes in a young person are thirst and loss of weight. These two symptoms are related and one leads to the other. The first thing to go wrong is the increased amount of urine. Normally we pass about $1^1/_2$ litres (just over 2 pints) of urine per day but a diabetic out of control may produce five times that amount. This continual loss of fluid dries out the body. The feeling of thirst is a warning that unless he drinks enough to replace the extra urine, he will soon be in trouble. Of course people who are not diabetic may also pass large amounts of urine. Every beer drinker knows the effects of 5 pints of best bitter. In this case the beer causes the extra urine whereas in diabetes the extra urine causes the thirst. The resulting thirst is usually mild in the early stages, and most people fail to realise its significance unless they happen to have a friend or relative with diabetes. An undiagnosed diabetic may take jugs of water up to bed, wake in the night to quench his thirst and pass water, and still not realise that something is wrong. It would be a good thing if more people knew that unexplained thirst can be due to diabetes.

2 Why do diabetics often lose weight before their condition is brought under control?

One reason for the weight loss is simply the result of the large urine output, since this urine is loaded with sugar. An uncontrolled diabetic may lose in 24 hours as much as 1000 grams (just over 2lb) of sugar. Anyone trying to lose weight knows that sugar = calories. These calories contained in the urine are lost to the body and are a drain on its resources – hence the loss of weight. The 1000 grams of sugar lost are equivalent to 20 currant buns. Lack of insulin is another cause of weight loss in a diabetic who is out of control.

3 Why do some diabetics experience itching and soreness in the genital area?

A woman whose diabetes is out of control may be troubled by itching around the vagina. The technical name for this distressing symptom is pruritus vulvae. The equivalent complaint may be seen in men when the end of the penis becomes sore (balanitis). If the foreskin is also affected, it may become thickened (phimosis), which prevents the foreskin from being pulled back. This makes it impossible to keep the penis clean.

These problems are the result of infection with yeasts which thrive on the high concentration of sugar in this region. If the urine is kept free from sugar by good diabetic control, the itching and soreness will normally clear up. Anti-yeast cream from a doctor may speed up the improvement but this is only a holding measure while sugar is cleared from the urine.

4 Can the eyesight be affected early on in diabetes?

Most of the serious eye problems caused by diabetes are due to damage to the retina (retinopathy). The retina is the 'photographic plate' at the back of the eye.

Even minor changes in the retina take years to develop and are never seen early on in the disease in younger diabetics. Older people may have diabetes for years without being aware of it, and in these cases the retina may already be damaged by the time the condition is discovered.

The lens of the eye which is responsible for focusing the image on the retina can also be affected in diabetes. However, this is usually a temporary change and causes blurred vision which can be corrected by wearing glasses. The lens of the eye becomes swollen when diabetes is out of control and this makes the person short-sighted. As the diabetes comes under control, so the lens of the eye returns to its normal shape. A pair of glasses fitted for a swollen lens at a time of uncontrolled diabetes will no longer be suitable when the diabetes is brought under control. A new diabetic with blurred vision should wait until a few months after things have settled down before visiting an optician for new spectacles. The blurred vision will probably improve on its own, and glasses may not be necessary.

In very rare cases the lens of the eye may be permanently damaged (cataract) when diabetes is badly out of control.

5   *Can diabetes be discovered by chance?*

In young diabetics the diagnosis is usually made because the patient feels unwell and goes to the doctor.

In older people with no obvious medical problems, diabetes is often discovered as a result of a routine urine test – sometimes during an insurance examination. Once the diagnosis is made, the person may admit to feeling slightly thirsty or tired or to having itching (pruritus), but these symptoms are often not very dramatic, and may be put down to 'old age'. So in older people diabetes can take a less obvious form. Even though this form of diabetes seems to be a minor problem, it must be taken very seriously, as so-called 'mild' diabetes can still lead to problems with vision and circulation. In any case, most people feel much better and more energetic once the diabetes is controlled. This can often be done by diet or by diet and tablets, although insulin injections are occasionally needed.

Types of diabetes

6   Are there different types of diabetes?

Yes. Diabetes exists in many different forms. Two main groups are recognised:

a Younger people (under 40 years old) in whom the condition develops in a fairly dramatic way and for whom insulin injections are nearly always needed. About 30% of all diabetics fall into this category, known as Insulin Dependent Diabetes (or IDD for short).

b At the other end of the scale is the older person who develops diabetes with less obvious symptoms and who is often overweight. In this group insulin by injection is not normally needed and these patients are described as having Non-Insulin Dependent Diabetes (or NIDD).

There are plenty of exceptions to this rule. Occasionally young diabetics can be well controlled with diet or tablets and quite a large number of people who develop diabetes late in life are much better off on insulin injections.

7   What is diabetes insipidus?

The only connection between diabetes insipidus and the usual form of diabetes (diabetes mellitus) is that people with both conditions pass large amounts of urine. Diabetes insipidus is a rare condition that is due to an abnormality in the pituitary gland and not the pancreas. One disorder does not lead to the other, and diabetes insipidus does not have the same potential for long-term complications as diabetes mellitus.

8   I have recently been given steroid treatment (prednisone) for severe arthritis. My joints are better but my doctor has now found sugar in my urine and tells me I am diabetic. Is this likely to be permanent?

Steroids are very effective treatment for a number of conditions but they may precipitate side-effects, as you have just discovered. One of these side-effects is to cause diabetes which can usually be controlled with tablets (e.g. glibenclamide) and insulin is not normally required. When

you stop steroid therapy there is a good chance that the
diabetes will go away completely. However, you *may* have
been a diabetic without knowing it before you started steroids
– in which case you will need to continue some form of
diabetic treatment indefinitely.

**9   *I am told that other hormones apart from insulin may
      cause diabetes.***

It is a deficiency of the hormone insulin that leads to diabetes.
If certain other hormones (chemical messengers) are produced
in excessive amounts then diabetes may result. Thus people
who produce too much thyroid hormone (thyrotoxicosis) may
develop diabetes which clears up when the thyroid is restored
to normal. Also thyrotoxicosis and diabetes tend to run
together in families, and people with one condition are more
likely to develop the other.

Sometimes a person will produce excessive quantities of
steroid hormones (Cushing's disease), and this may lead to
diabetes (see previous question). Acromegaly is a condition
where excess quantities of growth hormone are produced
and this may lead to diabetes.

10   *Can a severe illness cause diabetes?*

Any serious condition (e.g. coronary thrombosis or severe
injuries from a traffic accident) may lead to diabetes. This
is because most of the hormones produced in response to
stress tend to have the opposite effect to insulin and cause
the glucose level in the blood to rise. Most people simply
produce more insulin to keep the blood glucose stable.
However, in some cases, if the reserves of insulin are
inadequate the blood glucose level will climb. Such a person
is a temporary diabetic, and the glucose level will usually
return to normal once the stress is over. However, he or
she will have an increased risk of becoming a permanent
diabetic later on in life.

**11   *My wife has just given birth to a baby boy who weighed
      4.3 kg (9 lb) at birth. Apparently she may have been
      diabetic while she was pregnant. Is this likely to happen
      again with her next baby?***

Women who give birth to heavy babies (over 4 kg or 9 lb) may have had a raised blood glucose level during pregnancy. This extra glucose crosses into the unborn baby, which responds by producing extra insulin of its own. The combination of excess glucose and excess insulin makes the unborn baby grow fat and bloated. Once it has been born and cut off from its supply of glucose from the mother, the baby may then become hypoglycaemic (develop a low glucose concentration in the blood). These fat babies of diabetic mothers are definitely at risk. Mothers who become diabetic during pregnancy and who then return to normal after their babies are born are called *gestational diabetics*. Once the problem has been identified the mother will have to keep a close check on her blood glucose during any subsequent pregnancy. Providing it is kept strictly normal (usually insulin is needed for this), the baby will be a normal weight and will not be at risk.

Women who are diabetic during pregnancy are slightly more likely to become diabetic later in life.

12 I have had to go to hospital for repeated attacks of pancreatitis and now have diabetes. I am told these two conditions are related – is this true?

Pancreatitis means that the pancreas has become inflamed and this can be a very painful and unpleasant illness. The pancreas is the gland which, among other things, produces insulin and if it becomes badly inflamed and scarred it may not be able to produce enough of this hormone. Sometimes during or after an attack of pancreatitis a patient may become diabetic and need tablets or insulin to keep the blood glucose controlled. This form of diabetes is usually, but not always, permanent.

Causes of diabetes

13 Why have I got diabetes?

The short answer is that your pancreas is no longer making enough insulin for your body's needs. The long answer as to why this has happened to *you* is not so well understood.

However, there are a few clues. Diabetes may run in families (p. 14). Other possible causes are discussed in this section. It is not a rare condition. In England about 1 in 100 people have diagnosed diabetes and the chances increase with age. About 2 in 1000 children under 16 years of age are diabetic.

14 Is diabetes caused by a virus?

Despite a vast amount of research throughout the world the cause of diabetes is not known. It is known that in some families there is a tendency towards diabetes (p. 14) and that the disease in young people often develops when triggered off by some infection such as a cold. Some people suspect that a certain virus could actually cause diabetes but there is no proof. If a virus is the cause, it is probably a common one (like Coxsackie B) which leads to diabetes only in susceptible people (i.e. those who have inherited some diabetic tendency). There is no 'diabetes virus' and you cannot catch diabetes like chicken-pox. Research workers have suggested that full-blown diabetes may not be discovered for several years after the infection has occurred. Diabetes in older people is probably nothing to do with a virus infection.

15 Can fatness cause diabetes?

If the tendency towards diabetes is present, then fatness (obesity) may bring on the disease. This does not happen often in young people, but it is a common cause of diabetes in middle-aged or older people (p. 22). In most cases this type of diabetes can be controlled by dieting and weight loss. Many fat people with diabetes find it hard to stick to a diet; others find that strict dieting alone is insufficient to lower the blood glucose and have to take tablets or insulin injections. This is second-best as the sensible and safe treatment for an obese older diabetic is *weight loss*.

16 Can a bad shock bring on diabetes?

Sometimes diabetes develops soon after a major disturbance in life, such as a bereavement, a heart attack, or a bad accident and the diabetes is blamed on the upset. This is not really the case, as insulin failure in the pancreas takes a long time to develop. However, a bad shock may stress the system and bring on diabetes a bit earlier if the insulin supply is already running low.

17 Do large babies cause their mother to be diabetic?

No. It's the other way round. In pregnancy even very 'mild' diabetes, which may not be detected without special tests, may result in an overweight baby. In any woman who has given birth to a baby weighing more than 4 kg (9 lb), the possibility of diabetes should be considered by her doctors. If a mother is diabetic during pregnancy but recovers soon after her baby is born, she does carry a slightly increased risk of diabetes for the rest of her life. The baby itself does not carry this risk. (More details are given on p. 154.)

18 Can diabetes be prevented?

No. At the present time, if you are going to get diabetes, you get diabetes. It is possible, under certain circumstances, to identify some people who are not diabetic but who have a very high risk of becoming so within a year or so. Various drugs have been tried to prevent diabetes in these high-risk people, but so far with no success.

19 Can tablets or medicines cause diabetes or make diabetes worse?

Yes; there are several drugs in common use that either precipitate diabetes as an unwanted side-effect or make existing diabetes worse. The most important group of such medicines are hormones. Hormones are substances produced by special glands in the body and insulin from the pancreas is itself a hormone. Some hormones have an anti-insulin effect and one of these, a steroid hormone, is sometimes used in treating medical conditions, such as severe asthma or rheumatoid arthritis. The most commonly used steroid is prednisolone which opposes insulin and therefore tends to cause the level of sugar in the blood to rise. Steroids in large doses will often precipitate diabetes which usually gets better when the steroids are stopped (p. 9). The contraceptive pill is another type of steroid hormone with a very mild anti-insulin effect. Sometimes diabetics on insulin find they have to give themselves more insulin if they are on the pill.

Glucagon is a hormone from the pancreas with a very strong anti-insulin effect. It is used to correct a severe insulin reaction (p. 58). Apart from other hormones, certain medicines may have an anti-insulin effect. In particular, water tablets (diuretics) which make people pass extra amounts of urine sometimes precipitate diabetes. Cough syrups made up of a concentrated sugar solution are not recommended in diabetes, but in practice they do not seem to cause any harm unless taken to excess.

Inheritance

20   Does diabetes run in families?

Diabetes is a common disorder affecting about 1 out of 50 people. So in any large family more than one person may be affected, simply by chance alone. However, certain families do seem to carry a very strong tendency for diabetes. The best known example of this is a whole tribe of American Indians (the Pima); over half its members develop diabetes by the time they reach middle age. Genes are the parts of a human cell that decide which characteristics you inherit from your parents. The particular genes that you get from each parent are a matter of chance – in other words, whether you grow up with your father's big feet or your mother's blue eyes. Similarly it is a matter of chance whether you pass on the genes carrying the tendency for diabetes to one of your children. It is only the tendency to diabetes which you *may* pass on and the full-blown condition will not develop unless something else causes the insulin cells in the pancreas to fail. If you are a diabetic father there is probably a 1 in 20 chance that your child will develop diabetes at some stage. If you are a diabetic mother the risk lessens to about 1 in 50.

21   I am 16 and have been diabetic for 5 years. Why has my identical twin brother not got diabetes?

A large study has been carried out at King's College Hospital, London, where they have been collecting examples of identical twins for over 20 years. Their results show an interesting difference between young diabetics who need insulin and older diabetics who usually manage on diet or tablets. If you have an identical twin who is a young diabetic on insulin, then you only have a 50% chance of becoming diabetic yourself. On the other hand, the identical twin of a middle-aged diabetic who does not need insulin is almost 100% certain to get the same sort of diabetes. So in your case your twin brother has an evens chance of becoming diabetic.

Physiology

22 What is the pancreas?

The pancreas is a gland situated in the upper part of the abdomen connected by a fine tube to the intestine. It releases digestive juices which are mixed with the food soon after it leaves the stomach. They are needed for food to be digested and absorbed into the body. This part of the pancreas has nothing to do with diabetes.

The pancreas also produces a number of hormones which are released directly into the bloodstream – unlike digestive juices which pass into the intestine. The most important of these hormones is insulin, lack of which causes diabetes. The other important hormone produced by the pancreas is glucagon which has the opposite action to insulin and may be used in correcting serious hypos (p. 58). Both of these hormones come from a part of the pancreas known as the islets of Langerhans.

23 Is diabetes a disease of modern times?

No. The earliest detailed description of diabetes was made 2000 years ago. Diabetes appears to be more common now than in the past. This is partly because cases which would not have been picked up then are nowadays detected by routine check-ups. There is a suggestion that diabetes in younger people may be occurring more frequently.

24   Why does the body need insulin?

Without insulin the body cannot make full use of food that
is eaten. Normally, food is eaten, taken into the body and
broken down into simple units (one of which is glucose)
which then provide fuel for all the activities of the body.
These simple units also provide building blocks for growth
or replacing worn-out parts, and any extra is stored for later
use. In diabetes food is broken down as normal, but because
of shortage of insulin the excess glucose produced is not
stored but accumulates in the blood stream and spills over
into the urine. Insulin ensures the correct balance between
glucose production in the body and its utilization.

25   How does insulin control the supply of fuel?

Food is a mixture of complex materials which are absorbed
into the body and broken down to various simple chemicals.
This takes place in the liver which can be regarded as a
food processing factory. Glucose is one of the simple chemicals
made in the liver from all carbohydrate foods. In the absence
of insulin, glucose pours out of the liver into the bloodstream.
Insulin switches off this outpouring of glucose from the liver
and causes glucose to be stored in the liver as starch or
glycogen.

   Insulin also helps glucose to get inside some cells where
it is used as a fuel. So if there is not enough insulin, glucose
will pour out of the liver into the bloodstream and have
difficulty getting into some cells. This causes a build-up of
glucose in the blood. Insulin has a similar effect on amino
acids and fatty acids which are the breakdown products of
protein and fat respectively.

26   How do people who are not diabetic get their insulin?

Insulin is stored in the pancreas and is released into the
bloodstream immediately the blood glucose level starts to
rise after eating. It is taken straight to the liver where it
has the important effect of stopping glucose production and
the storage of glucose as glycogen. The level of glucose in
the blood then falls and as it does so insulin production is
switched off. So people who are not diabetic have a very

sensitive system for keeping the amount of glucose in the blood at a steady level.

The slightest rise in blood glucose causes insulin to be produced. This in turn brings down the glucose level, and the insulin is switched off. See figure 1.

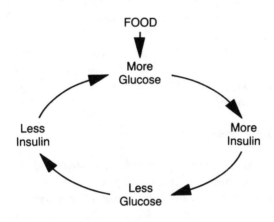

Figure 1: Insulin production system.

In diabetics this system is faulty. Less severe diabetics have some insulin but the pancreas cannot produce it fast enough or in sufficient amounts, so the blood glucose level goes up. Other diabetics have little or no insulin of their own and need injections of insulin to try to keep the blood glucose level normal.

Obviously, an injection of insulin once or twice a day is not as efficient at regulating blood glucose as the pancreas which can switch insulin supply on or off at a moment's notice in response to mild fluctuations.

27   Can a diabetic on insulin keep his blood glucose at a
     normal level?

Yes, although it may not be easy and can only be done by means of a balancing act. There are three main things which affect the blood glucose: (i) food (which puts it up); (ii) insulin; and (iii) exercise (which both bring it down). Any form of stress, in particular an illness like flu, puts up the blood glucose. The only way of learning how to balance the blood glucose level is by trial and error. This means making a lot of measurements and discovering how various foods and forms of exercise alter the blood glucose.

In the past, diabetics were brought into hospital to be 'stabilised' on a certain dose of insulin. Experience has shown that the insulin needed in the artificial surroundings of a hospital ward may bear little relation to the amount needed in someone leading an active, normal life in the outside world. Nowadays, diabetes can be 'stabilised' at home by the patient himself.

28   When was insulin discovered?

Insulin was discovered by Frederick Banting and Charles Best in the summer of 1921. The work was carried out in the Physiology Department of Toronto University while most of the staff were on their holidays. The first human diabetic to be given insulin was a 14-year-old boy, named Leonard Thompson who was dying of diabetes in Toronto General Hospital. This was an historic event, representing the beginning of modern diabetic treatment. It was then up to the chemists to transform the production of insulin into an industrial process on a vast scale.

Related conditions

29   Do other diseases increase the chances of getting diabetes?

Yes. These can be grouped as follows:

1 Glandular disorders
   Thyrotoxicosis (overactive thyroid)
   Acromegaly (excess growth hormone)
   Cushing's disease (excess steroid hormone)

2 Diseases of the pancreas
   Pancreatitis

Cancer of the pancreas
Surgical removal of the pancreas (for one or other of above)
Haemochromatosis (iron overload)
Cystic fibrosis (a childhood disorder)

3 Virus disease ⎫
  German measles ⎬ rarely lead to diabetes
  Mumps ⎭
  Coxsackie

4 Stress
  Heart attack
  Pneumonia
  Major surgical operation

The diabetes usually clears up when the stress is removed.

2
Treatment

Introduction

Here we describe different ways of controlling diabetes. In younger patients there is usually no choice and they need to start insulin injections fairly soon, but in older people found to be diabetic the eventual form of treatment they will need may not be obvious at the outset. Provided they are not feeling terribly ill this sort of patient is usually put on a diet and this alone will have a dramatic effect on their condition, especially in obese patients who manage to get their weight down. If diet on its own fails to control diabetes, tablets are usually tried next. These may be very effective but tablets do not always work and in such cases insulin is the only alternative.

Knowing about the right type of food and the amount that you can eat is important. Most of the questions we have included help explain the general principles but diet is very individual, so do ask for help and further explanations from your own diabetic advisers. It is particularly important to have an opportunity to review what you are doing about food about once a year.

The books below illustrate the range of recipes that individuals and their families can enjoy.

Recipe books with some explanation about diet:

Cooking for Diabetes By Jill Metcalfe (Thorsons)
The Complete Diabetic Cookbook by Joyce Margie and Dr P. J. Palumbo (Grafton)
Recipe books:
Diabetic Cooking for One by Sue Hall ((Thorsons)
Cooking for your Diabetic Child by Sue Hall (Thorsons)
Diabetic Desserts by Sue Hall (Thorsons)
Packed Lunches and Snacks by Sue Hall (Thorsons)
The Diabetic's Microwave Cookbook by Sue Hall (Thorsons)
Cooking the New Diabetic Way by Jill Metcalfe (BDA Publications) (For those needing to lose weight)
Better Cookery for Diabetics by Jill Metcalfe (BDA Publications)
The Diabetic International Diet Book by Sue Lousley (Macdonald Optima)
The Diabetic's Cookbook by Dr Jim Mann & Roberta Longstaff (Macdonald Optima)
Diabetic Delights by Jane Suthering & Sue Lousley (Macdonald Optima)
Diabetic Entertaining by Azmina Govindji and Jill Myers (Thorsons)

The section on hypos (*low* blood sugar) is one of the most important parts of this book. They usually affect diabetics on insulin but can happen to those taking tablets. It is the fear of hypos that prevents some diabetics from controlling their blood sugar carefully. Doctors are often criticised for not giving new diabetics enough information on hypos. So if you have just started insulin treatment, *read this section* (p. 55).

Most people with diabetes and, especially, parents of diabetic children long for a miracle cure and this explains why we have been sent so many questions about unorthodox methods of treatment. We have tried to answer these questions in a sensitive manner but there is no escaping the fact that for a diabetic child, insulin is the only miracle cure and that is how it was regarded when discovered in 1921.

Diet

1   *Why do diabetics not taking insulin injections need to control their weight?*

People who become diabetic later in life are often a little overweight. They rarely need insulin and treatment is by diet with or without tablets. In these cases, the insulin produced by the pancreas is less effective due to the increased fat (obesity). Once the excess weight is lost this so-called insulin resistance is overcome. In addition to the control of the diabetes there are other health risks associated with obesity such as high blood pressure and heart disease. This means that every effort should be made not to be overweight.

2   *Why do people put on weight?*

Your body needs energy (measured in calories) from food and drink to fuel the body processes, such as breathing, which go on even when you are sleeping. Any form of physical activity such as walking, shopping, typing etc. requires additional energy or calories. The ideal calorie intake should balance the amount of energy used by the body. When this happens you will neither gain nor lose weight. If the amount of food and drink you consume provides more energy (calories) than is used in your daily activities, the extra food will be converted into body fat and you will start to put on weight. If you are overweight you need to reduce your daily intake of calories so that you are eating less than your body needs, and you will then burn up body fat stores.

3   *What are calories or joules?*

Calories or joules are a measure of the energy and heat that your body can obtain from food and drink that you consume. Although calories are commonly referred to in this country, many countries refer to joules as the measure of energy. One calorie (or Kcal) = 4.2 joules.

4   *I eat very small amounts of food and am constantly on a diet but cannot seem to lose any weight. My friend who is the same age eats four times the amount of food and remains as slim as a reed. Why is this?*

This is because your rate of metabolism is different from that of your friend. The metabolic rate is the rate at which you burn up a given amount of food. The rate depends on your own make up and, although it seems unfair, some people burn up their food very fast and remain slim whilst others eat small amounts of food and put on weight easily. The metabolic rate can be altered under certain circumstances. For example, people subjected to long periods of starvation slow their metabolic rate right down to conserve energy, whilst those who take regular, vigorous exercise speed up their rate of metabolism so that they can eat more food and not put on extra weight. The only way you will lose weight is by eating less food than your body needs. It is important to remember that to lose about a pound a week your body needs to take in at least 500 calories *less* a day i.e. you need to save 3500 calories across the week. This is quite a difference for many people who have already been watching their diet, and that is why you should not have unrealistic expectations of weight loss. If you are losing a pound or slightly more a week you are doing very well.

5   *Do diabetics controlled by diet alone have to keep to strict meal times?*

The need for diabetics on medication to keep fairly closely to regular mealtimes is to avoid a low blood glucose. Since diabetics treated by diet alone are not at risk from hypoglycaemia they need not keep to strict meal times. Whilst this is so, all diabetics find their diabetes easier to control if they are having three or more small meals a day rather than one or two very large ones. It is for this reason that diabetics, whether on medication or not, are encouraged to space out their food.

6 *Are there any appetite suppressants on the market that are suitable for diabetics?*

Many of the 'slimming aids' on the market contain methyl cellulose, an artificial fibre which swells to a greater bulk to help fill the stomach. Although these 'slimming aids' will do no harm it is much more sensible to train your stomach to expect less food at mealtimes so that you do not feel hungry and therefore reduce your calorie intake.

7 *My husband's diabetes is controlled by diet alone. Since being diagnosed 2 years ago, he has kept strictly to his diet and in the past year he has not had a positive urine test and his clinic blood glucose measurements have been normal. Does this mean he is no longer diabetic?*

Once a diabetic, always a diabetic. This applies to almost everyone and exceptions to this are very rare. He should be commended for keeping to his diet so well because this is the reason his diabetes is obviously so well controlled. If he went back to his old dietary habits and started putting on weight, it is very likely that all the old symptoms would return and his blood sugars would be high again.

8 *Do diabetics on diet alone need to eat snacks in between meals?*

No. The reason that patients taking insulin injections are often advised to eat a snack in between their main meals is to balance the effect of the insulin they take. Patients on diet alone or diet and tablets do not have this problem and so do not necessarily need to have snacks. In some cases too many snacks might cause a problem with weight gain.

9 *Can I eat as much diabetic food as I like?*

No. Most foods labelled as 'diabetic' are unsuitable for the majority of people with diabetes. Their main selling point is that they replace sugar with a substitute. They therefore contain a similar amount of calories but are lower in sugar.

Nowadays the advice for most people with diabetes allows the inclusion of some sweetened foods and with the general improvement and interest in healthy eating many of these foods often have other benefits such as a higher fibre content or a lower fat content. The only special foods that we recommend for people with diabetes are the ones labelled as 'diet' or 'low calorie' and these are suitable for all, especially the drinks and reduced sugar preserves, and the sugar free jellies.

10 Where or how do I find out about the carbohydrate or calorie content of foods?

The BDA produces a booklet called *Countdown* which lists the carbohydrate and calorie content of most manufactured foods. It is divided into sections: green for foods which can be used regularly in the diet, amber for foods which can be used with a little more care, and pink for foods which should be used only on special occasions. There is also detailed information on alcoholic drinks.

11 I have just started tablets for my diabetes. Does this mean I can relax my diet?

No. Tablets are usually prescribed if diet alone is insufficient and the blood glucose level is not coming down to normal. If you start on tablets and relax your diet you are very likely to put on weight and the blood glucose levels may climb even higher. If it has been a while since you have been seen by the dietitian it might be worthwhile to review your diet now that you are on tablets to see if there are any changes that can be made.

12 I have many family celebrations in the summer and would like advice on the choice of drinks. I have managed to lose weight and my control has improved so much that I have been taken off my diabetic tablets.

With the exception of very sweet wines all wine, red or white, can be drunk. Alcohol is quite a major source of calories (one small glass of wine is equivalent to a slice of bread) but even on a weight reducing diet most people would be allowed some alcohol for social occasions. Long drinks

such as beers, lagers or cider can be drunk but you are best
to avoid the 'strong' lagers which are often labelled as being
low in carbohydrate. Remember that low alcohol or alcohol
free drinks do contain a lot of sugar. Spirits are sugar free
(although *not* calorie free) so could be used with suitable
sugar free mixers or soda water.

13   Which scales do you recommend for weighing food?

It really is quite unnecessary for diabetics to weigh their
food on a daily basis. In most instances enough accuracy
can be obtained by using handy household measures which
your diet adviser should have shown you at the time of
diagnosis. Some foods which are particularly difficult to judge,
such as pasta, might be worth weighing on one or two
occasions until you get an idea of the portion size but
thereafter scales should be quite unnecessary.

*14   I have a number of queries about my diet. Can you
      advise me how I can get advice about it?*

Good dietary advice is essential in the proper care of diabetics
and it needs to be tailored to fit every individual diabetic.
Most hospitals have a professional dietitian attached to the
diabetic clinic and some nurses and health visitors who are
specially trained in diabetes may also be able to give good
dietary advice. Some general practitioners who organise their
own diabetic clinic may arrange for a dietitian to visit this
clinic. The BDA offers helpful literature and advice but every
diabetic should receive personal advice from a properly
trained person.

*15   I have had diabetes for 22 years and have only recently
      come back under the care of my local hospital. When I
      talked about my diet to the dietitian she was keen to
      make some changes saying that there were quite a lot
      of new ideas and diet recommendations for diabetics.
      What are these and is it worth me changing?*

The diabetic cannot cope with rapidly absorbed carbohydrate
such as sweet or sugary foods and therefore high-fibre
carbohydrate foods which are absorbed slowly are more
suitable. Dietary fibre is of two main types: 'fibrous' fibres

typically found in wholegrain cereals, wholemeal flour or bran, and 'viscous' fibres found in pulses (peas, beans and lentils) and some fruit and vegetables. Viscous fibres (especially those found in beans) appear to be of particular benefit to the diabetic because they slow down food absorption and hence the rate at which carbohydrate present in a meal will be absorbed into the bloodstream. All plant foods, especially those which are raw or only lightly cooked, are digested very slowly because of the plant cell walls which have to be broken down before the carbohydrate contained within them is released. As well as the slow absorption and therefore the slower rise in blood sugar, the major benefit of encouraging more fibre-rich foods of course is the prolonged effect that these foods can have in maintaining the blood sugar, so helping to reduce unexpected hypos if meals or snacks are delayed or missed. The new recommendations are summed up as follows:

1. Excessive energy content (i.e. calories) in the diet worsens diabetic control. Each person therefore requires a diet, based on individual needs, which does not contain a surplus amount of food energy.
2. To lessen the risk of coronary heart disease and arterial disease the proportion of fat in the diet should be reduced. This means substituting semi-skimmed or skimmed milk for whole milk, using less butter or margarine, using low fat spreads, greatly reducing the intake of cream and cheese, grilling rather than frying foods, and having smaller portions of meat and buying the leanest you can afford.
3. Whilst sugar and sugary foods should still be avoided as much as possible, these can now be fitted into the diet plan on an occasional basis, preferably at the end of a meal where the carbohydrate content is rich in fibre and therefore more slowly absorbed. Carbohydrates you could choose would be fruit, vegetables and beans. Eat wholemeal bread rather than white whenever possible. Pick high-fibre breakfast cereals such as Weetabix, Shredded Wheat, Bran Flakes, All-Bran or porridge. Use wholemeal flour in baking, and substitute brown rice for white rice and wholemeal pasta for ordinary pasta.

4. The diabetic who needs to lose weight no longer needs to
   follow a diet low in carbohydrate. The high carbohydrate,
   low fat diet is particularly suitable as it is a bulky diet
   and hence less likely to cause hunger.
5. Special diabetic foods are not encouraged because they
   are expensive and are usually high in calories. Low calorie
   foods and drinks can be useful for those diabetics who
   need to lose weight.
6. Diabetics may have moderate amounts of alcohol provided
   its energy contribution is taken into account. Beers and
   lagers specially brewed for diabetics have a high alcohol
   and energy content and this must not be forgotten.

Lastly, the advice on a healthy diet for diabetes is exactly
what has been recommended for the whole population.
Changing to a diet with more fibre and a lot less fat is
certainly very worth while and may reduce your risks of
developing heart disease in later life.

16   As a diabetic taking insulin should I eat a bedtime snack?

Generally speaking, yes. As blood glucose tends to fall during
the night it is sensible to cover the injected insulin with a
snack before bed. Something like a bowl of cereal, bread or
toast, sandwiches, or wholemeal crispbreads will last better
through the night than a rapidly absorbed milk or fruit juice
drink with biscuits.

*17   My son has been putting on weight since being diagnosed
      diabetic 3 months ago. What are the reasons for this?*

Most people lose weight before their diabetes is discovered
and treated. This is because body fat is broken down for
'fuel' and protein. Also many calories are lost in the urine
as sugar when the diabetes is uncontrolled. As soon as the
control improves, the calories are retained, body fat and
protein is no longer broken down and the weight increases.
Food intake and insulin dose need to be carefully balanced
once insulin has been started to avoid the situation where
extra food is being given to prevent hypos.

18 *My 18-year-old daughter is diabetic and is trying to lose weight. She has an 80 gram carbohydrate diet and sticks to this rigidly. I cannot understand why she does not lose any weight.*

Just reducing the amount of carbohydrate will not necessarily result in weight loss. When trying to lose weight it is important to reduce total calories which will involve also reducing protein, fat and alcohol – particularly fat as it is a concentrated form of calories. Your daughter should avoid fried foods, sugary foods and alcohol, cut down her cheese intake, substitute skimmed milk for ordinary milk and allow only a scraping of butter or margarine on her bread. A diet that contains more carbohydrate, particularly of the higher fibre type, will be more satisfying and encourage less fluctuation in blood sugar and as a result will be easier to follow. Ask your daughter to seek help from the dietitian and diabetes nurse so that they can work together to prevent hypoglycaemia.

19 *What is the best thing to take when I have a hypo?*

What you take to treat a hypo very much depends at which stage you recognise the hypo is developing. In the early stages the best treatment would be to have a meal or snack if there is one due. If it is some time before a meal it is best to take something in the form of fruit, sandwiches, or biscuits. If however the hypo is fairly well advanced then you need very rapidly absorbed carbohydrate and this is best taken as sugar, sweets or, for even greater speed, a sugary drink such as ordinary Coke, lemonade, or Lucozade. The best things to carry in your pocket are glucose tablets such as Dextrosol as they are absorbed very quickly. They are also less likely to be eaten when not hypo than ordinary sweets! (3 tablets of Dextrosol contain 10 g of glucose.)

20 *My daughter has been diabetic for 4 years and has had no problems with her diet. She takes part in most school sports but since she has taken up running longer distances she finds that she has a hypo about 2 hours after she*

*has finished running. She has no problems during the
run so what should she do to counteract this?*

The effect of exercise on the body can last well after the
exercise has stopped. The muscles are restocking their energy
stores with glycogen. Any food taken lasts during the exercise
but runs out later on. She will benefit from taking an extra
carbohydrate snack, such as a sandwich or two, after the
run has finished. It may also be helpful to reduce the morning
dose of insulin on the days she is running.

*21   Should I increase my insulin over Christmas to cope
      with the extra food I will be eating?*

Certainly extra insulin can be taken to cover extra
carbohydrate that may be eaten at Christmas and on special
occasions. You will probably work out by trial and error
how much the insulin needs to be adjusted but to begin
with we would suggest that you do not increase the insulin
by more than 4 units at a time. Remember that if you do
this too often you will be very likely to put on too much
weight.

22   Why do thin people taking insulin injections need a 'diet'?

The word 'diet' is often misleading as many people think of
a diet as being a weight reducing diet. In fact the word diet
means a way of feeding or a prescribed course of food, and
for a diabetic simply means planned eating. The reason for
planning meals is to balance the amount of food against the
amount of insulin and exercise taken. When you take insulin
you need to consider the amount of carbohydrate eaten
throughout the day. Carbohydrate foods are starchy or sugary
foods such as bread, biscuits, potatoes, rice, fruit, ice cream,
etc. Proteins are an essential part of everyone's food intake
but the amounts eaten should not be excessive. Some of the
protein foods include meat, fish, eggs, pulses and nuts. Fats
are used for energy and are a more concentrated source of
calories than either carbohydrate or protein. Fats should
only be eaten in moderation as excess fat in the diet can
lead to being overweight or may contribute to heart disease

in later life. Examples of fats are butter, cream, margarine, cheese and cooking oil.

Most people eat roughly the same amount of food each day and so when trying to balance food, insulin and exercise it makes sense to keep the carbohydrate intake fairly constant – only the insulin or exercise needs to be adjusted. The aim of the diet is to eat roughly the same amount of carbohydrate every day at much the same time every day. When you are first seen by the dietitian she will assess your previous diet and then advise you on the essential changes that are needed whilst trying to retain as much as possible of your previous eating pattern.

23 Why do diabetics taking insulin need to eat snacks in between meals?

When the pancreas functions normally, insulin is produced in response to eating food and 'switches off' when the food has been used up. Injected insulin does not 'switch off' when the food has been eaten. As this insulin has a peak effect at certain times of the day it is important to cover its action with a certain amount of carbohydrate otherwise a hypo will occur. If you find it difficult to eat between meals it *may* be possible to cut down the number of snacks by changing from a short-acting insulin to an intermediate-acting insulin, but most diabetics still need to eat snacks even when taking a longer acting insulin. It is worth remembering that carbohydrate will last longer if it is rich in fibre as it is more slowly absorbed.

24 I have been told that I am going to have to start insulin after many years of diet and tablets. Will my diet need to change?

Before you start the insulin it would be helpful for you to have the opportunity to discuss your present eating habits with the dietitian. There are quite a number of cases where the diet has become a little neglected over the years and it may be that enough improvement can be made even to avoid the need to start insulin. If this is not the case, at the very least the dietitian can advise whether the gaps between meals or the choice of meals can be improved. If you have been trying to avoid insulin by restricting your carbohydrate the dietitian will want to make some recommendations about an increase.

25   I am gradually losing my desire for sweet foods. When I do have them I follow my dietitian's advice and make sure that it is at a time when they are least likely to result in a high blood sugar. However I really do not enjoy my selection of high-fibre breakfast cereals without some sweetener – I was a Sugar Puff fan before! Can I put a little sugar on?

Nowadays experts do accept that the food plan can include a little sugar. But rather than take sugar in this way why not use one of the granulated sprinkle-type sweeteners, e.g. Canderel, Sweetex granulated, Sweet 'n' Low 1 or 2, Hermesetas Sprinkle or Sweet 'n' Lite, as these will not have any effect on your blood sugar.

26   Why are both my dietitian and diabetes nurse so against my family buying me diabetic foods? I find my diet very hard to keep to and never lose weight anyway. So why can't I have diabetic foods as a treat?

In all probability the reason why you are not losing weight is that you are having a diet plus 'diet foods'! Unfortunately foods labelled as diabetic are, with very few exceptions, still high calorie foods. A bar of diabetic chocolate or a diabetic biscuit contain as many calories as the ordinary varieties. This is because the only change in the recipe is a swap, they use sorbitol or fructose in place of sugar (sucrose). But these substitutes contain as many calories as sugar. To make things worse, manufacturers often have to add a little more of the other ingredients such as fat, flour or milk powder to improve taste, and these again add extra calories. Why not ask the dietitian to increase your diet plan a little to make it easier for you to actually keep to it? Providing you do this and promise to avoid the diabetic foods in future, weight loss is a certainty.

27   I come from the Caribbean and rice is part of my way of life. Since I have developed diabetes my doctor has

*told me not to have it any more. If I wash it well, won't
I get all the 'fatness' out of it?*

I am afraid you are both wrong! Your doctor should let you
have some rice – it is no worse than bread and potatoes at
putting up the blood sugars and putting on the weight. The
key to the problem is how much you eat in any one go and
how you cook it. About a cupful of cooked boiled rice contains
only 150-200 calories, the same as a large potato or two
slices of bread and there are very few diets that could not
fit this in at a main meal. Of course you should not add
any extra oil or fat during the cooking.

Washing rice before or after cooking may remove a little
of the loose starch but it does not really reduce the overall
content by more than a fraction. For a change, why not try
brown rice instead of white?

28 *As a single parent I really find it hard to make ends
meet. I know that very often I do not buy the foods I
should to help my diabetic control. Is there any way I
can eat healthily but cheaply?*

The sort of food plan advised for most diabetics does not
cost more than the foods most people are eating before
diagnosis. There is no doubt that when people are on very
limited incomes the amount they spend on food is often less
than is required to buy a healthy diet.

A few tips that might help. For breakfast have porridge:
it is very cheap and it is an excellent breakfast cereal from
the point of view of your diabetic control. A sandwich lunch
can be very healthy and tinned fish such as sardines or
pilchards are excellent choices and can work out very
inexpensive. For main meals you do not need large helpings
of meat and you can often extend it with extra tinned, frozen
or fresh vegetables. Children love crisps as snacks but these
can work out expensive, which cuts down the money you
have to spend on main meals. A cheaper, healthier snack
for you all would be home-made popcorn. A half-pound bag
that you pop yourself would make well over the equivalent
of a dozen packets of crisps and still cost less than 75p.
For in between meals or desserts diet yogurts are excellent

and good value for money. You can cut costs further by buying a large pot of natural yoghurt and adding chopped or puréed fresh or tinned fruit in natural juice with a little extra sweetener if needed. A quick and healthy home-made dessert is a low sugar jelly (available from most supermarkets) made up with milk or yogurt.

Do ask your dietitian for some more ideas to help you. You are far from alone in wanting to eat well but cheaply nowadays.

29 *I am 18 now and go out a lot with my friends. I am careful never to drink and drive but when it is not my turn to drive I do drink quite a lot. I have had quite a few bad hypos recently though I am careful not to miss any meals and I am not increasing my insulin as I used to when I first started drinking.*

Alcohol blocks the release of sugar from the liver. If your blood sugar is dropping because it is a while since you have eaten or because you have been out and active longer than usual your body cannot come to the rescue as it normally does. Ideally it is better if you try not to have more than 3 or 4 units of alcohol (1 unit of alcohol being half a pint of beer or lager or cider *or* a glass of wine *or* a measure of spirits *or* a measure of sherry or aperitif) in any one session. If you are going to have more than this make sure you have your usual meal before you go out, have a snack while out and, very importantly, before you go to bed have a sandwich or even a take-away meal.

30 *My 16-year-old son has had diabetes since he was six. We have managed quite well but since he has been transferred to the diabetic clinic we have seen more of the dietitian. I am confused – why doesn't she seem to stress the exchanges? She spends time urging us to eat more fibre-rich foods and cut down the fats. He's not overweight and has never had a problem with his bowels.*

This is a case of the right advice but not enough explanation. Nowadays we know that it is not just the number of exchanges that matter (an exchange = 10 g of carbohydrate). Different foods or meals affect the blood sugar in varying ways even when the carbohydrate content is the same. There is now a lot more emphasis on the type and quality of the carbohydrate foods. Carbohydrates that are rich in fibre usually take longer to digest, do not raise the blood sugar quite so much and have a more prolonged effect which helps to prevent hypos. They also contain more vitamins and minerals and are believed to prevent the build up of excess fat in the arteries. The amount of heart disease amongst diabetics (and the general population) worries the experts and this is why there is much more emphasis on the whole diet, particularly in eating more of the fibre-rich foods and cutting back on fatty foods.

31 *Since I went onto multiple injections to improve my control and fit in with my hectic work schedule I have put on quite a lot of weight. I am really pleased with my control but I know in part it is because I take my insulin now whereas I often didn't before because of the fear of hypos. I really can't go on getting fatter.*

The new system is helping you control your diabetes in a hectic lifestyle but it is important to realise that now you have insulin at the right time any food you eat is going to be used, and the excess is going to be stored as fat! Try to cut back on fatty foods, i.e. have fruit or diet yogurt in place of crisps or biscuits, and choose less fatty meat. Also have a look at how much alcohol you drink. Fats and alcohol are very rich sources of calories. A weight loss of between 1 or 2 pounds ($^1/_2$ - 1 kg) a week is quite reasonable. If things slow up or stop then be prepared to trim back a little on your starchy foods. Before you start to notice the drop in weight your control might well improve further, so do be prepared to monitor your blood sugars and reduce your insulin as necessary. Regular exercise will help burn off some of the fat and stop the problem developing in the future. If weight gain continues to be a problem be prepared to record all your meals and snacks for 3 or 4 days and ask the dietitian to go over them with you to see where further changes can be made.

Overweight (obesity)

*32   I have just been told that I have diabetes. Is it true that
      if I lose weight I will probably not need insulin injections?*

Most people with diabetes in the UK do not need insulin,
especially those over 40 years old who are overweight. People
who are of normal weight at the time of diagnosis are more
likely to need insulin or tablets. In overweight diabetics, it
is impossible to predict how much weight a particular patient
will need to lose in order to control the diabetes. Sometimes
the loss of half a stone (3 kg) is enough to restore the blood
glucose to normal while other patients remain diabetic after
losing several stones by dieting. Such people may then need
tablets or insulin, but provided they do not become *too* thin,
they will be better off for shedding the excess weight.

*33   I have been a diabetic on insulin for 8 years and over
      this time I have put on a lot of weight. My doctor says
      that insulin does not make you fat, but if that is so why
      have I put on so much weight?*

People tend to lose weight if their diabetes is badly controlled.
This is mainly because they are losing a lot of sugar which
is equivalent to calories in their urine. Once the diabetes
is controlled, sugar is no longer lost in the urine and so
there will be a tendency for a diabetic starting treatment
to put on weight. Insulin in the right dose does not make
people fat but anyone having too much insulin will have to
eat more to prevent hypos, and these extra calories will
cause an increase in weight. If a diabetic on insulin does
become too fat, losing the extra weight can be a slow business.
People taking insulin cannot afford the luxury of sudden,
drastic dieting but can only lose weight by careful reduction
of both food and insulin. This can be a delicate balance but
many diabetics manage it successfully.

It is best not to put on weight in the first place. There
is a particular risk of this at the time when children stop
growing. Children need enormous amounts of food when they
are actually growing taller but once fully grown a conscious
effort must be made to reduce the total food intake. Girls
usually stop growing a year or two after their first period

and unless they eat a lot less at that stage they will almost certainly become fat – and it is much easier to put on weight than to take it off.

34   I have heard that tablets for diabetics can make you fat. Is this true?

Tablets can only make you fat if used wrongly. Sulphonylureas (e.g. chlorpropamide and glibenclamide) work by making the failing pancreas produce more insulin. An overweight diabetic who is not in urgent need of insulin should first of all get down to his normal weight and only then take tablets if the blood glucose is still raised. If an overweight diabetic is started on tablets straightaway without first trying the effect of diet, that person will find it difficult to lose weight and may become even fatter. In other words, tablets should not be used as a substitute for diet and weight reduction.

Tablets

35   I understand that there are two different sorts of 'diabetic' tablets. Can you tell me what they are and what the difference is between them?

The two different groups of tablets which may be used for certain diabetics are (a) sulphonylureas which include chlorpropamide (Diabinese), glibenclamide (Daonil, Euglucon) and tolbutamide (Rastinon) and (b) biguanides, e.g. metformin (Glucophage). The two groups of drugs work in different ways. Sulphonylureas act mainly by increasing the amount of natural insulin from the pancreas; biguanides increase the uptake of glucose by muscle and also reduce absorption of glucose by the intestine. Tablets are only effective when a reasonable amount of natural insulin is produced, so they cannot be used in most young diabetics in whom the pancreas makes very little insulin or even none.

Tablets should always be used in conjunction with a diet restricting sugars. In elderly, overweight diabetics the first line of treatment is generally diet, and tablets should be kept in reserve. The sulphonylurea group of tablets tend to cause weight increase.

36 What are the lengths of action of the various 'diabetic' tablets?

The two commonly used tablets in the same group (sulphonylureas) are glibenclamide and chlorpropamide. Glibenclamide tablets act for about 18 hours and are taken once or at the most twice daily. Chlorpropamide has a very long action of 36 hours or more. For this reason it never needs to be taken more than once a day. This long action of chlorpropamide can be dangerous in the elderly; if for some reason they are unable to eat, they may have a very low blood glucose level for several days.

37 Can taking too much glibenclamide cause slight dizziness?

Glibenclamide could be causing your blood glucose level to be too low and your dizziness could be a mild hypo particularly if you get this feeling when taking exercise or before meals. You can easily find out by checking your blood glucose at a time when you feel dizzy. If your blood glucose level is above 4 mmol/l then something apart from the glibenclamide must be causing the dizziness.   There are of course other causes of dizziness which have nothing to do with diabetes!

38 I find I am dropping off to sleep all the time and never feel refreshed. I take 500 mg Diabinese and 500 mg Metformin a day. Could I be taking too much?

Diabinese 500 mg is quite a large dose and your sleepiness *could* be due to a hypo. You should check that your blood glucose is not too low (below 4 mmol/l). On the other hand, people with a *high* blood glucose often feel drowsy and lacking in energy. So your complaint could be due to either a low or a high blood sugar, and the best way of finding out is to do a blood glucose test.

39 Can one get withdrawal symptoms when taken off Diabinese?

Some medicines, especially certain sleeping tablets and painkillers, become necessary to the body if taken regularly for long periods of time. When these drugs are stopped the body reacts violently, causing withdrawal symptoms. Diabetic tablets are not like this and can be stopped quite safely – provided, of course, that they are no longer necessary to keep the blood glucose under control. If the blood glucose begins to rise, symptoms of thirst, itching, and so on will return but these cannot be described as withdrawal symptoms.

40 My chemist tells me that some diabetic tablets react badly with alcohol. Can you please enlarge on this?

A number of people who take chlorpropamide (Diabinese) experience a hot flush in the face when they drink alcohol. It seems that flushing caused by chlorpropamide and alcohol runs in families and it has been used by research workers to study the genetics of diabetes. Fortunately none of the other anti-diabetic tablets have this effect of causing flushing when combined with alcohol. If you are taking chlorpropamide and are troubled with the problem you could take instead an equivalent dose of glibenclamide. Alcohol may have other effects on the blood glucose in diabetics (p. 129).

41 Since taking Glucophage (metformin) I have had feelings of nausea and constant diarrhoea and have lost quite a lot of weight. Is this due to Glucophage?

Nausea and diarrhoea are possible side-effects of Glucophage. The loss of weight could either be due to poor food intake because Glucophage has reduced your appetite or else because your diabetes is out of control. Either way you should stop Glucophage or at least reduce the dose and see if the nausea and diarrhoea disappear. If your diabetes is then poorly controlled with high blood glucose levels (more than 10 mmol/l) you may need a different sort of tablet or perhaps insulin injections in addition to diet, and you should consult your doctor.

42 What is the cause of a continuous metallic burning taste in the mouth? I am 62 years of age and diabetic, controlled on tablets for the last 4 years.

You are probably taking metformin (Glucophage) tablets as these sometimes do cause a curious taste in the mouth. If the taste is troublesome (and it sounds unpleasant) you should stop taking these tablets. Other tablets for diabetes (e.g. glibenclamide or chlorpropamide) do not cause this side-effect. You should consult your doctor for advice.

43   I am a diabetic controlled on tablets. My dose was halved, and my urine was still negative to sugar. Would it be all right to stop taking my tablets altogether to see what happens? Obviously I would restart the tablets if my urine showed sugar.

Your idea is probably a good one but you should also check your blood glucose level as urine tests can sometimes be misleading. Provided the blood glucose remains controlled (less than 8 mmol/l) you would be better off without any tablets. If you no longer need tablets, diet becomes even more important for controlling your diabetes and you must avoid putting on weight. Some people think that if they come off tablets they are no longer diabetic but this is not so. There is always the chance that they will need tablets or even insulin at some stage in the future.

44   I have been taking Euglucon tablets to control my diabetes for the past 3 years. This week my doctor gave me Daonil instead and the chemist tells me it is the same substance. Could you please let me have a list of the tablets for diabetes?

Your chemist is correct in saying that Daonil and Euglucon are identical. It is confusing because different manufacturers market the same substance under different trade names. The different tablets used in the treatment of diabetes are listed below. The main difference between them is their length of action which varies from a few hours (e.g. gliquidone) to chlorpropamide which usually lasts for about 36 hours and may last even longer. Metformin (Glucophage) is from a different group of drugs and is not included in the list.

NAME	TRADE NAME	DOSE RANGE (mg)
gliquidone	Glurenorm	15-180
glipizide	Glibenese, Minodiab	2.5-40
acetohexamide	Dimelor	250-1500
tolbutamide	Rastinon, Pramidex	500-2000
glymidine	Gondafon	500-2000
gliclazide	Diamicron	80-320
glibenclamide	Daonil, Euglucon, Libanil	2.5-15
glibornuride	Glutril	12.5-75
tolazamide	Tolanese	100-1000
chlorpropamide	Diabinese, Melitase	100-500

45 Please tell me what is the maximum dose of tablets before insulin is required?

The previous table gives the minimum and maximum dose of tablets that you can take each day.

Many diabetics continue to use the maximum dose of tablets for years with rather poor diabetic control (blood glucose consistently greater than 10 mmol/l). Although these people often feel *fairly* well in themselves they are usually much better off when they change to insulin. After the change to insulin people notice that they have more energy and can usually manage on a less strict diet.

46 My doctor has advised me to change from tablets to insulin. Would I be right in thinking that I could avoid doing this if I cut down my intake of carbohydrate?

No, you would probably not be right. If you are overweight you *might* be able to avoid insulin by dieting strictly and losing weight but only if you are eating more than you need at the moment. If your present food intake is the amount you need, then reducing this will only make you lose weight and in due course become weak – and you may already be suffering from thirst, weight loss and fatigue. So if you are eating too much, eat less and try to improve your control that way. If you are already dieting properly do not try to starve yourself. Accept insulin and you will probably be very grateful.

47 *My diabetes has been treated with tablets for 2 years and now my doctor has said I need insulin injections. Is my diabetes getting worse?*

If your blood glucose can no longer be controlled with tablets, then your pancreas is becoming less efficient in producing insulin, and in that sense your diabetes is worse. However, it does *not* mean that you are going to suffer any new problems from the disease. Once you have got over the initial fear of injecting yourself (and most people manage this very quickly) then going on to insulin should not alter your life – in fact it will probably make you feel much better.

Insulin

48 *Where does insulin come from?*

Since the discovery of insulin in 1921, countless people with diabetes have injected themselves with insulin extracted from the pancreas of cows and pigs. In the last 10 years or so human insulin has become widely available. This human insulin cannot be taken from human beings in the same way as beef and pork insulin is extracted. A great deal of research went into producing 'human' insulin by means of genetic engineering. This means that the genetic material of a bacterium or a yeast is reprogrammed to make insulin instead of the proteins it would normally produce. The insulin manufactured in this way is rigorously purified and contains no trace of the original bacterium. Human insulin has also been made on a commercial scale by making a chemically altered pig insulin so that it becomes identical to the human variety. However the method using genetic engineering will probably become standard as it is cheaper in the long run and does not depend on a supply of pigs' pancreases.

49 *How is long-acting insulin made?*

The first insulin to be made was clear soluble insulin. Injected under the skin, this lasts for about 6 hours and is called short-acting insulin. Various modifications were made to this original insulin so that it would last longer after injection. By incorporating protamine or zinc into the insulin a single injection could last from 12 up to 36 hours. For many years a single daily injection was advised by many doctors but people realised that this was not a good way of controlling the variations in blood glucose that occur during the day. Nowadays most people who need insulin have a mixture of short- and long-acting insulin twice a day and an increasing number have insulin four times a day (see NovoPen regimen on p. 53).

50   *I have been on ordinary pork insulin for 7 years and my doctor has just changed me over to human insulin. I feel upset because I was given no real explanation. Can you please help?*

There has been a gradual switch to human insulin since it was introduced in 1982. Many doctors felt that human insulin was generally better because it led to less antibody formation than pork insulin. However, these antibodies probably do no harm and they may even be of some benefit by making the insulin injection last longer. There are also commercial pressures as insulin manufacturers would prefer to make only the human variety which would in turn reduce production costs.

Most people are able to swap from pork to human insulin without any difficulty but it is usual to reduce the dose by about 10% to compensate for the reduction in antibodies. This is a gradual process that lasts up to 6 weeks. Obviously during this transition period you will need to be especially careful to do frequent blood checks and if necessary to adjust the dose of insulin.

If the new type of insulin causes any problems, you can always ask to go back on pork insulin.

51   *Since changing to human insulin my hypos have changed. There is less warning and on several occasions I needed help from my wife to get me back to normal. Have other people had the same experience?*

This is a common complaint and is very worrying because people rely on their warning signs to help them cope with the problem of hypos. Before human insulin was introduced, exhaustive tests were performed to try and find ways in

which it differed from animal insulin. By and large these
tests failed to show any significant differences apart from
the lower levels of antibodies to insulin. It came as a surprise
when a few people reported that their hypos were different
on the new insulin and no real explanation has been found
for this observation. (Please see the section on hypos (p. 55)
for more information.)

52 *I have had problems with human insulin and would
    like to go back to pork insulin. However my chemist tells
    me that Actrapid is only available in the human form.
    Any suggestions?*

It is true that pork Actrapid and Monotard are no longer
manufactured. However the same company still makes
Velosulin in both pork and human form. This is a highly
purified soluble insulin comparable to Actrapid. You should
be able to substitute porcine Velosulin for your original dose
of porcine Actrapid.

There is no pork zinc insulin the same as Monotard but
Insulatard is often a good substitute, and this can be either
human or pork. For the record, Mixtard and Initard also
come in both forms.

53 *My diabetes has been well controlled on beef insulin
    (soluble and isophane) for the past 22 years. Should I
    use human insulin instead?*

Provided you are doing well on your present insulin, there
is no need to change anything. Although the major insulin
companies have not been making beef insulin for the past
few years, there is a firm called Fisons Pharmaceuticals
which supplies beef insulin under the brand name Hypurin.
They give soluble insulin the name Hypurin Neutral and
also provide Isophane, Lente and Protamine Zinc Hypurin.

54 *I have seen a programme on television which says that
    human insulin may be dangerous. My 14-year-old son
    has just become diabetic and I see that the doctor has
    put him on human insulin. You can imagine how worried
    I am about it.*

Yes it is unfortunate that this programme appeared at such a bad time for you. The people who make these programmes do not realise the fear and anxiety they can cause.

First you must believe that your son needs insulin – without it he would soon become very ill. It does not really matter at this stage what sort of insulin he has though most doctors in this country start patients who need insulin on the human variety.

The only problems with human insulin seem to be caused by the change over from pork to human insulin. As your son has been on human insulin from the start he should not run into any difficulties. Perhaps you should talk to a family in which one of the children has had diabetes for a few years. They would probably be able to give the reassurance you need.

55 *I was changed from pork to human insulin 4 years ago and I have not really noticed any difference. I have recently heard that human insulin can be dangerous. Should I be worried?*

There has been adverse publicity about human insulin, which has been mentioned in the preceding questions. A number of people changing from pork to human insulin have noticed that they get less warning of hypos. This change of awareness may result from other factors (see section on hypos on p. 55) but some people are convinced that the problem was caused by human insulin.

There have also been reports of unexpected deaths in people changed to human insulin. These deaths *may* have been due to hypoglycaemia but this has not been proved. Nor has it been shown that the numbers involved have increased since human insulin was introduced. The British Diabetic Association is carrying out research into these vital questions.

56 *Can I get AIDS from human insulin?*

Definitely not. Human insulin is either made from bacteria 'instructed' to produce insulin that has the same structure as human insulin or from pork insulin modified to resemble human insulin.

*57 My doctor is considering changing me from one to two
insulin injections per day. Will the second interfere with
my social life – eating out, etc?*

No. The second injection should make life more flexible.
Most people on one injection a day find they need a meal
in the late afternoon, around 6.00 to 7.00 p.m. With a second
injection, this meal can be delayed for several hours with
the insulin given shortly beforehand. With modern plastic
syringes or an insulin pen, it is easy to give oneself insulin
even when eating out.

58 Is it possible to be allergic to insulin?

Very occasionally diabetics may develop an allergy to one
of the additives to insulin such as protamine or zinc, but
the insulin itself is unlikely to cause an allergy.

*59 I have been taking insulin for 20 years. Recently, I noticed
red lumps after injecting into my legs. These lumps do
not appear anywhere else. Have you any idea what they
can be?*

In the past when insulin was not as highly purified as it
is nowadays, it was quite common for red itchy lumps to
appear at the site of injections. This was probably due to
impurities in the insulin and is not often seen nowadays.
Another cause of painful lumps at the injection site is that
the needle is not going in deeply enough so that the insulin
is being forced *in between* the layers of skin rather than
into the fat below. This may happen when people change
to new plastic syringes with very short needles. These really
have to be injected straight down at right angles to the
skin rather than at an oblique angle. However, after 20
years on insulin, neither of these explanations seems very
likely so there is no simple answer to your question.

*60 Is it possible for a diabetic to take his insulin injection
immediately after a meal rather than before?*

People who are not diabetic start to produce insulin at the
very beginning of a meal. Since it takes some time for injected
insulin to be absorbed, it is usual to have an insulin injection

about 20-30 minutes before a meal. This is the best way of
keeping the blood glucose balanced.

61   How long before eating should I have my insulin injection?

With the older, less purified insulin, diabetics were often
advised to have their insulin more than 30 minutes before
eating. However, highly purified insulins tend to be absorbed
more rapidly, and if the delay between insulin and food is
so long you run the risk of a hypo (p. 55). Now that most
diabetics are measuring their own blood glucose they are
able to keep this level closer to normal, so there is less
leeway before the blood glucose falls too low. Therefore it
is sensible to inject your insulin and start eating within
20-30 minutes.

*62   When I was first diagnosed I was put on insulin but
      now the dosage has been decreased. The doctor tells me
      I am in the honeymoon period of diabetes. What does
      this mean?*

Most people need a reduction in their insulin dose soon after
diagnosis is made. This is due to partial recovery of the
insulin-producing cells of the pancreas. During this period
hypos are often a problem but on the whole it is easy to
control the blood glucose during the 'honeymoon'. The
honeymoon period usually comes to a sudden end within a
few months, often during a bad cold or some other stress
to the insulin-producing cells. However, the honeymoon period
is a good thing and improves the chances of successful
long-term diabetic control.

*63   When I developed diabetes I was started on insulin but
      kept having hypos and 3 months ago I came off insulin.
      Why was I given it in the first place?*

Presumably you were given insulin because your doctors
thought you needed it. Most diabetics under 40 years old
who have ketones in their urine are likely to need insulin
and tend to be started on this without any delay. After
having insulin for a week or so, it is quite common for the
diabetic to be troubled by hypos, in which case the insulin
has to be reduced. Sometimes even tiny doses of insulin

cause hypos during this 'honeymoon period' (see previous question) and the injections have to be stopped completely. The honeymoon period may occasionally last as long as a year.

64   I am on two injections a day. Sometimes I find it inconvenient to take my evening injection. Can I skip it and have a meal containing no carbohydrate?

No, you cannot skip the evening injection. When the effect of your morning injection wears out your blood glucose levels will rise even if you have no carbohydrate to eat. Nowadays by using a plastic syringe or an insulin pen, injections are much less inconvenient.

65   What should I do if I suddenly realise I have missed an injection?

It is quite easy to forget to give your injection or – even worse – to be unable to remember whether or not you have had your injection. If this happens you should measure your blood sugar to help you decide what to do next. If the blood sugar is high (more than 10 mmol/l) you probably did forget your injection and you should have some insulin as soon as possible. The dose depends on how close you are to the *next* injection time. If your blood glucose is normal or low (7 mmol/l or less) you probably did have your injection even if you have forgotten doing it. It would be safest to check your blood sugar again before the next meal and if it is high have an extra dose of short-acting insulin.

66   Does the timing of the injections matter? Can a diabetic who is on two injections a day take them at 10.00 a.m. and 4.00 p.m.?

It is best to have insulin shortly before a meal (p. 46) and if you have your main meals in the middle of the morning and in the afternoon then you could try giving insulin at these times. You may find that an afternoon injection may not last the 18 hours until the next morning and that is why most diabetics try to keep their two injections approximately 12 hours apart.

67 *I have unsighlty lumps on my thighs where I inject my insulin. Could I have plastic surgery to make my thighs smooth again?*

If insulin is injected into the same area every time there is a strong chance that these lumps will appear. Some people have similar lumps on their abdomen from repeated injections into the same spot. If you carefully avoid the lumps and inject insulin somewhere else the lumps will eventually disappear although this may take a long time. Apart from looking odd these lumps may cause problems with blood sugar control by altering the rate at which insulin is absorbed. Sometimes it can be difficult to persuade people to avoid these lumps as injecting into them is less painful. Unfortunately they will tend to get larger. Plastic surgery would leave a scar and is not recommended.

68 *Should I increase my insulin over Christmas to cope with the extra food I shall be eating?*

At Christmas everyone (including diabetics) eats more and it is best to accept this. Extra food does need extra insulin and it is up to you to try to discover how much to increase your dose. The extra insulin is best taken in a quick-acting form shortly before the meal.

Don't forget the effect of exercise on the blood sugar – the traditional afternoon stroll after Christmas lunch is probably a good idea.

69 *I have been a diabetic for 9 months and attend the diabetic clinic every month to have my insulin dose adjusted. How long does it usually take before doctors get you balanced?*

This is an interesting question as it assumes that it is up to the *doctors* to balance *your* diabetes. Of course the doctors and nurses in the clinic must provide you with all the help and information you need but, in the end, it is *your* diabetes for *you* to control. Good diabetic control depends not just on the dose of insulin but the site of the injection, the timing and type of food and the amount of exercise. These are things over which the doctor has no direct control. Most diabetics begin to get their blood glucose under control in a few weeks.

70   Is my insulin requirement likely to vary at different times of the year because of the weather?

Several diabetics have remarked that their dose of insulin needs to be altered in very hot weather – some need to give themselves more insulin and others less. This is probably because people react in different ways to a heatwave. There is a tendency to eat less and take less exercise in tropical conditions. However, because blood flow to the skin is increased in warm temperatures this could speed up the absorption of the injected insulin and mean that a given dose will not last as long. Everyone is different and you will have to find out for yourself how hot weather affects your own blood glucose.

71   Is it all right for me, as a diabetic on insulin, to have a lie-in on Sunday or must I get up and have my injection and breakfast at the normal time?

Like many of the answers in this book, the best advice is try it and see on a couple of occasions. Try the effect of missing out your morning injection and breakfast and measure your blood glucose when you get up 3 or 4 hours late. If it is well below 10 mmol/l, all well and good, but if the blood glucose is higher than 10 mmol/l it means that you should not have missed your insulin. Alternatively try to persuade someone else to give you your morning injection and bring you breakfast in bed.

72   When one's insulin requirements decrease over the years, does this mean that the pancreas has gradually started to produce more natural insulin than when one was younger?

No. It is most unlikely that after many years of diabetes the pancreas will start to produce natural insulin. However, this reduction in dose in older people is well recognised. It could be that you were having more insulin than you really needed in the past. Since the introduction of blood glucose measurement many diabetics are found to be having too much insulin – or sometimes too much at one time of the day and not enough at another. Other possible explanations for older people needing less insulin are that they eat less food or because of hormonal changes.

73 *I have two injections a day: morning and evening. I keep regular times for breakfast and evening tea but I would like to vary the time I take lunch. What effect would this have on my diabetic control?*

This is a difficult problem for a diabetic on insulin. Because of the morning injection, people often tend to feel hypo if they are late for lunch. If the morning injection is mainly intermediate-acting insulin (e.g. Monotard or Insulatard), you may be able to delay your lunch a little provided you have a mid-morning snack. Have you thought of the NovoPen regimen (see p. 53)?

74 *Sometimes I suffer from a poor appetite. Is it all right for me to reduce my insulin dose on such occasions?*

Yes, that is perfectly acceptable provided that you do not miss out completely on a main meal. You will have to find out for yourself (by measuring blood glucose) how much you should reduce the insulin for a particular amount of food. If you are underweight do not reduce your food intake too drastically. On the other hand, overweight diabetics need to reduce both food intake and insulin.

75 *I have heard about insulin pumps for treating diabetics. Doctors in my own clinic never seem very keen on the idea. How do pumps work and are they a good form of treatment?*

First, an explanation of why insulin pumps have been developed. People who are not diabetic release a very small amount of insulin into the bloodstream throughout the day and by night. This insulin prevents the liver from pouring glucose into the bloodstream. Whenever the glucose level rises after a meal the pancreas immediately releases extra insulin to damp the level down. This is a simple feedback system designed to keep the level of blood glucose steady. Without the 'background' insulin in between meals, the level of blood glucose would slowly rise. Insulin pumps are an attempt to copy this normal pattern. They consist of a slow motor driving a syringe containing insulin which is pumped down a fine-bore tube and needle. This is inserted under the skin and strapped in place. There is also a device for giving meal time boosts of insulin.

Many hundreds of diabetics have successfully controlled their blood glucose with an insulin pump. However, they are cumbersome devices which have to be carried about all day long. Pumps take a lot of looking after and centres where pumps are widely used usually provide 24-hour professional back-up.

You will see that pumps are not all plain sailing and require extra blood tests and adjustments in the dose of insulin. They are a good way of achieving tight control of diabetes in people with a high degree of commitment. Since the introduction of pen injection devices (see p. 53) pumps have become less popular.

76 *My diabetes is well controlled. Should I be thinking of buying a pump?*

Probably not, if your diabetes really is well controlled. The pump is only used in a small number of diabetic clinics throughout the UK. Insulin pumps can only be used in conjunction with an expert team who can provide 24-hour cover in case of emergencies. Without such technical back-up, it is not really feasible to embark on pump therapy.

Research has shown that, if you are the sort of person who achieves good control by giving insulin with a standard insulin syringe, then you would probably be able to do *slightly* better by using a pump. However, if your control is normally erratic then equipping you with a pump is not likely to improve matters.

77 *What are the main difficulties of using a pump for giving insulin?*

The main problem with pumps is that, like all machines, they are capable of going wrong. One reason for the high cost of insulin pumps is the need to build into the design a warning system to alert the user to a mechanical fault.

If the pump suddenly stops, the user will rapidly go into a state of complete insulin lack and may quickly develop ketoacidosis.

Because the needle remains under the skin it acts as a foreign body and may set up a focus of infection leading to an abcess. The needle must only be inserted after careful cleaning of the skin.

From the user's point of view, the main disadvantage of the pump is the fact that it has to be worn day and night. This is obviously more inconvenient than the ordinary injections which are over and done with. Many people dislike the pump which they find a constant reminder of their diabetes.

78 What is the advantage of taking four injections a day with a NovoPen?

When using a multiple injection regimen the idea is to try to mimic the normal pancreas and to give small doses of short-acting insulin to cover meals, with a longer-acting insulin taken at bedtime to act as a background insulin. Some people who lead rather erratic lives find this regimen more convenient as they have a little more flexibility over the timing of their meals, as the insulin is not taken until just before the meal is eaten. In practice they may also need some longer-acting insulin taken in the morning to act as a background insulin. The advantage of using a NovoPen is that bottles of insulin do not need to be carried around during the day, and it is easy to give the injection very discreetly (see p. 72).

79 There seem to be a lot of different types of insulin on the market. Can you give me some details?

The range of insulins is confusing although they do fall into three separate groups. Please note that the times of insulin action vary greatly from one person to another and those given here must only be regarded as a rough guide.

1 SOLUBLE INSULIN which is clear and lasts from 4-6 hours with a peak action at 2-3 hours.

NAME	MANUFACTURER	SOURCE
Actrapid	Novo Nordisk	human
Actrapid Penfill	Novo Nordisk	human
Velosulin	Novo Nordisk	human & pork
Humulin S	Lilly	human
Hypurin Neutral	Fisons Pharmaceuticals	beef
Pur-In Neutral	Fisons Pharmaceuticals	human

2 MEDIUM-ACTING INSULIN which is cloudy and lasts 6-12 hours with a peak at 8-10 hours.

Insulatard	Novo Nordisk	human & pork
Monotard	Novo Nordisk	human
Ultratard	Novo Nordisk	human
Protaphane	Novo Nordisk	human
Protaphane Penfill	Novo Nordisk	human
Semitard	Novo Nordisk	pork
Humulin I	Lilly	human
Humulin Lente	Lilly	human
Humulin Zn	Lilly	human
Hypurin Isophane	Fisons Pharmaceuticals	beef
Hypurin Lente	Fisons Pharmaceuticals	beef
Pur-In Isophane	Fisons Pharmaceuticals	human

3 MIXED INSULIN containing both short- and medium-acting insulin. This is designed to have an early peak of action at 2 hours with a total action of more than 12 hours.

Mixtard 30/70	Novo Nordisk	human & pork
Penmix 10/90 Penfill	Novo Nordisk	human
Penmix 20/80 Penfill	Novo Nordisk	human
Penmix 30/70 Penfill	Novo Nordisk	human
Penmix 40/60 Penfill	Novo Nordisk	human
Penmix 50/50 Penfill	Novo Nordisk	human
Initard 50/50	Novo Nordisk	human & pork
Actraphane 30/70	Novo Nordisk	human
Humulin M1 10/90	Lilly	human
Humulin M2 20/80	Lilly	human
Humulin M3 30/70	Lilly	human
Humulin M4 40/60	Lilly	human
Lentard	Novo Nordisk	beef & pork mixture
Rapitard	Novo Nordisk	beef & pork mixture
Pur-In Mix 15/85	Fisons Pharmaceuticals	human
Pur-In Mix 25/75	Fisons Pharmaceuticals	human
Pur-In Mix 50/50	Fisons Pharmaceuticals	human

Hypos

80 Since my wife has been started on insulin she has had 'funny turns'. What is the cause of this?

Your wife's funny turns are due to a low blood glucose. The medical name for this is hypoglycaemia and most people call it *hypo* for short. The feelings people have when they are hypo are due to two things: (i) the brain itself cannot work properly as the blood glucose falls below a certain level – usually 3 mmol/l – and (ii) the body reacts to a low blood sugar by producing hormones (mainly adrenaline) which increase the blood glucose. When the brain is affected by a low blood glucose level, it may cause weakness of the legs, double or blurred vision, confusion, headache and, in severe cases, loss of consciousness and convulsions. The adrenaline causes sweating, rapid heartbeat and feelings of panic and anxiety. Children often describe a 'dizzy feeling in the tummy' or just 'tiredness' when they are hypo. Most diabetics find it hard to describe exactly how they feel when hypo but the proof is that the blood glucose is low (less than 3 mmol/l) and the feeling is quickly put right by taking some form of glucose or sugar.

81 I am taking soluble and isophane insulin twice a day and am getting hypos 2-3 hours after my evening meal. As I live alone this has been worrying me. What can I do?

Anyone who is having frequent hypos at a particular time of day can easily put this right by adjusting their insulin. In this case you are having hypos at the time when the evening dose of soluble insulin is working. You should reduce the amount of soluble insulin you take in the evening until you have stopped having hypos at that time. Hypos *before* the evening meal could be corrected by reducing the dose of morning intermediate-acting (isophane) insulin.

82 My daughter is a diabetic and sometimes turns very nasty and short-tempered. Is this due to the insulin?

Yes, probably – although it is not the only cause of bad moods in teenage girls! The only way to find out is try to persuade her to have a blood glucose measurement during her bad moods. If it is low (3 mmol/l or less) then some glucose should restore her good nature. Because the brain is affected by a low blood glucose level, irrational behaviour is common during a hypo. Your daughter may forcibly deny that she is hypo and resist taking the glucose her body needs. If you are firm and do not panic you will be able to talk her into taking the glucose (Lucozade can be useful here) and she will soon be back to normal.

Children can also become irritable if their blood glucose is very high.

83 *My 8-year-old son often complains of feeling tired after recovering from a hypo. Is this usual and what is the best way to overcome it?*

There are many different warnings of an oncoming hypo. These include shaking, sweating, pins and needles around the lips and tongue, palpitation, a sense of hunger, headache, double vision, slow thinking and, in some children, vomiting. To this list may be added a sense of tiredness and heaviness, and some people yawn repeatedly when hypo. There are other feelings which individuals recognise for themselves – often the parent or spouse of a diabetic can tell by a certain characteristic expression or gesture.

Apart from headache, these feelings usually vanish within 5 minutes of taking glucose. It is unusual to feel tired for a long time after a hypo but if your son does so, you should first check his blood glucose. If this is more than 3 mmol/l you will just have to let him rest until he is back to normal.

84 *My teenage son refuses to take extra carbohydrate when he is hypo and insists that we let him sleep it off. Is this all right?*

Hypos should always be corrected as quickly as possible. Your son is right in thinking that the insulin will eventually wear off and that his blood glucose will return to normal. However, if the blood glucose falls to very low levels it could cause problems and he may even become unconscious. His refusal to take sugar is part of the confusion that occurs during a hypo and if he can be persuaded to take glucose he will get better more quickly.

85 *I have been a diabetic on insulin for 38 years and my hypos have always been mild. Recently I suffered two blackouts lasting a minute which I presume were hypos. Why has this started?*

Blackouts tend to occur in children who have not yet learned to recognise the warning signs of a hypo but on rare occasions anyone on insulin can be caught unawares and have a sudden hypo which makes them black out. Sometimes as people get older the 'adrenaline' warnings of hypo fail to operate. The failure may be due to the natural ageing process or to diabetic damage of the involuntary nerve supply which transmits the warning signs.

A number of people have reported that after changing to human insulin they have less warning of hypos. So far there is no explanation for this but research is being carried out by the BDA to answer the question (see p. 43).

86 *My father has been a diabetic for 20 years. Recently he had what his doctor calls epileptic fits. Would you tell me how to help him and if there is a cure?*

A bad hypo may bring on a fit and it is important to check your father's blood glucose during an attack. If it is low then reducing insulin should stop the fits. If the fits are not related to diabetes then it should be possible to control them by taking tablets regularly.

87 *Can insulin reactions eventually cause permanent brain damage?*

This question is often asked and is a great source of anxiety to diabetics. The brain quickly recovers from a hypo and there is unlikely to be permanent damage, even after a severe attack with convulsions. Very prolonged hypoglycaemia can occur in a patient with a tumour that produces insulin and if someone is unconscious for days on end then the brain will not recover completely. This is not likely to occur in diabetics, in whom the insulin wears off after a few hours.

*88   I have heard that there is an opposite to insulin called
      glucagon. Is this something like glucose and can it be
      used to bring a diabetic round from a hypo?*

Glucagon is a hormone which, like insulin, is produced by
the pancreas. It causes glucose to be released into the
bloodstream from stores of starch in the liver. It can be
used to bring a diabetic round from a hypo if he is too
restless or unconscious to swallow glucose. Glucagon cannot
be stored in solution like insulin but comes in a vial in a
plastic pack. This contains the glucagon powder plus a syringe
and sterile fluid for dissolving the powder. The process of
dissolving the glucagon and drawing it into the syringe may
be a bit fiddly especially if there is a bit of a panic going
on. It is worth asking the diabetes nurse to show you and
your likely helper how to draw up glucagon.

It is usually stated that glucagon only has a short-lasting
effect and it is therefore important to follow it up with some
glucose to prevent a relapse of coma. However, in children
the blood glucose may rise very high after glucagon and as
they often feel sick it seems silly to force more sugar down
them. It is best to do a blood test to help decide whether
more   glucose   is   needed   immediately.   Longer-acting
carbohydrate (such as bread or biscuits) should be given as
soon as they feel well enough to eat it as the blood sugar
can fall again later.

89   Is it normal to vomit shortly after a glucagon injection?

Some people do vomit after regaining consciousness after a
glucagon injection, particularly children. If only half the
contents of the vial are given, it will usually be enough to
correct the hypo but is less likely to cause sickness.

*90   My diabetes was controlled by tablets for 20 years but
      2 years ago my doctor recommended that I begin insulin
      treatment. I am well controlled but my sleep is often
      disturbed by dreams, or I wake up feeling hungry. Can
      you advise me what to do if this happens?*

It sounds as though you are going hypo in the middle of
the night. It has been shown that many diabetics have a

low blood glucose in the early hours of the night and provided they feel all right and sleep well this probably does not matter. However, if you are regularly waking with hypo symptoms (such as hunger) or having nightmares you should first check whether you are hypo by measuring your blood glucose at around 3.00 a.m. If the reading is low you need to reduce the evening dose of medium-acting insulin. If the blood glucose is then high before breakfast the next day, an injection of medium-acting insulin taken before going to bed instead of before the evening meal may solve the problem.

91 What can I do if my diabetic son has a bad hypo and is too drowsy to take any glucose by mouth?

You should try giving your son Hypostop. This is a jelly loaded with glucose which comes in a container with a nozzle. It can be squirted onto the gums of someone who is severely hypo and in many cases it leads to recovery within a few minutes. Hypostop can be obtained from Diabetic Care Ltd: address is at the back of the book. If Hypostop fails you should next try glucagon (see p. 58).

92 Am I correct in thinking that only diabetics on insulin can have hypos?

No. Some of the tablets used for diabetes cause hypos. The commonly used ones are glibenclamide (Euglucon, Daonil) and chlorpropamide (Diabinese). These hypos will improve with glucose in the normal way but because the tablets have a longer action than insulin the hypo may return again after several hours.

Chlorpropamide is particularly dangerous in this respect as the hypos may return at any time for up to 36 hours. Anyone having hypos on tablets probably needs to reduce the dose. Metformin does not cause hypos.

93 I am a diabetic on diet alone and have headaches and a light-headed feeling around midday if I have been busy in the morning. I am all right after eating something. Why is this?

It seems surprising but some diabetics on diet alone can go hypo if they go without food. This is because they produce their own insulin but too late and sometimes too much. Ideally you should try to arrange a blood sugar measurement at a time that you feel odd in order to prove that you are actually hypo. If so, you could avoid the problem by eating little and often, especially on days when you are busy.

94 *My daughter aged 21 is a diabetic on insulin and is moving down to London where she hopes to rent a flat on her own. In view of the risk of hypoglycaemic attacks, would you advise against this?*

By the age of 21 your daughter should be quite capable of looking after herself and this includes living in a flat by herself – in London or anywhere else for that matter. Most parents worry when their diabetic children leave home, but sooner or later they will have to be independent. People always recover from hypos as the insulin eventually wears off. The only time when hypos are potentially dangerous are during such activities as driving and swimming.

If your daughter is sensible she will tell close friends and workmates that she is diabetic and explain that she must be given sugar if she behaves oddly. Diabetics often fail to take this simple precaution which can avoid a lot of worry to their friends who may find them hypo and yet have no idea how to help.

Practical aspects

95 *When I was discharged from hospital as a new insulin dependent diabetic I was given a few disposable syringes and needles for my injections. How do I obtain more?*

Disposable insulin syringes and needles are available free on the drug tariff. Your GP can supply you with a prescription for any make of insulin syringe you choose and they can then be obtained free from the chemist. Alternatively you can buy them directly from the chemist without a prescription (although you will have to pay for them), or you can send for them by post from suppliers such as Owen Mumford (Medical Shop), Hypoguard, or Mariner Medical.

96 What is the best way of disposing of insulin syringes and needles?

There is a device available called the B-D Safe-Clip which cuts the needle off the top of the syringe and retains it in the device. The clipped syringes can then be disposed of in a used bleach bottle (or similar) which should have the cap replaced and sealed with tape before being thrown into the dustbin. The B-D Safe-Clip is obtainable on prescription from your GP.

97 I have recently heard that disposable syringes and needles can be reused. How many times can they be reused and how can they be kept clean in between injections?

Although the manufacturers state that disposable syringes and needles are for single use only they may be reused. (The Department of Health has recently stated that insulin syringes should be marked for Single Patient Use to avoid the confusion about reuseability of syringes.) The most commonly used insulin syringes come complete with a fixed needle on the end of the syringe and therefore will only last as long as the needle. We do not recommend that these are used for more than about 4 or 5 injections as the needles become blunt. Some cloudy insulins tend to clog the fine gauge needles when reused frequently. Disposable syringes should be kept dry between injections with the protective cover placed over the needle, preferably in a clean place. They must never be boiled and should not be kept in any type of spirit as the marks rub off.

98 There is a bewildering array of syringes and needles on the market. Which are the best types to use?

In this country there are three sizes of syringe for use with U100 insulin: the more commonly used 0.5 ml (millilitre) syringe marked with 50 single divisions for those taking not more than 50 units of insulin in one injection, the 1 ml syringe marked up to 100 units in 2 unit divisions for those taking more than 50 units of insulin in one injection; and the most recently introduced (from B-D) 0.3 ml syringe which has been designed for children, or those taking less than 30 units of insulin in one injection. All these syringes are marked with the word INSULIN on the side of the syringe, and no other type should be used when giving an insulin injection. (See figure 2.)

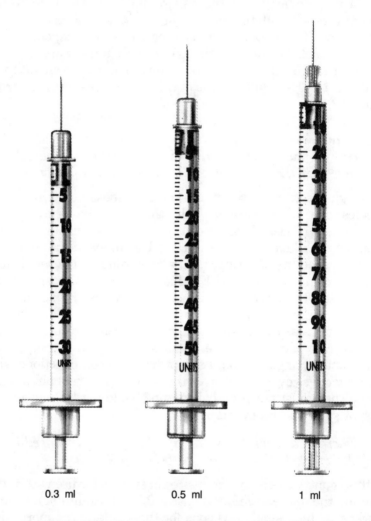

Figure 2: Insulin syringes – 0.3 ml, 0.5 ml and 1 ml.

Note that one division on the 0.3 ml and 0.5 ml syringe is equal to 1 unit of insulin and on the 1 ml syringe is equal to 2 units of insulin.

The most popular syringe is the B-D syringe which comes complete with a fixed microfine $\frac{1}{2}''$ needle, but there are several other makes available.

99 What syringes are available for the blind or partially sighted diabetic?

There is a pre-set syringe which has an adjustable locking nut on the syringe plunger which can be altered by a sighted person so that the plunger can only be drawn back to a certain point. The disadvantage with this syringe is that the nut can move out of place unless screwed up very tightly and then the wrong amount of insulin will be drawn up. It is also impossible to mix two types of insulin in the same syringe. This syringe is available on prescription from your GP.

A more practical glass syringe is the Click-Count syringe which is made by Hypoguard Ltd. This syringe clicks for every mark on the syringe and has two positions, a free position where the plunger moves freely up and down, and a clicking position where the plunger clicks into place for every mark. It requires practice, but there is less chance of error than with the pre-set syringe, and two types of insulin can be mixed in the same syringe. It is also available on prescription from your GP.

Two useful pieces of equipment to be used with either of the above syringes are a location tray that lines up the syringe/needle and insulin bottle, and the Centre Point Needle Guide. These are available from Hypoguard Ltd.

For people using disposable syringes the Count-a-Dose enables blind or partially sighted people to draw up insulin. By fixing the syringe in a plastic holder and by the use of a thumb wheel it enables the user to hear and feel how much insulin is being drawn up, as each click represents two units of insulin. Two types of insulin can be drawn into the same syringe, but the Count-a-Dose only uses B-D 1ml syringes. Printed instructions and an audio cassette are supplied with each Count-a-Dose which is obtainable from Owen Mumford (Medical Shop).

B-D, Sherwood, and Mariner Medical can supply magnifiers which clip over their plastic syringes which may make the marks easier to read. Terumo and B-D also supply plastic gauges for use with their syringes but as they have to be cut off at the correct dose by a sighted person they would be of little use for people requiring frequent changes in the dose of insulin.

The use of an insulin pen (see p. 72) may be an advantage to the blind or partially sighted person once the technique has been mastered, and if the insulin pen regimen suits the person concerned. This should be discussed with your physician or diabetes specialist nurse.

100 I am using a glass click/count insulin syringe but do not know the best way of sterilising it. I have been told that boiling is out of date.

We do not recommend that you boil glass syringes as they may crack after being boiled several times. It also takes time and the syringes wear out more quickly. It is better to store the glass syringe (and needle) in a syringe carrying case that is half filled with industrial methylated spirit *(not* surgical spirit) and change the spirit in the case about once a week. Before drawing up the insulin the plunger should be worked up and down several times to remove the spirit. Industrial methylated spirit and syringe carrying cases are obtainable on prescription from your GP.

101 My son has trouble giving himself injections and has asked me if he can use an injector. What type of injector should he use?

With modern syringes and fine gauge disposable needles injections are rarely a problem if the correct technique is used. Most people find injectors more trouble than they are worth, and they are something extra to carry around, but they may help people through a difficult patch. There are several injectors around which work on a similar principle of pushing the needle very quickly through the skin, whilst hiding the needle from view. The Injectomatic is for use only with Monoject syringes, comes in two sizes (one specifically for 1 ml and one for $1/2$ (0.5) ml syringes) and is obtainable from Mariner Medical. The Instaject II (which can also be used as a finger pricking device) can be used with any brand of insulin syringe and is obtainable from Owen Mumford (Medical Shop). As well as offering fast needle penetration the Auto-Injector also automatically delivers the insulin at speed using a conventional syringe. Its disadvantages are that it is rather noisy and oversized. It is obtainable from Owen Mumford (Medical Shop). None of these injectors is available on prescription.

Another aid for injection is a small plastic catheter called Insuflon. It is introduced under the skin using a needle and can theoretically be left in place for about a week, thus cutting down the number of injections needed. Insulin is introduced using a conventional syringe and needle (or an insulin pen) by piercing the membrane at the end of the catheter. Its disadvantages are that it is likely to increase the risk of infection at injection sites, may impair the effect of insulin absorption if the same sites are used too frequently, and it is expensive. It is not available on prescription but is obtainable from Viggo-Spectramed (see address at the back of the book).

102 What is the 'jet' injector?

This is an injector which works by firing liquid, such as insulin, through the skin from very high pressure jets. It is not entirely painless, is very bulky, very expensive, unsuitable for those who mix insulins and has not yet been proved to be harmless when multiple injections are given, i.e. by a diabetic giving twice daily insulin for several years. Until more is known about the long-term effects we would not advise its use.

103 Is it necessary to use spirit before or after injecting myself?

To reduce the chance of transferring infection from one patient to another, doctors and nurses swab the skin with spirit (alcohol) when giving injections in hospital. For a long time diabetics were taught to do the same but it is now realised that it is unnecessary as infection is unlikely to be introduced from normal skin. We advise against the use of spirit as it tends to harden the skin. If you feel you must clean the injection site (say after playing football) use soap and water only.

104 Is it dangerous to inject air bubbles that may be in the syringe after drawing up insulin?

The only reason you are taught to get rid of large air bubbles from the syringe after drawing up insulin is because the air takes the place of the insulin and therefore the dose will not be accurate. *Very large* quantities of air injected directly into the circulation could be dangerous and produce an airlock in the bloodstream, but these amounts are far larger than could possibly be introduced when injecting insulin. Tiny air bubbles, even when introduced into a vein, would not do any harm and would quickly be absorbed.

105 Can two types of insulin be mixed in the same syringe?

Yes, many people these days are taking mixtures of insulin. Unless instructed otherwise by your doctor you should inject mixtures of insulin immediately after they are drawn up, particularly if you are using a zinc based insulin such as Monotard, Ultratard, or ZN. The rule when drawing up two types of insulin is to draw up the clear (short-acting) insulin first followed by the cloudy (long-acting) insulin. The reason for this is to prevent the clear bottle of insulin becoming 'contaminated' by the cloudy insulin. If this happens the clear or short-acting insulin loses its quick-acting properties. The correct way of mixing insulins in the same syringe is illustrated in plate 2.

106 When drawing up my insulin I sometimes find that the insulin gets 'sucked back' into the bottle. Why is this?

This is due to not putting air into the bottle before drawing up the insulin. You should inject the same volume of air into the bottle as the amount of insulin you intend to draw out. If you do not do this a vacuum will develop and either the insulin will be sucked back into the bottle or it will be difficult to get the insulin out. So remember to prime the bottle with air from your syringe before trying to draw up insulin (see plates 1 and 2). It has recently been shown that this traditional advice to prime the bottle with air before drawing up insulin may not be necessary, but our patients continue to use this technique.

107 I have been giving my insulin injections at an angle of about 45 degrees for many years but have recently been told that this is incorrect. What do you advise?

Insulin is designed to be given into the deep layer of fat under the skin but not into the muscle. In the past, when using longer needles, people taking insulin injections were taught to pinch up the skin and then inject at an angle of 45 degrees. With the introduction of shorter $\frac{1}{2}''$ needles teaching gradually changed and the majority of diabetics now give their injections at right angles without first pinching up the skin. This encourages the injection to be given more quickly and can be given with one hand. However, recent reports have suggested that thin people who use this perpendicular injection technique may sometimes inject into the muscle leading to an erratic absorption of insulin, and as a result teaching methods have changed yet again. The current advice is to give the injection by first pinching up a generous amount of skin (do not squeeze too tightly as this may cause bruising), and then pushing the needle in quickly at right angles to the skin. If the needle is pushed through the skin quickly the injection should be virtually painless. We recommend that people who are injecting into a flat area of skin and who have stable diabetes should continue to use this technique if they find it easier. Injection technique is shown in plate 3.

108 My young daughter spends a very long time giving her injection and complains that it is painful. Is there any advice you can give?

One of the reasons that she finds it painful is because she is probably pushing the needle slowly through the skin. The sensitive nerve endings lie virtually on the surface of the skin and are more likely to be stimulated if the needle enters the skin very slowly. Try to encourage her to push the needle through the skin as quickly as possible. The use of disposable 'microfine' needles will also make things easier. If she still experiences difficulty then the ice cube technique may be helpful. A cube of ice can be held against the skin for about 10 seconds and this 'freezes' the skin just long enough for the injection to be given. This method can be used until confidence has been gained in the giving of injections.

109 Sometimes after giving my injection I find that a small lump appears just under the skin. What is the cause of this?

It sounds as though you are giving the injection at too shallow a depth. If the insulin is injected into the skin (intradermally) a small lump will appear. Apart from being more painful, the insulin will not be absorbed properly. Try giving the injection more deeply by injecting at right angles to the skin (see plate 3) and this will not happen.

110 Should I draw back on the plunger after inserting the needle to check for blood?

It used to be common practice to teach diabetics to draw back on the plunger before injecting insulin to check that the needle has not entered a blood vessel. These days we do not teach this as the chances of insulin entering a blood vessel are extremely slight and pulling back on the plunger may make the injection more difficult for some people. If you are in the habit of drawing back before giving insulin by all means continue but it is not strictly necessary.

111 Sometimes after giving my injection I notice that the injection site bleeds a lot. Does this do any harm?

This may happen if you puncture a blood capillary (very small blood vessel) which means that the needle goes straight through the capillary. You may then bleed from the injection site and probably see a bruise the following day, but it does no harm. It helps to press quickly with your finger or a tissue over the site.

112 When I have given my injection I sometimes see some insulin leaking out from the injection hole after taking out the needle. Should I give myself extra insulin later and how much should I give?

Insulin does sometimes leak out immediately after having given the injection. This can often be avoided by moving the skin to one side immediately after withdrawing the needle or alternatively moving the skin to one side *before inserting* the needle. This effectively means that the needle channel closes after the needle has been withdrawn. If either of these methods fail then have a tissue handy at injection time ready to press straight on the spot after giving the injection. Extra insulin should not be given if you lose a little because you will not know how much has been lost and will probably overcompensate, give too much and risk hypoglycaemia. Having taken too little insulin may mean that your urine tests or blood sugar levels will be just higher than normal that day.

113 The layer of fat beneath the surface of the skin of my thighs is very hard and I find it difficult to inject myself. Have you any suggestions?

This could be due to not rotating injection sites and reusing the same place too many times. This causes the flesh to become hard and as a result leads to erratic absorption of the insulin. These over-used areas should not be injected for about a year and new areas should be found instead. Another possible cause for hard skin is the use of spirit for swabbing the skin which makes the skin tough and difficult to inject. Stop swabbing the skin (p. 65) and try softening it by rubbing in hand cream at night. If the needle still appears to be resisted by the skin try stretching the skin before giving your injection.

114 I have been taking insulin for 18 years and have unsightly bulges at the top of my thighs where I give my injections. How can I get rid of them?

These bulges which are known as lipohypertrophy are due to the build-up of fat below the skin. This is almost certainly caused by constantly injecting insulin into the same site over several years. Insulin will not be absorbed properly from these areas and the sites should not be used for at least a year. Inject into your abdomen, buttocks and upper arms until the thighs have been 'rested'. When you return to the thighs use a much larger area than before, and try to avoid the top of the thighs.

115 Where is the best place to give an injection of insulin?

Insulin is designed to be given into the deep layers of fat below the skin and basically can be given in any place where there is a reasonable layer of fat. The recommended places are the fronts and sides of the middle or upper thighs, the abdomen and the buttocks. The upper arms may also be used, but some women prefer not to use the arms in the summer months in case they have marks at the injection sites which may be noticeable when wearing summer dresses. It is very important not to develop 'favourite' injection areas, and to change to new sites regularly. Suitable sites for injection are shown in figure 3.

116 I have to increase my dose of insulin by 4 units when injecting into my arms and by 6 units when injecting into the abdomen to maintain control. Can you tell me why this is, and should I inject only into my thighs?

It is known that insulin is absorbed at different rates from different areas of the body. The fastest rate of absorption is from the abdomen and arms, and the slowest from the thighs and buttocks. For many people this will not make much difference to their control, but for others the difference will be significant. You may wish to see if injecting into different areas affects your control by measuring several blood sugars at different times of the day each time a new area is chosen. Insulin is also more quickly absorbed from the thighs and buttocks if exercise is taken immediately after the injection. Heat also influences the rate of absorption of insulin (p. 50) and will be more quickly absorbed following a hot bath or after sunbathing in a hot country.

117 After using the tops of my thighs for my injection for many years I have recently started using my abdomen but now seem to have hypos every day. Why is this?

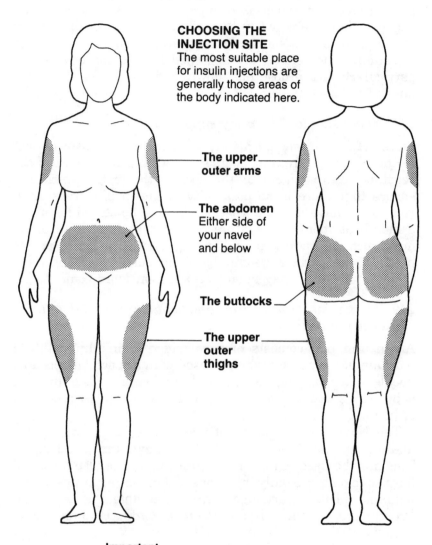

CHOOSING THE INJECTION SITE
The most suitable place for insulin injections are generally those areas of the body indicated here.

The upper outer arms

The abdomen
Either side of your navel and below

The buttocks

The upper outer thighs

Important
Do not give injections in the same small area.
This may lead to pitting or lumpiness of the skin.

Figure 3: Injection sites.

This is probably due to insulin being poorly absorbed in the past from your much-used injection areas. We normally suggest that diabetics reduce their dose of insulin when changing to a new or rarely used area because the insulin is usually more effectively absorbed from these new areas, particularly if the dose has slowly increased over the years due to the injection being given in the same place continually.

118 Where should I keep my supplies of insulin?

Stores of insulin should ideally be kept in a refrigerator not in the freezer or freezing compartment. The best place is the vegetable compartment or the door of the fridge which will ensure that there is no possibility of the insulin freezing. If you do not have a fridge, the insulin may be stored for about a month at room temperature but keep it away from direct heat such as radiators and strong sunlight. Many people prefer to keep their insulin bottle in current use at room temperature as it may make the injection more comfortable.

119 What is an insulin pen, and what are the advantages of using one?

An insulin pen consists of a cartridge of insulin inside a fountain pen type case which is used with a special disposable needle. After dialling the required number of units of insulin, a button is pressed and the pen releases the correct dose of insulin.

The NovoPen II is made of plastic and has a system for dialling up the dose of insulin to a maximum of 36 units. This may be used with Human Actrapid but is also intended for people on twice daily injections of long-acting or pre-mixed insulins. Thus cartridges are available for Human Protaphane, Penmix 10/90, Penmix 20/80, Penmix 30/70, Penmix 40/60, and Penmix 50/50.

NovoPen II is available free on request (no prescription needed) from Novo Nordisk. Also on the market is the Autopen which can be purchased from Owen Mumford (Medical Shop), the B-D Pen which is obtainable from Becton Dickinson and uses Lilly insulin cartridges Humulin S, Humulin M1, M2, M3, and M4, and the Pur-In Pen from Fisons Pharmaceuticals which uses Pur-In Neutral, Pur-In

Isophane, and the Pur-In Mix 15/85, Mix 25/75, and Mix 50/50. Insulin cartridges can be prescribed by your doctor but unfortunately pen needles are not yet available on prescription. A disposable insulin pen injector is already in use on the continent and will be released by Novo Nordisk as soon as it has satisfied the licensing authorities.

The great advantage of the pen is that you do not need to carry around syringes and bottles of insulin. It is easy to give an injection away from home, e.g. in a restaurant or when travelling. For the visually impaired the dial-a-dose clicking action may be easier than drawing up insulin in a conventional syringe.

All these pens rely on ordinary finger pressure for the injection, i.e. they are not automatic injectors.

120 Should I wipe the top of the insulin bottle with spirit before drawing up the required dose?

Although many clinics teach people to clean the tops of the insulin bottles, we do not think that it is necessary.

Unproven methods of treatment

121 Recently I saw a physical training expert demonstrating a technique of achieving complete relaxation. She concluded by saying 'Of course, this is not suitable for everyone, for example diabetics'. Is this true and, if so, why?

This sounds like an example of ignorant discrimination against diabetics. There is no reason why diabetics should not practise complete relaxation if they want to. If the session went on for a long time you might have to miss a snack or even a meal but as you are burning up so little energy in a relaxed state, perhaps it would not matter.

122 My back has troubled me for many years and a friend has suggested that as a last resort I should try acupuncture. Would there be any objection to this, given that I am a diabetic? Might it even help my diabetes?

Acupuncture has been a standard form of medical treatment in China for 5000 years. In the last 20 years it has become more widely used in this country. In China acupuncture has always been thought of as a way of preventing disease and is less effective in treating illness. In the UK acupuncture tends to be used by people who have been ill (and usually in pain) for a long time. It is most often tried in such conditions as a painful back, where orthodox medicine often fails to help. Even practitioners of the art do not claim that acupuncture can cure diabetes.

123 I have heard that there are herbal remedies for diabetes. Could you enlarge on these?

There are many plants which have been said to reduce the high level of blood glucose in diabetics. One of these is a berry from West Africa and another a tropical plant called Karela or Bitter Gourd. These only have a mild effect on lowering the blood glucose and as the Bitter Gourd lives up to its name and tastes disgusting, you would find conventional tablets more convenient, more reliable and much safer. Herbal remedies have no effect on diabetics who need insulin.

124 My little girl has just contracted diabetes at the age of three. I would do anything to cure her. Would hypnosis be worth a try?

Most parents have a desperate desire for a cure when their child becomes diabetic. In one sense, insulin injections are a cure in that they replace the missing hormone. This fact is not much consolation to the parent. Although a sense of desperation is natural, it is best for your child's sake to try to accept that she will remain diabetic. In this way she is more likely to come to terms with the condition herself. It is normal to grieve but at some stage you must face facts as a family and make use of all the help that is available for you and your daughter. In that way she will be less upset about her diabetes than you are. Hypnosis will not help her insulin cells to regenerate.

125 An evangelistic healing crusade claims to heal among other diseases 'sugar diabetes', malignant growth and multiple sclerosis, etc. Are these claims correct?

There are of course a handful of reports of miracle cures of various serious diseases like cancer but these are few and far between. A mild overweight diabetic might be persuaded to lose weight by a faith healer and it might appear that his diabetes was 'cured' but no diabetic on insulin has benefited from a healing crusade except in the strictly spiritual sense.

126 I recently read an article on ginseng which said it was beneficial to diabetics. Have you any information on this?

Ginseng comes from Korea and the powdered root is said to have amazing properties. You may come across glossy leaflets extolling the virtues of ginseng and implying that it will cure all conceivable ailments, as well as increasing your sexual prowess. The cost of these lavish booklets is passed on to any customer gullible enough to buy them. Ginseng does not help diabetics – or anyone else for that matter.

3
Monitoring and control

Introduction

The key to a successful life with diabetes is achieving good blood glucose control. The degree of success can be judged only by measurements of the body's response to treatment. Unfortunately, the fact that a diabetic feels well does *not* mean that he or she is well controlled. It is only when control goes *badly* wrong that the person is aware that something is amiss. If the blood glucose is too low the diabetic may be aware of hypo symptoms and if untreated may progress to unconsciousness (hypoglycaemic coma). At the other end of the spectrum, when the blood glucose concentration rises very steeply, the diabetic will be aware of increased thirst and urination, and if untreated this may progress to nausea, vomiting, weakness, and eventual clouding of consciousness (and coma). It has long been apparent that relying on how one feels is too imprecise, even though some people may be able to 'feel' subtle changes in their control. For this reason, many different tests have been developed to allow precise measurement of the goodness (or badness) of control and as the years go by these tests get better and better. The involvement of the patient in monitoring and control of their own condition has always been essential for successful treatment. With the development of blood glucose monitoring this has become even more apparent; it allows diabetics to measure precisely how effective they are at balancing the conflicting forces of diet, exercise, and insulin, and to make adjustments in order to maintain this balance. In the early days after the discovery of insulin, urine tests were the only tests available and it required a small laboratory even to do these. Urine tests have always had the disadvantage that they are only an indirect indicator of what the diabetic really needs to know, which is the level of glucose in the blood. Blood glucose monitoring first became available to patients in 1977 and since then has become widely accepted. As anyone who has monitored glucose levels in the blood will know, these vary considerably throughout the day as well as from day to day. For this reason, a single reading at a twice yearly visit to the local diabetic clinic is of limited value in assessing long-term success or failure with control. The introduction of haemoglobin A_1 (glycosylated haemoglobin or HbA_1) and fructosamine measurements (p. 96) has given the patients and doctors a very reliable test for longer-term monitoring of the average blood glucose level (taking into account the peaks and troughs) over an interval of 2 to 3 weeks in the case of fructosamine, and of 2 to 3 months with HbA_1. Attainment of a normal HbA_1 or fructosamine level indicates that the blood glucose concentration has been contained within the normal range, and indicates to the patient and doctor alike that providing there are not unacceptable attacks of hypoglycaemia, balance is excellent and no further changes are required. It can be seen that attaining a normal HbA_1 or fructosamine level and maintaining it at normal is an important goal for patient and doctor. Not all can achieve it, but this is undoubtedly the most effective way of eliminating the risk of long-term diabetic complications.

Monitoring of other aspects of health are an important part of long-term diabetic care. Regular checks on eyes, blood pressure and feet are a good way of picking up conditions that require treatment at a stage before they have done any serious damage (see the chapter on long-term complications p. 183). The control of your diabetes is important and so is the detection and treatment of any complications, so make sure you are getting the medical care and education you need to stay healthy. The British Diabetic Association have published a guide called *What Diabetic Care to Expect*. This is reprinted on p. 102.

Control and monitoring

1   *I am an 18-year-old diabetic on insulin. When my sugar is high I do not feel any ill effects. Is it really necessary for me to maintain strict control?*

It is quite true that some diabetics do not develop the typical thirst or dry mouth, frequency of passing water, or tiredness which usually occur if the blood glucose is high and diabetes out of control. Of course it is much more difficult for a diabetic in this situation to sense when control is poor and take steps to improve it. Yet even without these symptoms, blood glucose control is still important because the development of complications after many years is much less likely and possibly even eliminated if you can maintain blood glucose concentrations within the normal range.

2   *In the past 12 months I have had to increase my insulin dosage several times yet I was still unable to get a blood test result that was near normal. I have been a diabetic for 25 years and until last year I have always been well controlled. What has gone wrong?*

Here are a few reasons why your blood sugars may have crept up and why you need more insulin after many years of good control: (a) less exercise will mean that more insulin is needed for your food intake; (b) an increase in your diet;

c) increased stress or emotional upsets; (d) any illness which tends to linger on may lead to a need for more insulin; (e) technical problems with injections such as the appearance of lumps from repeated doses of insulin into the same site; (f) increase in weight and middle-aged spread. Having said all that some people do find that their dose of insulin changes by quite large amounts for no obvious reason.

3   Can stress influence blood glucose readings?

Yes, but the response varies from one person to another. In some people stress tends to make the blood glucose rise whereas in other people it may increase the risk of hypoglycaemia.

4   Would I be able to achieve better control if I went on to three injections a day?

Some people on multiple injections use the NovoPen which was introduced because it was felt that giving insulin before each meal would reflect the normal situation and would improve the control of blood sugars. In some cases this has been so, but studies carried out so far show that people have not necessarily shown a dramatic improvement in diabetic control. However people like the NovoPen because it makes mealtimes more flexible and frees them from having to eat at fixed times.

Blood glucose

5   What is the normal range of blood glucose in a non-diabetic?

Before meals the range is from 3.5 to 5.5 mmol/l. After meals it may rise as high as 7-10 mmol/l depending on the carbohydrate content of the meal. However long a non-diabetic person goes without food the blood glucose concentration never drops below 3 mmol/l and however much they eat it never goes above 10 mmol/l.

6   My blood glucose monitor is calculated in millimoles. Can you tell me what a millimole is?

Formerly blood glucose was measured in milligrams per 100 millilitres (mg%; mg per dl) of blood. To conform with a Système Internationale adopted by the common market the unit was changes to millimoles per litre (mmol/l of blood). The conversion is as follows:

```
 1 mmol/l =  18 mg%
 2 mmol/l =  36 mg%
 3 mmol/l =  54 mg%
 4 mmol/l =  72 mg%
 5 mmol/l =  90 mg%
 6 mmol/l = 108 mg%
 7 mmol/l = 126 mg%
 8 mmol/l = 144 mg%
 9 mmol/l = 162 mg%
10 mmol/l = 180 mg%
12 mmol/l = 216 mg%
15 mmol/l = 270 mg%
20 mmol/l = 360 mg%
22 mmol/l = 396 mg%
25 mmol/l = 450 mg%
30 mmol/l = 540 mg%
```

7   *Is blood glucose monitoring suitable for tablet controlled diabetics?*

All diabetics, whether controlled by diet, tablets or insulin, should strive for perfect control. Traditionally this has been achieved by regular urine tests at home. Since 1977 there has been a move towards encouraging patients to do their own blood glucose measurements. This form of monitoring was thought to be most suitable for insulin-treated patients. However, further experience has shown that it is equally suited to tablet and diet treated patients. The disadvantage of having to prick one's finger to obtain a drop of blood is more than compensated for by the increased accuracy and reliability of the readings so obtained.

8   *Should I keep my sticks for blood glucose monitoring in the fridge with my insulin?*

No. It is important to keep them dry as any moisture will impair their activity. You must put the lid back on the container immediately after removing a strip. The strips contain enzymes which are biological substances that do not last forever, and the sticks should never be used beyond their expiry date. The bottle of sticks should be kept in a cool, dry place, and should not be exposed to extremely high temperatures. If you have any reason to suspect the result of a blood test the best thing is to repeat the test using a new bottle of strips.

9   How are the enzymes on the test strip made?

Enzymes are biological substances extracted from living cells, sometimes plants, sometimes animals, sometimes bacteria. The enzymes on the test strips are a mixture obtained from plants.

10   How can I obtain supplies of blood testing strips?

Blood glucose reagent strips are available on prescription from your own GP. Alternatively you can buy them directly from the chemist, but they are expensive.

11   I had a glucose tolerance test and my highest blood sugar was 17 mmol/l. However my urine analysis was negative for sugar. Is there a way I could test my blood for sugar without going to the laboratory?

You appear to have a 'high renal threshold' to glucose (p. 95) which means that it is only at very high concentrations of sugar in the blood that any sugar escapes into the urine. In your case urine tests are unhelpful and blood tests essential. Self-monitoring of blood glucose by diabetic patients first started in 1977 and has rapidly spread. There are several different techniques, most of them based on reagent strips containing enzymes that react to the glucose in the blood and produce a colour which is deeper as the concentration of glucose in the blood rises. Although the colour that develops on the strip can be read by eye, it is possible to make this reading more effective by use of a specially designed meter. Some people prefer the objectivity of a meter. The meters are not available on prescription and cost about £40. Most hospital diabetic clinics will be able to show the various strips and meters that are available, and the selection should be made after discussion with the specialist nurse or physician in the clinic. All the different methods give good results provided they are used sensibly and after proper instruction (see plates 5-7).

12 When I am in a hypo I cannot read the colours on the blood test strips. What do you advise?

In your case it would be preferable for you to have a meter that will read the colour of the sticks for you and give you a direct reading of the blood glucose. People vary in their ability to read the colours on the strips, but when the blood glucose levels are low, colour vision often deteriorates. Concentration also fails which makes the timing of the procedure less accurate and increases the risk of error.

13 I feel hypo when my blood glucose is normal and only well when it is high. I feel very ill when my doctor tries to keep my blood glucose normal. Am I hooked on a high blood sugar?

In a diabetic patient with poor control for several years, the brain and other tissues in the body can adjust themselves to a high concentration of glucose in the blood. As a result they may feel hypo at a time when their blood glucose is normal or even high. The long-term outlook for such patients is poor unless they can be re-educated to tolerate normal blood glucose levels without feeling unwell. This is possible but requires determination on behalf of the patient and an understanding of the long-term dangers of a high blood glucose. This problem can be overcome by regular measurement of blood glucose, and the person must accept that however unwell he feels no harm will be done if the blood glucose remains above 3 mmol/l. It may take up to 6 months of good control for this feeling to wear off.

14 Apart from the initial day or two after diagnosis I have had no glucose in my urine at any time since I have been on treatment with a diet and metformin tablets. I

feel lost without an occasional blood sugar for guidance,
so can you suggest any guidelines for me?

If you check your urine 2 hours after a meal and the tests consistently remain negative for glucose, you need to ascertain what sort of levels the blood glucose reaches before you show any sugar in the urine. You can do this either by making a note of the results of the blood tests that you had when you went to the diabetic clinic or to your GP and relate those to urine tests or by learning how to do your own blood glucose readings and making a study yourself at home. Consistently negative urine tests used to be regarded as an indication of satisfactory diabetic control. We now know that this is not always the case and that some people can still have negative urine tests at a time when their blood glucose is quite high. Our criteria for good diabetic control at present is blood glucose readings within the range 3-10 mmol/l with an average of approximately 5 mmol/l and a haemoglobin A_1 of less than 8.5%. If you can achieve this by monitoring your urine then that is all that is strictly necessary but it sounds as if you would feel happier if you gave up urine testing and adopted blood testing as your regular monitoring routine.

15 Is there a way of knowing how much extra Actrapid insulin to give depending on my blood glucose level so I can maintain a better blood glucose?

The answer is yes, but it will require some experimenting on your behalf. The particular type and dose of insulin most suited to you can best be judged by repeated measurements of your body's response to the insulin you are taking. If you find, for example, that your blood glucose always goes very high after breakfast then you may be able to prevent this by taking more Actrapid before breakfast, but before making any adjustment in insulin dosage it is important to see that the blood glucose changes you see are part of a regular pattern. This is part of the process of balancing insulin, diet and exercise and we would caution against taking an extra dose of insulin if you come across a rather high blood glucose reading as an isolated finding. It is usually far better to try to work out a routine whereby you can prevent the blood glucose from rising too high rather than to take an extra injection of insulin when it has happened. There are exceptions to this rule, of course. If you suddenly become unwell and your blood glucose goes very high, repeated extra injections of a short-acting insulin such as Actrapid is the most effective way of preventing the development of ketoacidosis (p. 235).

16   *I find that my control is only good for one week and that is the week before my period. Why is this and what should I do about it?*

In some people the dose of insulin required to control diabetes varies in relation to the menstrual cycle. Your question implies that you become more sensitive to insulin in the week before you menstruate and you probably require more insulin at the other times in your cycle. There is no reason why you should not try to work out a pattern where you reduce the insulin dose the week before your period and increase it at other times. This variation is due to different hormones coming from the ovary during the menstrual cycle. Some of these hormones have an anti-insulin effect. The same sort of effects may occur when taking oral contraceptive tablets or whilst pregnant. The correct thing to do is to make adjustments in the insulin dose in order to compensate for these hormonal changes and to keep the balance of the blood glucose where it should be.

17   *Where is the best place to obtain blood for measuring blood glucose levels?*

It is usually easiest to obtain blood from the fingertips. You can use either the pulp, which is the fleshy part of the fingertip, the sides of the fingertips or some people like to use the area just below the nail bed. Most people find it easier to use the tip but the sides of the fingertips are less sensitive than the pulp. It may be necessary for some people such as guitarists, pianists or typists to avoid the finger pulp.

The fleshy ear lobes are also suitable areas for obtaining blood and are less sensitive than the fingers but they can be difficult to use as the blood has to be applied to the reagent stick with the use of a mirror. The ear lobes are a useful area for children if the parents are obtaining the blood for the child.

18   Which is the best finger pricker?

We recommend the use of Monolet, Unilet, Ames Lancet, Autoclix, or B-D blood lancets. The lancets may either be used on their own or in conjunction with an automatic device. These lancets usually obtain a good drop of blood without leaving a painful wound, and they are obtainable on prescription from your own GP. Alternatively they can be bought from a chemist, or sent for by post from companies such as Hypoguard, Owen Mumford (Medical Shop) or Mariner Medical. If you have trouble pricking your fingers without an automatic finger pricker there are now a wealth of devices that make the task much easier. The most popular amongst our patients seem to be the Soft Touch (from Boehringer Mannheim), the Ames Glucolet (from Bayer Diagnostics), the Monojector (from Mariner Medical), the Hypolet (from Hypoguard), and the Autolet 2000 (from Owen Mumford, Medical Shop). They are all very similar and work on the principle of hiding the lancet from view whilst piercing the skin very quickly and at a controlled depth. They are not available on prescription, but can be obtained from chemists, or by post from the companies named. They cost about £5-£9. Before buying any automatic finger pricker check that you are using the correct lancets with the appropriate finger pricker, as some are not interchangeable.

19   Should I clean my fingers with spirit or antiseptic before pricking them?

We do not recommend the use of spirit for cleaning the fingers as its constant use will lead to hardening of the skin of the fingertips. It can also interfere with the reagent strips. We suggest that you wash your hands with soap and warm water and thoroughly dry them before pricking your finger.

20   Will constant finger pricking make my fingers sore?

You may find that your fingers feel sore for the first week or two after starting blood sugar monitoring but this soon disappears. We have seen many diabetics who have been measuring their blood glucose levels regularly three or four times a day for more than 10 years and who have no problems with sore fingers. Always try to rotate to different fingers.

21   *As I am a diabetic, will my fingers take a long time to heal after finger pricking and am I more likely to pick up an infection of the finger?*

Your fingertips should heal as quickly as a non-diabetic but make sure you are using suitable blood lancets. We have seen only one infected finger among many thousands of finger pricks. We suggest that you keep your hands socially clean and wash them before collecting your blood sample.

22   *There are a bewildering number of blood glucose sticks and meters on the market. Which are the best to use?*

This is purely a matter of preference and may depend on the type of strips or meters used in your local clinic. The most popular strip is the BM-Test 1-44 made by Boehringer Mannheim. This strip has a double colour block, the blood is wiped from the strip with cotton wool, and the total timing takes 2 minutes. They can easily be read visually or can be used in a meter. The Reflolux S meter is the latest from Boehringer and is designed to read BM-Test strips. It costs about £29 and is obtainable from Boehringer Mannheim UK. The Ames Glucostix reagent strips have a double colour block, the blood is removed by blotting with a tissue, and the total timing takes 50 seconds. These can also be read visually or can be used in the Ames Glucometer GX meter. This Ames meter currently costs about £40 and is obtainable from Bayer Diagnostics Ltd. Hypoguard GA strips are probably the least known strips and they are usually used with the Hypo-Count GA meter, although they can be read visually. The blood is wiped from the strip with a tissue, and the total timing takes 90 seconds. The Hypo-Count GA meter costs about £20 and is obtainable from Hypoguard. The blood testing reagent strips mentioned are all obtainable on prescription from your GP. All these meters have an automatic timing device, are small and portable, and have a built in memory that enables the user to recall blood glucose readings.

A system that is fast gaining in popularity is the ExacTech Blood Glucose Sensor which uses totally different test strips that do not change colour according to the blood glucose value. These strips cannot be read visually and must be read in either the pen sensor or the companion sensor. The advantages of the system are that both the sensors are very small (one the size of a pen, and the other the size of a credit card), the blood does not need to be wiped off, and the timing only takes 30 seconds. The ExacTech strips are available on prescription from your GP and the sensors are available from MediSense who offer personal tuition. They currently cost £39. Another meter using non-visually read strips is the One Touch II with a 250 test memory (from LifeScan). Hypoguard have produced a meter which uses strips that do not require wiping, blotting or washing but can be used with a colour comparison chart. It is the Hypocount Supreme and is available from Hypoguard (UK) Ltd at £49. Although we have made every effort to be up to date with our information sooner or later the latest technology will be replaced by something else. The magazine *Balance*, produced by the British Diabetic Association, usually carries advertisements of the latest strips and meters and their use should be discussed with your diabetes specialist nurse or diabetes physician.

23   I have recently started using BM-Test strips but have been told that my results do not compare well with the hospital results. What is the reason for this?

The first thing is to make sure that your technique is absolutely correct. Inaccurate results will be obtained if the correct procedures are not followed completely (see plate 5). If your technique is not at fault it could be that you are not able to interpret the colour chart correctly. If this is so you would be advised to use a meter which reads the colour for you.

*24   My blood glucose meter appears to give slightly different
      results compared with the hospital laboratory. Are the
      meters accurate enough for daily use?*

Most results obtained when using a meter will be slightly
different from the hospital laboratory results because different
chemical methods are used. These slight differences do not
matter and the strips and meters are quite accurate enough
for home use. If your results are very different from the
laboratory it could be that your technique is incorrect. The
most common fault is not applying a large enough drop of
blood to the strip. The other fault is smearing the blood on
the strip, or taking too long to apply the blood to the strip.
The reaction must also be timed accurately and the blood
removed sufficiently (unless using ExacTech). The insert or
carrier of the meter must be kept clean, and you should
follow the maker's instructions for cleaning the carrier. Also
check that the reagent strips are not used past their expiry
date. If all else fails, read the instructions!

*25   I have trouble obtaining enough blood to cover the whole
      pad on my BM-Test 1-44 strips and have heard that
      these BM strips can be cut in half. Are they as accurate?*

Although the manufacturers would not necessarily agree,
they can be cut in half lengthwise. This means that you
need less blood to apply to the test pad area, and if you
have been having trouble covering the pad completely, it is
likely to make the test more accurate when using a half
width strip. The use of a half width strip is often very useful
for children. When cutting them in half it is easier to start
at the reagent pad end, and always use a sharp pair of
scissors. These half width strips cannot be used in a meter.
If you are having trouble obtaining enough blood you might
find the use of an automatic finger pricker makes this easier.
Also try to warm your hands by washing them in warm
water before you start, and drying them thoroughly before
pricking your finger. Finally, when squeezing the blood out
of the finger try 'milking' the blood out gently, allowing the
finger to recover in between each squeeze. Do not squeeze
so hard that you end up 'blanching' the finger.

26   *I would like to measure my own blood glucose levels,*
     but as I am now blind I do not know if this is possible.
     Can it be done?

Yes, it is possible but it is very difficult, and the results
would not always be reliable. Hypoguard make two blood
glucose meters which are designed to be used by the blind:
one is the Audio Hypo-Count II B which buzzes in six different
reporting blocks, and the other is the Talking Hypo-Count
B which uses a built-in voice synthesizer. However, the
greatest difficulty is knowing whether there is sufficient blood
covering the correct part of the strip. Hypoguard make a
strip guide that assists blind diabetics to place a blood sample
on to a reagent strip, but it is by no means foolproof. These
meters use only Boehringer BG strips which are not
obtainable on prescription. Both the meters and the strip
guide are obtainable from Hypoguard, but they are expensive;
the Audio Meter costs £80 and the Talking Meter costs £130.
The Audio Hypo-Count is due to be phased out shortly.

Urine

27   *I have been told to ignore my urine tests because I have*
     a low renal threshold. Can you tell me what this means?

A low renal threshold means that glucose escapes into the
urine at unusually low blood glucose levels. This is
particularly common during pregnancy. The presence of a
low renal threshold can only be established by careful
comparison of simultaneous blood and urine glucose tests.
If your renal threshold is low (or indeed high), then urine
tests can often be misleading. There is no real way round
this problem so it is important to establish where your own
renal threshold lies if you are going to rely on urine tests
alone as an indication of diabetic stability and control.

28   *I do not understand why it is that the glucose from the*
     blood only spills into the urine above a certain level. I
     gather this level is known as the renal threshold – could
     you explain it for me in a little more detail?

Urine is formed by filtration of blood in the kidneys. When the glucose concentration in the blood is below about 10 mmol/l, any glucose filtered into the urine is subsequently reabsorbed into the body. When the level of glucose exceeds approximately 10 mmol/l (the renal threshold) more glucose is filtered than the body can reabsorb and the result is that it is passed in the urine. Once the level has exceeded 10 mmol/l, the amount of glucose in the urine will be proportional to the level of glucose in the blood. Below 10 mmol/l, however, there will be no glucose in the urine and since in non-diabetics the blood glucose level never exceeds 10 mmol/l, a non-diabetic has no glucose in his urine, unless they have renal glycosuria (p. 94). You can test your urine with strips such as BM Ketur-Test, Ames Ketostix or Ketodiastix, which are all available on prescription from your GP.

29   How do you know if you have ketones in your urine? What are they and are they dangerous?

Ketones are breakdown products of fat stores in the body which are present in small amounts even in non-diabetics particularly when they are dieting or fasting and therefore relying on their body fat stores for energy. In diabetics small amounts of ketones in the urine are commonly found. They become dangerous only when they are present in large amounts. This is usually accompanied by thirst, passing large amounts of urine, and nausea. If ketones are present in the urine together with continuous 2% glucose, or blood glucose levels higher than 13 mmol/l, then they are dangerous as this is the condition which precedes the development of ketoacidosis; under these circumstances you should seek urgent medical advice.

30   What does it mean if I have a lot of ketones but no glucose on urine testing?

Testing for ketones in the urine can be rather confusing and unless there are special reasons for doing it, we do not recommend it for routine use. Some diabetics seem to develop ketones in the urine very readily, especially children, pregnant women and people who are dieting strictly to lose weight. Usually if glucose and ketones appear together it indicates poor diabetic control, although this may be transient and sugar and ketones which are present in the morning may disappear by noon. If they persist all the time then diabetic control almost certainly needs to be improved, probably by increasing the insulin dose. Ketones do sometimes appear in the urine without glucose although not very frequently. It is most commonly seen in the first morning specimen and probably occurs as the insulin action from the night before is wearing off: it occurs because in some people the ketone levels increase before the glucose levels. Under these circumstances it is not serious and no particular action is needed. Lastly, ketones without glucose in the urine are very common in people who are trying to lose weight through calorie restriction. Anyone who is on a strict diet and losing weight will burn up body fat which causes ketones to appear in the urine. Provided there is not excess sugar in the urine, these ketones do not mean that the diabetes is out of control.

31   When ketones and glucose are present in the urine at the same time, what does this indicate?

When this occurs in only one sample of urine and is gone by the next one, it indicates some slight imbalance in diabetic control. If, on the other hand, the ketones and glucose are present in a series of urine samples passed one after the other and accompanied by increasing thirst and tendency to make urine, then they are an indication that the diabetic control is severely out of balance and may be followed by diabetic ketoacidosis. In this case you should contact your doctor urgently.

32   My son tests his urine once a week. Is this enough or should he do his tests more frequently?

Only one test a week is not anything like enough and is of little value. When one is starting treatment for the first time or when some illness has upset diabetic control, a urine sample should be tested before each main meal and before going to bed, and continued until the balance is restored. These times of testing are the most useful because they tend to reflect the peaks and troughs of blood glucose control. When testing is carried out in a well stabilised patient we recommend that these four time points are still used and two tests should be completed at each of these points each week. This can either be in the form of 2 days in which a full profile test is made, or the tests done in such a way that at the end of the week there are two results available at each testing time. Most people prefer blood testing these days. The same guidelines are recommended with the addition that many diabetics find it very helpful to do occasional blood glucose readings at 3.00 a.m. to detect hypoglycaemia even if this means setting the alarm clock to wake them up! This only needs to be done occasionally and at times when the balance is unstable.

33   Why do we not always get a true blood sugar through a urine test (as in my case)?

In most people urine only contains glucose when the glucose concentration in the blood is higher than a certain figure (usually 10 mmol/l), so below this level urine tests give no indication at all to the concentration of glucose in the blood. The level at which glucose spills out into the urine (renal threshold) (p. 89) varies from one diabetic to another and you can only assess it in yourself by making many simultaneous blood and urine glucose measurements. If you undertake this exercise you will undoubtedly find, like most other people, that the relationship between the blood and urine concentrations is not very precise. For this reason most diabetics nowadays prefer to do blood tests rather than urine tests as they find that the increased precision of blood tests outweighs any disadvantage that may stem from having to prick your finger to get a drop of blood.

34   I have been using Clinitest tablets for many years for testing my urine for glucose but I know that there are strips around that are more convenient. Which are the best to use?

There is little to choose between them. They are all easy to use and can either be dipped into the urine, or urine can be passed directly onto the strip, and they must then be timed accurately. Bayer Diagnostics make a strip called Diastix for testing glucose in urine, and a strip called

KetoDiastix for testing glucose and ketones in the urine. Boehringer make a strip called Diabur Test 5000 specifically for testing glucose in urine, which has the advantage of retaining its colour for some time after the test has been made, although the timing of the reaction must be for at least 2 minutes. All these strips are available on prescription.

35   If you are testing urine four times a day is it necessary to empty the bladder each time before the test? In my experience this is easier said than done.

The 'double voiding' technique that you describe is not essential for every test and we agree with your comments. It is only necessary if many hours have elapsed since the previous bladder emptying which in practice means the first morning specimen only. Otherwise it is only required if one is attempting to compare blood glucose tests with urine tests.

36   At what time of day should I test my urine? I am on diet only.

If your first test in the morning before breakfast is continually negative, as it should be if you are on diet only –you can test your urine occasionally before lunch, before your evening meal or at bedtime, and you should find it negative at these times. If these are all negative you should try checking it 2-3 hours after breakfast which is the most likely time when you will find glucose in the urine. If this is negative too then there is nothing further that you can do to monitor your control more accurately by urine tests. You should check that your fasting blood glucose values are 6 mmol/l or less and that your routine haemoglobin A_1, is less than 8.5%. If you can achieve these goals then by all criteria your diabetes is exceptionally well controlled.

37   For some time now I have suffered from diabetes. I am always curious to know what type of tests are made on

*my urine specimens when they are taken off into the
laboratory.*

Urine specimens are tested for several things but the most
common are glucose, ketones and albumin (protein). These
tests serve only as a spot check and are meant to complement
your own tests performed at home. Clinics like to know the
percentage of sugar in samples taken at different times of
day as giving some measure of control at home. The detection
of ketones is of rather limited value since some patients
make ketones very easily and others almost not at all, but
the presence of large amounts of ketones together with 2%
glucose shows that the patient is very badly out of control.
The presence of protein in the urine can indicate either
infection in the urine or the presence of some kidney disease
and in diabetics this is likely to be diabetic nephropathy,
one of the long-term complications (see p. 202).

38   *I have a strong family history of diabetes. My daughter
     recently tested her urine and found 2% glucose. However,
     her blood glucose was only 8 mmol/l. She underwent a
     glucose tolerance test and this was normal. Could she
     have diabetes or could there be another reason why she
     is passing glucose in her water?*

It is very unlikely that she has diabetes if a glucose tolerance
test was normal. If she had glucose in her urine during the
glucose tolerance test when all the blood glucose readings
were strictly normal, then this would indicate that she has
a low renal threshold for glucose (p. 89). If this is the correct
diagnosis then it is important to find out whether she passes
glucose in her urine first thing in the morning while fasting
or only after she has eaten. In people who pass glucose in
the urine during the fasting state, there is not known to
be any increased incidence of development of diabetes and
the condition (renal glycosuria) is inherited. If on the other
hand she only passes glucose in the urine after meals
containing starch and sugar, this condition sometimes
progresses to diabetes.

39   Many doctors seem to prefer negative urine tests. I encourage my son to ensure that there is a low glucose level in his urine. What is the ideal test?

Doctors prefer to see negative urine tests because it is only under these circumstances that they can be sure that blood glucose is close to normal which is everyone's goal in therapy. You undoubtedly encourage your son to show the presence of some glucose in his urine to reduce the risk of hypoglycaemic attacks. Unfortunately this attitude is potentially dangerous in the long term because although you may avoid the short-term problems with hypoglycaemia you expose your son to the longer term risks of diabetic complications (retinopathy, neuropathy, nephropathy) which develop gradually over many years as a result of persistently high blood glucose levels. In answer to the last part of your question, the ideal test is to measure blood glucose and not to rely on urine tests. Unfortunately blood cannot be obtained without pricking a finger.

40   If my urine tests are regularly blue (negative) can my blood sugar levels be high?

Yes, they can. It all depends on where your renal threshold lies, i.e. at what blood glucose level you begin to pass glucose in the urine. The best way of checking this is to do a series of simultaneous blood and urine samples over a period of several weeks to find out for yourself at what level of glucose in the blood you begin to have glucose in the urine. Having once discovered this renal threshold, it tends to stay constant for many years. Having once done the comparison between blood and urine tests you will know approximately your blood glucose values from the urine test result. You may find like many patients that having done these simultaneous blood and urine tests you would rather continue in the future with the blood test.

41   A colleague has asked me whether all diabetics should be tested for colour blindness in case this might impair their ability to test urine.

You draw attention to a real and not uncommon problem. 20% (1 in 5) of males are affected by some form of red/green colour blindness and it has been shown that this impairs their ability to read the results of urine sticks, and probably the same problem applies also to reading sticks used for blood testing. There is another form of colour blindness that affects both males and females who have diabetic retinopathy and it has been shown that this form of colour blindness also impairs the ability to read the colours on the urine sticks and probably the blood sticks. We do not recommend the routine testing of all diabetics for colour blindness but when they are being taught either blood or urine monitoring their ability to read the colours accurately should be checked by the person (doctor or nurse) who is instructing them.

42   Is it possible to test my urine as a blind diabetic?

Yes. Hypoguard make a meter that measures results obtained from using Diastix. It is called the Hypo-Test Audio urine test meter and costs about £80 (October 1990).

Haemoglobin A₁ and fructosamine

43   What is haemoglobin A₁ and what are the normal values?

Haemoglobin A_1 is a component of the red pigment (haemoglobin A; HbA) present in the blood to carry oxygen from the lungs to the various organs in the body. Using a variety of laboratory methods the HbA_1 can be measured as a percentage of all the haemoglobin present. HbA_1 consists of HbA combined with glucose by a chemical link. The amount of HbA_1 present is directly proportional to the average blood glucose during the 120-day life span of the HbA-containing red blood corpuscles in the circulating blood.

It is the most successful of all the tests so far developed to give an index of goodness (or badness) of diabetic control. The blood glucose tests which we have used for many years fluctuate too erratically with injections, meals and other events for an isolated sample taken at one clinic visit to give much information about the degree of diabetic control since the last clinic visit. HbA_1 averages out all the peaks and troughs of the blood glucose over the 2-3 months before the test is done.

The normal values vary a little from laboratory to laboratory but in a non-diabetic person HbA_1 values usually run between 6% and 8.5%. In a poorly controlled diabetic, or in one who has only recently been diagnosed the values can go as high as 20% or 25% which reflects a consistently high average blood glucose over the preceding 2-3 months. On the other hand, in somebody who has perfect control, blood sugars averaging in the normal range, the HbA_1 will be in the range of 6-8.5% and in the occasional patient who runs his blood sugars too low due to taking too much insulin then the values will actually be subnormal, i.e. below 6%.

Some clinics use haemoglobin A_1C as the routine measurement. This is a sub-component of haemoglobin A_1 and has a lower normal range. The approximate normal values of HbA_1C are 3-5.5%.

44 What is fructosamine and what are the normal values?

Fructosamine is the name of a new test that is gaining increasing use; it is similar to HbA_1 in that it is an indicator of the average level of glucose in the blood in the 2-3 weeks before the test is done (compared with 2-3 months for HbA_1). It measures the amount of glucose linked to the proteins in the blood plasma (the straw-coloured fluid in which the red cells are suspended); the higher the blood glucose concentration, the higher will be the fructosamine. Its advantages are that it is usually quicker and cheaper for the laboratory to do and this may mean that it is possible for you to have it done at your hospital clinic visit and have the result ready by the time you see the doctor. The normal values may vary from one laboratory to another depending on the way the analysis is performed; in general, a value of less than 2.9 mmol/l is considered normal. It is likely that the current analysis may be replaced by an even newer one known as Fructosamine Plus (abbreviated as FTP) and just to be confusing the normal values are different for this one, with less than 300 micromol/l being a typical laboratory's normal value. In order to make sure you don't get confused

we suggest you pay particular attention to what is done in
your clinic and find out if it has plans to change; please
don't hesitate to ask and make quite sure you do know
what is going on!

45   How often should fructosamine tests be done?

Like HbA$_1$, there is no point in doing them too often; we
normally recommend doing one routinely at the time of each
clinic visit. If metabolic control is under close scrutiny and
therapy being adjusted, for example in pregnancy, then it
may be sensible to do one more often to check that things
are going according to plan.

46   I am 25 years old and have had diabetes since I was 15. I have been attending the clinic regularly every 3 months and do regular blood sugar tests at home with my own meter. At my last clinic visit the doctor I saw said he did not need to see me again for a whole year because my HbA$_1$ was consistently normal – why did he do this?

It sounds as though your specialist has tremendous confidence
in you and your ability to control your diabetes. As long as
you can keep it this way he clearly feels that seeing you
once a year is sufficient. He can then spend more time on
other patients who are not as successful as yourself. You
should feel very proud of this.

47   I am a diabetic treated only by diet. I find it very difficult to stick to my diet or do the tests between the clinic visits but I am always very strict for the few days before I am seen at the clinic and my blood glucose test is usually normal. At my last clinic visit my blood glucose was 5 mmol/l but the doctor said he was very unhappy about my diabetic control because the HbA$_1$ was too high at 12% – what did he mean?

Your experience shows very nicely the usefulness of HbA$_1$
testing, because quite clearly you have been misleading
yourself as well as your medical advisors about your ability
to cope with your diabetes. The HbA$_1$ has brought this to
the surface for the first time. Because the HbA$_1$ reflects

what your blood glucose has been doing for as long as 2 months before your clinic visit, your last minute attempts to get your diabetes under control before you went to the clinic were enough to bring the blood glucose down but the HbA₁ remained high.

48 *My recent HbA₁ was said to be low at 6%. Blood sugar readings look all right, on average about 5 mmol/l. The specialist asked me to set the alarm clock and check them at 3 o' clock in the morning – why is this?*

A low HbA₁ suggests that at some stage your blood sugars are running unduly low. If you are not having hypoglycaemic attacks during the day then it is possible they are occurring at night and you are sleeping through them. By doing 3.00 a.m. blood glucose tests you should be able to determine whether this is so.

49 *My diabetes is treated with diet and glibenclamide tablets. By strict dieting I have lost weight down to slightly below my target figure and all my urine tests are negative. My HbA₁ test, I am told, is still too high at 11% and does not seem to be falling despite the fact that I am still losing weight. I cannot be any stricter with what I eat. At the last clinic visit the doctor said that I am going to have to go on to insulin injections. I have been dreading these all my life – is he right?*

It sounds very much as if you have reached the stage where diet and tablets aren't strong enough to keep your diabetes properly under control. Even in the absence of any sugar in your urine a consistently high HbA₁ indicates that your blood sugar is running too high and that you need to move on to the next stronger form of treatment which is insulin injections. You have been given sound advice and I am sure it will not turn out to be as bad as you imagine – you will feel a great deal better which will make it all worthwhile.

50 *At my last visit to the hospital diabetic clinic they told me that I had an abnormal haemoglobin but that it was nothing to worry about and then went on to ask me if*

*my ancestors came from near the Mediterranean which
is true – how did they know and what does it all mean?*

At the time that you had your HbA₁ measured they were
probably able to detect the presence of another component
in your blood which is common in some countries, particularly
those around the Mediterranean. This is usually present in
such small amounts that it does not do any harm and it
sounds as if this is what is happening in your case.

Diabetic clinic

51 *They have just appointed a new young consultant at my
    hospital and I am told they are going to start a special
    diabetic clinic – will this offer any advantage to me?*

Most hospitals these days have at least one senior doctor
who specialises in diabetes. By running a special diabetic
clinic they can bring together all the specially trained doctors,
nurses, dietitians and chiropodists and this should mean a
better service for you and other diabetics attending the clinic.
You will have the benefit of seeing people who have special
training in diabetes, and most patients find this a big
advantage.

52 *My GP is starting a diabetic clinic in the local group
    practice and tells me that I no longer need to attend the
    hospital clinic. It's much more convenient for me to go
    to see my GP but will this be all right?*

You are very fortunate that your general practitioner clearly
has a special interest in diabetes and has gone to the trouble
of setting up a special clinic in the practice for this. Quite
a number of GPs have had special training in diabetes and
it is becoming quite fashionable to set up these
general-practice-based 'diabetic mini-clinics'. I am sure your
hospital specialist will know about this. If you have any
anxieties why not discuss it with him; he may even attend
the mini-clinic from time to time.

53 *Although they do a blood test every time I go to our
    local diabetic clinic, they now only test the urine once a*

*year when they look at my eyes and check my blood
pressure – why is this?*

With the introduction of HbA₁ and fructosamine measurement
and blood glucose monitoring the value of urine testing is
really for the detection of proteinuria (albumin) as an
indicator of possible kidney damage. This does not need to
be done more often than once a year in people who are
quite well and free from albumin in their urine. As a general
rule all diabetics should have their urine, eyes and blood
pressure checked annually.

**54   *Why do I have to wait such a long time every time I
go to the diabetic clinic?***

If you think about it, you probably have quite a lot of tests
done and it takes time to get the answers back and the
results all together before you see the doctor. This is
particularly likely to be so if you have had a blood glucose
and the HbA₁ or fructosamine levels measured in the clinic
which take time to process. Although it may be irritating
to have to wait for these results, they are very important
as they can be used in a two-way discussion between you
and the doctor to review your control and progress with
diabetes. Many clinics use this waiting time for showing
educational films or videos about diabetes and for meeting
the dietitian and/or chiropodist, as well as the specialist
nurse.

**55   *What determines whether my next appointment is in 1
month or 6 months?***

Generally speaking, if your control is consistently good you
will not need to be seen very often; on the other hand, if
your control is poor it is likely that you will be seen more
often. This is not, as you may perhaps think, a subtle form
of punishment but it will give both of you more opportunity
to sort out what is wrong.

**56   *At my clinic we have a mixture of patients from young
children to very old pensioners – why do they not have
special clinics for young people?***

Young people with diabetes do have special needs which are not usually met in an ordinary diabetic clinic. Growing up and learning to be independent places extra strains on diabetic control and young people prefer a more informal approach from members of the diabetes team. Some hospitals find it difficult to make these changes and there may be extra costs. However clinics for young people have been set up in many parts of the country and you could ask your GP if you could be referred to one of them.

57 We have a specialist nurse in diabetes working in the diabetic clinic that I attend. What does she do?

Many clinics in this country now employ specialist nurses who spend their whole time working with diabetic patients. They may work in the community and/or the hospital and have a variety of titles – Diabetic Health Visitor, Diabetic Community Nurse, Diabetic or Diabetes Liaison Nurse, Diabetes Nurse Specialist, Diabetic Sister, Diabetes or Diabetes Care Sister, etc. These senior nurses spend most of their time educating patients, giving advice (much of it on the telephone), making decisions about patient management and teaching other members of the medical and nursing staff about diabetes. They are experts in their field and are very valuable members of the diabetic team.

58 As a newly diagnosed diabetic patient what diabetic care should I expect?

The British Diabetic Association issued a document in May 1990 called *What Diabetic Care to Expect* and as it explains clearly what care to expect we are reprinting it here.

When you have just been diagnosed you should have:

(1) A full medical examination. (2) An explanation of what diabetes is and what treatment you are likely to need: diet alone, diet and tablets or diet and insulin. (3) A talk with a dietitian, who will want to know what you are used to eating and will give you basic advice on what to eat in future. A follow-up meeting should be arranged for more detailed advice. (4) If you are on insulin: frequent sessions for basic instruction on injection technique, looking after insulin and syringes, blood glucose and urine ketone testing

and what the results mean. Supplies of relevant equipment. Discussion about hypoglycaemia, when and why it may happen and what to do about it. (5) If you are on tablets: discussion about the possibility of hypoglycaemia and how to deal with it. (6) If you are on tablets or diet alone: instruction on blood or urine testing and what the results mean, and supplies of relevant equipment. (7) A discussion of the implications of diabetes on your job, driving, insurance, prescription charges, etc, and the need to inform the DVLC and your insurance company, if you are a driver. (8) Information about the BDA and its services and any local groups. (9) Ongoing education about your diabetes and the beneficial effects of exercise and assessment of your control.

You should be able to take a close friend or relative with you to these sessions, if you wish.

Once your diabetes is reasonably controlled, you should: (1) See a specialist nurse, doctor and dietitian at regular intervals – annually or more often if necessary. These meetings should give time for discussion as well as assessing your control. (2) Be able to contact any member of the health care team for specialist advice when you need it. (3) Have more education sessions as you are ready for them. (4) Have a formal medical review once a year by a doctor experienced in diabetes. At this review:

Your weight should be recorded
Your urine should be tested for protein
Your blood should be tested to measure long-term control
You should discuss control, including your home monitoring results
Your blood pressure should be checked
Your vision should be checked and the back of your eye examined with an ophthalmoscope. A photo may be taken of the back of your eyes. If necessary you should be referred to an ophthalmologist.
Your legs and feet should be examined to check your circulation and nerve supply. If necessary you should be referred to a chiropodist. Your injection sites should be examined if you are on insulin. You should have the

opportunity to discuss how you are coping at home and at work.

The control of your diabetes is important, and so is the detection and treatment of any complications. Make sure you are getting the medical care and education you need to ensure you stay healthy.

Brittle diabetes

59   What is brittle diabetes and what treatment does it require?

The term brittle diabetes is applied to an insulin dependent diabetic who oscillates from one extreme to another, i.e. from severe hyperglycaemia (blood sugar much too high) to severe hypoglycaemia with all the problems that are encountered with a hypo. A diabetic with this problem is frequently admitted to hospital for restabilisation. The term brittle is not a good one because to some extent the blood sugar of all diabetics taking insulin swings during the 24 hours from high to low and back again. The term brittle is therefore restricted to those diabetics in whom the swings of blood sugar are sufficiently serious to cause inconvenience with or without admission to hospital. It is important to realise that brittle diabetes is *not* a special type of diabetes and only applies when the instability is severe. This normally occurs at a time when perhaps a diabetic may be emotionally unsettled. It is therefore particularly common amongst teenagers, especially girls. It is most encouraging that as emotional stability and maturity are reached so brittle diabetes disappears and most of these patients will become reasonably stable and frequent admissions to hospital cease. During any particularly difficult period it is well worth remembering that it will not last for ever.

60   I am a 'brittle diabetic' and my doctor has advised me to stop working. Am I entitled to any benefits?

The term brittle diabetes is used rather too loosely. It is usually taken to mean someone whose blood sugar rises or falls very quickly and the diabetic may develop unexpected hypos. Many conditions may contribute to this but one of the most common factors is an inappropriate dose of insulin. Other factors which may contribute include irregular meals and lifestyle, poor injection technique, and general ignorance about the problems of balancing food, exercise and insulin. Few patients have such difficulty in controlling their diabetes that they have to give up work, but welfare benefits are available to diabetics in the same way that they are to anyone else.

61 I have noticed that there are much greater fluctuations in my blood sugar level when I am having a period. I have great difficulty in keeping blood sugar balanced then. I have read many books on diabetes but I have never seen this mentioned – is it normal?

It is quite normal for the blood sugar control to fluctuate during the monthly cycle. Most patients find the blood sugar is highest in the premenstrual phase and returns to normal during or after the period. Some diabetics need to adjust their dose of insulin during the cycle but rarely more than a few units. Every woman has to discover for herself the extent of this effect and how much extra insulin, if any, is needed. Your diabetic clinic doctor or specialist nurse is the best person to turn to for exact advice on how to make these adjustments.

4
Life with diabetes

Introduction

This chapter is meant to answer all the questions that affect daily living when you are diabetic. It covers a broad sweep from sport to holidays to surgical operations and illness.

Some questions are trivial ('Can I use a sunbed?'), and others are of great importance ('Do I stop my insulin if I am sick?'). At the end of the chapter is a miscellaneous section with questions that we cannot find a place for elsewhere (e.g. Social Security benefits, ear piercing and identity bracelets).

The section on other illnesses (p. 120) should be read early on by all diabetics, so that they know how to react if they are struck down by a bad attack of flu. All car drivers should read the section on driving (p. 125).

106

After reading this chapter, you will realise that there are very few activities that are barred to diabetics. Provided that you understand the condition, you should be able to do almost anything you wish.

Sports

1 *My 13-year-old son is a keen footballer and has just been diagnosed as diabetic. Will he be able to continue football and other sports? If so, what precautions should he take?*

Your son can certainly keep on with his football. There is a very well known First Division football player who is a diabetic on insulin. If your son is good enough at the game, diabetes should not stop him becoming another great diabetic footballer. Diabetics have reached the top in other sports, such as rugby, cricket, tennis, sailing, orienteering and mountaineering. Certainly all normal school sports should be encouraged. There is of course the difficulty that the extra energy used in competitive sports increases the risk of a hypo. Before any period of sport your son should take some extra carbohydrate, e.g. sandwiches, biscuits or chocolate wafers. Another snack at half-time is usually necessary and he must carry glucose tablets in his pocket. Very often following a prolonged sports period the blood sugar may drop 2 or more hours after the exercise has finished. Therefore a slightly larger meal or snack may be required and it is usually good practice if having exercise in the afternoon or evening to take a bigger than usual bedtime snack.

Another way of preventing a hypo during exercise is to reduce the amount of insulin beforehand. Thus if you are playing football in the morning, you could reduce by half the morning dose of quick-acting insulin. By trial and error you will discover how much to cut your insulin for a given amount of exercise.

A hypo during athletics and most team games can be inconvenient and may reduce your son's ability, but a hypo whilst swimming can be more serious. There are certain rules all diabetics on insulin should follow before swimming:

a never swim alone;
b tell your companions (or teacher) to pull you out of the water if you behave oddly or are in difficulties;
c keep glucose tablets on the side of the pool;
d get out of the water immediately if you feel the first signs of hypo.

By following these simple rules, diabetics can swim with complete safety.

Unfortunately diabetics on insulin are discouraged from scuba diving by the British Sub-Aqua Club, although each case is judged on its individual merits.

2   *As a diabetic can I take part in all or any forms of sport?*

The vast majority of sports are perfectly safe for diabetics. The problem lies in those sports where loss of control due to a hypo could be dangerous, not only to the diabetic but to fellow sportsmen or onlookers. Swimming is an example of a potentially dangerous sport but by taking certain precautions (see previous question) it is safe to swim. However in other sports (e.g. scuba diving, motor racing) the risk of serious injury in the case of hypo are even greater. For this reason the governing bodies of these high-risk sports discourage diabetics from taking part.

3   *I understand that diabetics are banned from all forms of parachuting because of the risk of hypos. Surely if one was sensible and took extra carbohydrate before a jump the risk would be minimal as a jump only takes a few minutes. Please give your views on the subject.*

We fully agree that it should be perfectly easy for a diabetic to ensure that he does not go hypo during the short time taken over a parachute jump. However the British Parachute Association would not be able to enforce restrictions for diabetics to jump only if their blood glucose were 7 mmol/l or more and that is probably why they have made the harsh decision of generally banning diabetics on insulin. Diabetics can obtain official sanction for a one-off parachute jump for charity. They will need a letter of support from their doctor.

4 As a 30-year-old insulin-dependent diabetic can I join a keep fit class or do a work-out at home?

Yes, certainly. Keeping fit is important for everybody. If you are unused to exercise you should build up the exercises slowly each week so that you do not damage any muscles or tendons. Remember that exercise usually has the effect of lowering blood glucose so you may need to reduce your insulin dose or take extra carbohydrate before exercising. *The Diabetics' Get Fit Book* by Jacki Winter (published by Macdonald Optima) is an excellent, well illustrated book that gives many suitable exercises for all ages and abilities.

5 I am a diabetic on insulin and do quite a bit of jogging. I would like to try running a marathon. Have you any advice on the subject?

Dr Matt Kiln, himself a diabetic on insulin, has considerable experience of long distance running. He has passed on the following suggestions to other diabetics wishing to take up this sport.

a Wear comfortable clothes and proper running shoes. Watch out for blisters. Shorts should have a pocket for Dextrosol.

b Start with very short runs and build up slowly to longer distances. This should take $1^1/_2$ – 2 years in young, fit people and even longer if you are older – perhaps as long as 4 years.

c Aim at training 3 times a week.

d Regular running reduces the average daily insulin dose by about 25%. Once in training, you will probably need less insulin even on days that you are not running. Conversely more insulin will be needed once you get out of training.

e During the run you will need to take carbohydrate. Dextrosol is less likely to cause stomach cramps than a bar of chocolate.

f Measure blood sugar levels before and after each run and keep a careful record of the blood sugar values, distance, time taken, carbohydrate intake and time since last insulin injection. In this way you can build up a pattern of your likely glucose requirements for future runs.

g On the day of a long run, if you reduce the insulin dose you will need to take less glucose while exercising. This lessens the risk of stomach cramps.

h After the end of a long run the blood glucose tends to rise and you will probably need a small dose of insulin to counteract this.

Before one London Marathon, Matt Kiln only gave himself 2 units of short-acting insulin. During the 26.2 miles run, which he achieved in 204 minutes, he only needed to take 30 g of carbohydrate (10 Dextrosol tablets). His blood sugar was 7 mmol/l at the start of the race and 4 mmol/l at the end. This perfect control was only possible because of careful measurements during the long training period.

Dr Kiln stresses that these hints are the result of his own personal experience and other diabetics may behave differently. Only 10% of the population as a whole is capable of finishing a marathon and nobody should run just for the glory. The activity should be enjoyable and also help towards a better understanding and control of your diabetes.

Further advice is available from the BDA who will supply a copy of Dr Kiln's notes on the subject.

Eating out

6   *My wife and I entertain a great deal and we often go out to meals in a friend's house or in restaurants. I have recently been started on insulin for diabetes. How am I going to cope with eating out?*

It is sometimes difficult when eating out with friends who have made a special effort to prepare delicious food which is quite unsuitable for diabetics. Do you refuse a syrupy pudding and offend your hostess or have a large helping and to hell with your diabetes? It is probably less embarrassing to warn your hostess in advance that you are diabetic and have to avoid food containing high concentrations of sugar. Restaurants should be less of a problem as you can select from the menu dishes that are suitable.

People on two doses of insulin a day sometimes worry about how they are going to give their injections away from home. Nowadays with plastic syringes there should be no difficulty. You can retire to the lavatory just before sitting down to eat. Diabetics who are less shy discreetly give themselves insulin into their abdomen or calf whilst at the table waiting for the first course to arrive. The use of an insulin pen (p. 72) may also make the injection simpler as bottles of insulin do not need to be carried around. Do not take the evening dose of insulin before leaving home in case the meal is delayed.

Holidays/travel

7   *Do you have any simple rules for diabetics going abroad for holidays?*

Here is a checklist of things to take with you.

a Insulin
b Syringes
c Test strips (and finger pricker)
d Identification bracelet/necklace/card
e Dextrosol tablets
f Longer-acting carbohydrate in case of meals being delayed.
g Glucagon
h Medical insurance
i Inside EC – form Elll from the DSS.

8   *Is it safe for a diabetic to take travel sickness tablets?*

Travel sickness pills do not upset diabetes though they may make you sleepy so be careful if you are driving. On the other hand vomiting can upset diabetes so it is worth trying to avoid travel sickness. If you do become sick the usual rules apply. Continue to take your normal dose of insulin and take carbohydrate in some palatable liquid form (p. 228). Test blood or urine regularly.

9   *We are going on holiday and wish to take a supply of insulin and glucagon with us. How should I store them both for the journey and in the hotel?*

If travelling by air you should keep insulin in your hand luggage: temperatures in the luggage hold of an aircraft usually fall below freezing and insulin left in this luggage could be damaged. Insulin is otherwise very stable and will keep for one month at room temperature in our temperate climate. However insulin does not like extremes of temperature and can be damaged if kept too long at high temperatures or if frozen. Insulin manufacturers say it is stable for one month at 25° C (77° F), so it is perfectly safe to keep insulin with your luggage on the average holiday. Avoid the glove compartment or the boot of your car where very high temperatures can be reached. In tropical conditions your stock of insulin should be kept in the fridge. It is best to carry your supplies in more than one piece of luggage in case one suitcase goes astray and you lose everything!

Storage of glucagon is no problem as this comes as a powder with a vial of water for dilution. It is very stable and can survive extremes of heat and cold.

10 Many airports now X-ray baggage for security reasons. Does this affect insulin?

Fortunately not.

11 I would like to go on a skiing holiday. Is it safe for diabetics to ski, skate and toboggan? Should I take special precautions?

It is as safe for a diabetic to ski as it is for a non-diabetic. Accidents do occur and it is essential to take out adequate insurance to cover all medical expenses. Read carefully the small print in the insurance form to ensure that it does not exclude pre-existing diseases like diabetes, or require them to be declared. In this case you should contact the insurance company and if necessary take out extra medical cover for your diabetes. Physical activity increases the likelihood of hypos so always carry glucose and a snack as you may be delayed, especially if you are injured. Never go without a sensible companion who knows you are a diabetic and understands what to do if you have a hypo.

12 Is sunbathing all right for diabetics?

Plate 1 ONE DOSE INJECTION TECHNIQUE

Wash your hands thoroughly and dry them.
Check the label on the insulin bottle and make sure that the expiry date has not passed.

1 Gently tip the bottle to and fro and make sure that the insulin is properly mixed. Do not shake the bottle.

2 Remove the plunger cap and the needle protection cap. Pull back the plunger of the syringe to measure an amount of air equivalent to the amount of insulin you require.

3 With the bottle standing upright, insert the needle straight through the centre of the rubber cap of the insulin bottle and push the plunger down. This pushes air into the bottle, which makes it easier to draw the insulin out of the bottle.

4 Turn the bottle upside down. Make certain that the point of the needle inside the bottle is well beneath the surface level of the insulin. Pull back the plunger until you have measured slightly more than your correct dose of insulin.

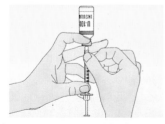

5. If there are any air bubbles in your syringe, remove them. Flick or tap the syringe with your finger. When the bubble goes to the top of the syringe, push the plunger up to expel the bubble back into the bottle. If any air bubbles persist expel all the insulin back into the bottle and start again. Air bubbles are not dangerous if injected, but their presence means that the dose of insulin is inaccurate.

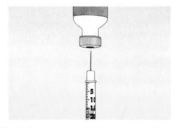

6. Push the plunger up to measure the exact insulin dose. Take the needle out of the bottle. You are now ready to inject.

Plate 2 MIXING INSULINS

Wash your hands thoroughly and dry them.
Check the labels on the insulin bottles for the expiry date and any special instructions.

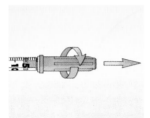

1 Remove the plunger cap. Remove the needle protection cap completely by twisting it and then gently pulling it.

2 Pull back the plunger of the syringe to measure the amount of air equivalent to the amount of *cloudy* insulin that you require.

3 With the bottle standing upright, insert the needle straight into the rubber cap of the cloudy insulin bottle and inject the air into the bottle.

4 Keep the bottle upright and the syringe plunger fully pressed down and remove the needle from the bottle. You are *not* going to draw up any of the cloudy insulin yet.

5 Now pull back the plunger of the syringe to measure the amount of air equivalent to the amount of *clear* insulin that you require.

6 Insert the needle straight through the rubber cap of the clear insulin bottle and inject the air into the bottle.

Plate 2

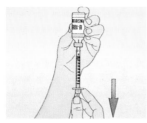

7 Turn the bottle upside down with the syringe needle still in it. Make certain that the point of the needle is well beneath the surface level of the insulin.
Pull down the plunger until you have measured slightly more than your correct dose of clear insulin.

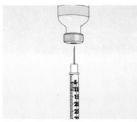

9 Adjust the plunger to measure the exact dose of clear insulin. Withdraw the needle from the bottle.

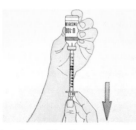

11 Holding the bottle of cloudy insulin upside down, put the needle through the rubber cap, making certain that the point of the needle is well beneath the surface level of the insulin. Carefully pull back the plunger until you have measured your exact dose of cloudy insulin. N.B. If you accidentally measure too much cloudy insulin do *not* push the plunger up into the bottle of cloudy insulin because you will also inject some clear insulin into the cloudy bottle and your dose will be incorrect. Remove the needle from the bottle and discharge all the insulin from the syringe into the sink. Then start again.

8 If any air bubbles have entered the syringe, flick and tap the syringe at the bubble with your finger. When the bubble goes to the top of the syringe, push the plunger up to expel the bubble back into the bottle. If any air bubbles persist, expel all the clear insulin back into the bottle and start again. Air bubbles are not dangerous if injected but their presence means that the dose of insulin is inaccurate.

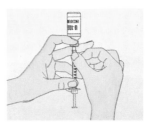

10 Gently tip the cloudy insulin bottle to and fro to make sure that the insulin is properly mixed.

12 Withdraw the needle from the cloudy bottle and check again for bubbles. It is rare to see them at this step, but if you do, discard all of the insulin into the sink and start again. N.B. Always measure your two insulins in the same order every day, and give the injection immediately after drawing the insulins into the syringe.

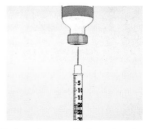

Plate 3 INJECTION TECHNIQUE

Your doctor or the nursing staff at the hospital are the final authorities regarding precisely how you should inject and where you should give your injection. Follow their advice carefully.

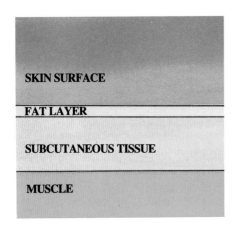

SKIN SURFACE

FAT LAYER

SUBCUTANEOUS TISSUE

MUSCLE

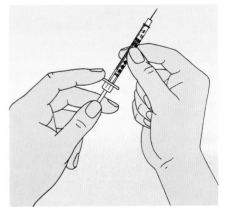

1 Choose an injection site where there is subcutaneous tissue. This type of tissue is located between the fat layer under the skin and the muscles which are below that.

2 Make absolutely certain once again that you have measured your insulin dose correctly.

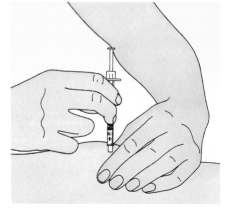

3 Taking care not to touch the sterile needle, hold the syringe firmly near the top, as if you were going to write with it like a pencil.

4 Using the other hand, pinch up a large mound of clean skin and quickly push the needle straight into the mound as far as it will go.

Plate 3

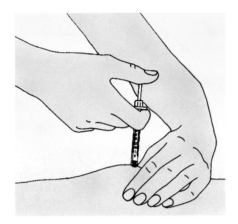

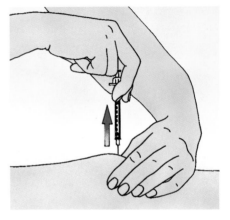

5 Holding the pinched mound throughout the injection, with your thumb on top of the plunger quickly and smoothly inject all of the insulin from the syringe. The injection of insulin should be completed in 3 to 5 seconds.

6 Withdraw the needle slowly straight out of the mound of skin, then release the mound and if necessary gently wipe the site with a clean piece of tissue or cotton wool. Your injection is now completed.

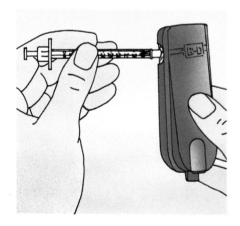

7 Dispose of your syringe carefully. Clip the needle off the syringe body using a B.D. Safe Clip. Put the now unusable syringe into a sealable household container, such as a bleach or washing-up liquid bottle – kept out of the reach of children. When full, seal the lid securely and place in the refuse.

Plate 4 USING A NOVOPEN II

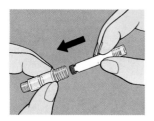

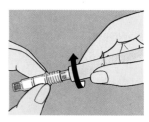

1 Insert the Penfill cartridge into the clear casing, metal-capped end first. Push the cartridge into place until it is fully inserted.

2 Screw the clear casing and the pen barrel together firmly. This is important to ensure that your NovoPen operates correctly.

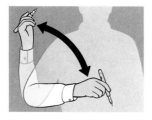

3 If using a Penfill cartridge containing a longer-acting insulin turn the NovoPen device up and down gently at least 10 times until the liquid appears uniformly white and cloudy.

4. When you are ready to give the injection screw the needle into place on the end of the cartridge.

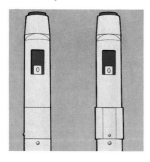

| Unlocked for carrying and dialling a dose. | Locked for delivering an insulin dose. |

5 Always keep the locking ring of your NovoPen in the unlocked position until you are ready to operate the push button.

6 Return the locking ring to the unlocked position before turning the dosage selector either up or down.

Plate 4

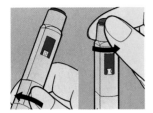

7 The dosage selector should be reset to zero with the locking ring in the unlocked position before you dial the number of insulin units you wish to inject.

8 Always give your NovoPen an air shot prior to each injection. Set the locking ring to the unlocked position and the dosage selector to zero, then dial the dose to 2 units. Twist the locking ring to the locked position, point the needle upwards and remove the needle cap. Press the push button and a drop of insulin should appear at the needle tip. Dial the number of units you wish to inject as in pictures 6 and 7.

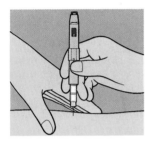

9 Stretch flat an area of clean skin and quickly push the needle in as far as it will go.

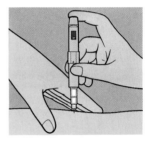

10 Depress the push button with your forefinger and wait for 2 seconds before withdrawing the needle straight out of the skin.

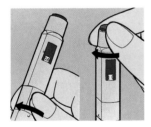

11 After giving yourself an injection always return the locking ring to the unlocked position. The dosage selector may either be returned to zero so that you are ready for your next injection, or may be left in position as a reminder of the last dose taken.

12 After the injection replace the plastic outer cap on the NovoPen needle, unscrew and discard the needle carefully and replace the NovoPen cap securely.

The NovoPen and Penfill cartridges should not be exposed to extremes of temperature, e.g. do not store your NovoPen in the refrigerator and do not leave it in the car in summer or winter.

Plate 5 BLOOD GLUCOSE MONITORING USING

1 Wash your hands and dry them thoroughly. Remove the test strip from the tube and place it on a clean, dry surface. Replace cap on the tube.

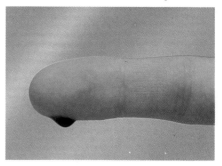

2 Take a sterile lancet and prick the side of a fingertip. Gently squeeze the finger and obtain a large suspended drop of blood.

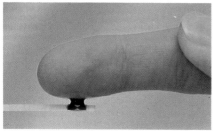

3 Apply blood to cover both test pads but do not allow skin to touch test pads. Be careful not to spread or smear the blood, and time for exactly 60 seconds.

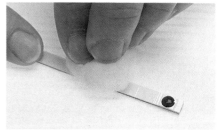

4 Hold the strip against a clean flat surface and wipe away blood with fresh cotton wool. Wipe twice more with clean area of cotton wool, and time exactly for another 60 seconds.

5 Compare the strip with colour blocks on tube. (The colours remain stable for ample reading or checking time.) If *upper* pad remains a buff colour the blood glucose level is below 9 mmol/l. Compare *lower* (blue) pad with lower blue colour block on the tube to read your blood glucose level. Record the result in your record book.

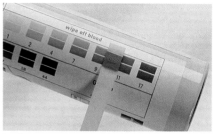

6. If *upper* pad changes to green, the blood glucose level is above 9 mmol/l. You should therefore compare the upper (green) pad with the upper (green) colour block on the tube to read the blood glucose level. Record the result in your record book.

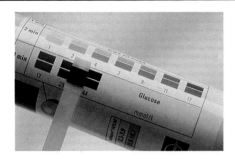

(a)   (b) and (c)

7 N.B. If result is above 17 mmol/l after 2 minutes, the reaction is not complete. Wait for a further 60 seconds and read again using only the upper (dark green) colour block on the tube. Record the result in your record book.

8 Good technique is vital.
(a) The proper drop size: ideally the drop of blood should *completely cover* both test pads.
(b) *Inadequate wiping away of blood* will leave blood stains on test pads, and make reading impossible.
(c) *Smearing* the blood: this will produce uneven colours and unreliable results.

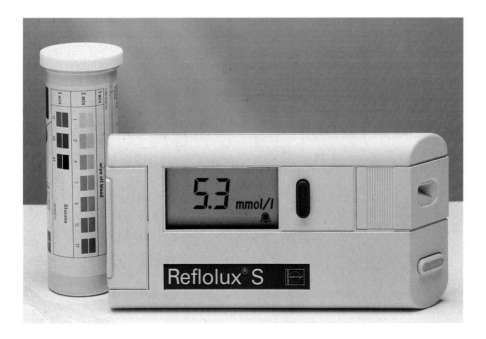

9 BM Test 1-44 may be read visually or by the Reflolux S blood glucose meter. This has a built-in timer, a digital read-out, and a memory for recalling previous blood test results.

Plate 6 BLOOD GLUCOSE MONITORING USING

Wash your hands and dry them thoroughly. Remove the test strip from the tube and then replace the cap.

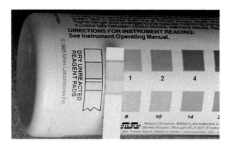

1 The unused strip should match the negative colour block on the side of the tube.

2 Take a sterile lancet and prick the side of a fingertip.

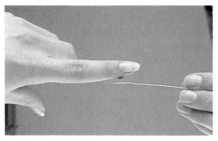

3 Gently squeeze the finger and obtain a large suspended drop of blood.

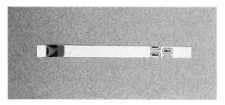

4 Apply blood to cover both test pads but do not allow skin to touch test pads. Start timing.

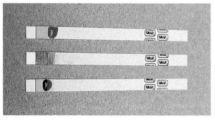

5 Good technique is vital.
Poor blood coverage: blood must completely cover both test pads. Do not smear blood on pads.

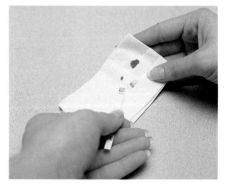

6 After exactly 30 seconds remove blood by doubling over an absorbent tissue and blotting firmly for 1-2 seconds (pads up).

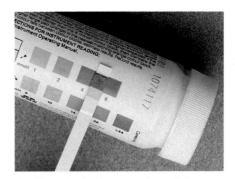

7. Poor blot (too much blood remaining).

Good blot (some blood will remain at edge).

8 After a further 90 seconds read the green pad by holding it against the colour scale on the side of the tube. If green pad is equal to or lighter than 6 mmol/l, ignore any slight orange colour which may develop. If green pad is darker than 6 mmol/l compare orange pad to nearest matching colour. Record the result in your record book.

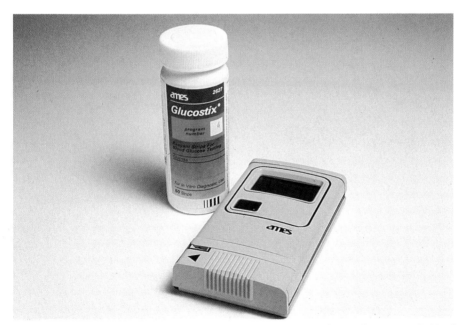

9 Glucostix may be read visually or by using the Glucometer GX or Glucometer II blood glucose meters both of which have a built-in timer, digital read-out and memory for recalling previous blood test results.

Plate 7 BLOOD GLUCOSE MONITORING USING EXACTECH

1 Wash your hands and thoroughly dry them. Remove part of the foil package to expose the end of the test strip with the silver bars. Insert the end into the sensor until it is secure. Give the packaging a quarter turn and remove it from the strip. Do not touch the target area at the end of the strip.

2 Take a sterile lancet and prick the side of your fingertip. Gently squeeze the finger and obtain a large suspended drop of blood.

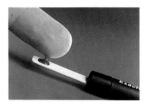

3 Collect a suspended drop of blood and place it on the test strip. The blood drop will naturally spread over the target area on contact.

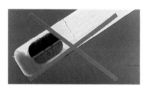

4 As soon as the drop of blood touches the target area, press the button. The sensor counts down from 30 to 1. The blood glucose result will now appear in the display window. Record this result in your record book.

5 Good technique is vital.
The proper drop size: the blood should form a small dome that completely covers the target area.

6 Smearing the blood: a thin covering wiped over the target or outside the target will give you incorrect results.

7 Not enough blood: the drop of blood must completely cover both halves.

8 Too much blood: the drop of blood should stay within the perimeter of the target area.

Of course diabetics can sunbathe. Lying around doing nothing may put your blood glucose up a little, especially if you overeat as most people do on holiday. So keep up your usual tests and you may need extra insulin. On the other hand, increasing the temperature of the skin may speed up the absorption of the insulin and can precipitate hypos, so be prepared for changes.

13 *Is vaccination more necessary in diabetics going abroad than non-diabetics?*

Diabetics are no more or less likely to contract illnesses abroad but if they do become ill the consequences could be more serious. Diabetics should have exactly the same vaccinations as anyone else. In addition to the necessary vaccinations it is very important to take protective tablets against malaria if you are going to a tropical area where this disease is found. More cases of this potentially serious disease are being seen in this country, usually in travellers recently returned from Africa or the East.

14 *I am going to work in the Middle East for 6 months. What can I do if my insulin is not available in the country where I am working?*

If you are only working abroad for 6 months it should be quite easy to export with you enough insulin to last you this length of time. Kept in an ordinary fridge it should keep – but make sure you are not supplied with insulin which is near the end of its shelf life. The expiry date is printed on each box of insulin.

Most types of insulin are available in the Middle East but you may have to make do with a different brand name or even insulin from a different animal (pig, cow or human).

Strict Muslim countries regard pork and products from the pig as 'unclean' and porcine insulin may be hard to obtain in these countries. We have heard of customs officials in Saudi Arabia confiscating supplies of porcine insulin. To avoid this awkward situation it would be worth changing to human insulin before you try to enter such a country. The change may affect your diabetic control, and you should therefore make it in good time to allow yourself to stabilise before travelling. U100 insulin may be difficult to obtain outside the UK, Australia, New Zealand, South Africa and parts of the Far East. Many European countries only stock insulin in 40 units/ml and special syringes for use with U40 insulin will have to be obtained.

15 *My husband has just been offered an excellent post in Uruguay which he would love to accept. He is worried about my diabetes there and especially about the availability of my insulin. Can you let me know if my insulin can be sent by post?*

It should be possible to obtain an equivalent type of insulin to your own in most parts of the world. If you are keen to keep up your normal supplies, Hypoguard Ltd are prepared to despatch syringes and equipment for testing blood and urine to all parts of the world. Unfortunately Hypoguard are not able to handle insulin. You might be able to make arrangements with a high street chemist who would be prepared to send insulin by post. Alternatively the Diabetes Care Department of the BDA can supply names of chemists who are prepared to send insulin abroad.

16 *My friends and I are going to Spain to work next year. One of my friends and I are diabetics. Can you tell me what I should take with me and whether I would have to pay if I needed to see a doctor?*

Before you go abroad prepare yourself well – take spares of everything such as syringes, insulin, testing equipment and keep spare supplies separate from the main supply in case your luggage is lost.

Medical attention is free in all EC countries although you should obtain certificate number Elll obtainable from your local Social Security office. For countries outside the EC you should insure your health before you go. The Diabetes Care Department of the British Diabetic Association can help with this.

17 *I am a diabetic on insulin and need to fly to the USA. How do I cope with the changing time zones?*

Flying from east to west (or vice versa) can be a bit confusing at the best of times and makes it difficult to know which meal you are eating. Here are some typical schedules for travelling from London to the East and West Coasts of the USA plus the return trip.

1 London – New York

Get up as normal and have your usual dose of insulin and breakfast. The departure for New York is usually around 12.00 noon so have a good snack before boarding the plane. During the flight you will be served lunch and an afternoon snack. You will arrive at about 2.00 p.m. local time but your body thinks it is 7.00 p.m. Eat soon after arrival with your normal evening dose of insulin. If you then go to bed at 10.00 p.m. local time (3.00 in the morning to you) you will need a small dose of long-acting insulin before a well-earned sleep.

2 New York – London

The problem here is that the flights are usually in the evening and the night seems to be very short. Assuming that you are going to try and sleep on the plane, you should reduce your evening dose of insulin by one-third and have this at about 6.00 p.m. New York time followed by a reasonable meal. After take off at 8.00 p.m. you should be served with a meal and should then sleep. You will arrive at London at about 7.30 a.m. local time although it will feel to you like 2.00 a.m. Most people have another journey followed by a good meal and then a sleep. You should have a dose of long-acting insulin before this sleep and try and get back into phase by the evening (local time).

3 London – Los Angeles

This is an 11 hour flight usually leaving around midday and arriving on the West Coast at 3.30 p.m. local time which feels to you like 11.30 p.m. During this long flight you will have to have an injection of insulin on the plane and this is best if taken before dinner served at 6.00 p.m. London time. It would be safest to give half your normal evening dose as short-acting insulin and then try and sleep.

On arrival at the other side you will need to travel to your destination and will probably have an evening meal at what will feel to you like the early hours of the morning. A small dose of long-acting insulin before this meal would cover your subsequent sleep.

4 Los Angeles – London
Leave 6.30 p.m. and after a 10 hour flight you will arrive in London just after midday local time which will feel to you like 2.00 a.m. Meals on this flight are usually served about an hour after take off and an hour before landing, in the hope that you have a good sleep between these two meals. One way round this arrangement would be to have a dose of insulin immediately before the first meal, giving normal dose of short-acting insulin and half the normal dose of long-acting insulin. Immediately before the second meal you could have a small dose of short-acting insulin alone. This should last you through until the normal evening meal at your destination which would be preceded by a routine evening insulin dose.

When travelling keep to the following rules:
a Do not aim at perfect diabetic control. You have to be flexible especially on international flights. A hypo whilst travelling can be very inconvenient.
b Be prepared to check your blood glucose if you are at all worried and not sure how much insulin you need.
c In general, airlines are prepared to make special allowances for diabetics and cabin crew will do their best to help. Airlines say that they like to be warned in advance but in practice this should not be necessary.

Work

18 Can I undertake employment involving shift work?

Yes, certainly. Many diabetics combine shift work with good control of their blood glucose. Shift work however does need a little extra care as most insulin regimens are designed round a 24 hour day. Shift workers usually complain that they are just settling into one routine when everything changes and they have to start again. It is hard to generalise about shift work as there are so many different patterns but if you follow these rules things should work out all right:

a Aim at an injection of short and medium acting insulin every 12 to 16 hours.

b Try to eat a good meal after each injection.

c Eat your normal snacks between meals every 3 hours or so, unless you are asleep.

d If there is a gap of 6-8 hours when you are changing from one shift to another, have some short-acting insulin on its own followed by a meal.

e Because the pattern of insulin and food is constantly changing shift workers have to do more blood glucose measurements than normal as they cannot assume that one day is very much like another.

f If the blood glucose results are not good be prepared to make changes in your dose of insulin. Soon you will know more about your diabetes than anyone else.

19 How can I cope with my diabetes if I work irregular hours as a sales rep?

Just as with shift work many diabetics manage to combine an irregular lifestyle with good diabetic control. Of course if you have had an injection of insulin in the morning and normally have a fairly low blood glucose before lunch, then you will go hypo unless you eat at the right time. So a well controlled diabetic cannot afford the luxury of missing meals completely. However it is always possible to have a few biscuits or even a sweet drink if you are getting past your normal time of eating. The occupational hazard of all sales reps, diabetic or otherwise, is the mileage they clock up each year on the roads. The dangers of hypoglycaemia while driving cannot be over-emphasised and there is really no excuse for this now that instant blood glucose measurement is available. Remember (i) if driving before a meal, check your blood glucose; (ii) if it is low eat before driving; (iii) carry food in your car and have some immediately if you feel warning of a hypo. Many people who lead an erratic lifestyle find that the NovoPen regimen gives them the freedom they require (p. 53).

20 *Should I warn fellow employees that I might be subject to hypos?*

Definitely. Hypos unfortunately can happen, especially when a person first starts using insulin. Warn your workmates that if they find you acting in a peculiar way they must get you to take some sugar. Warn them also that you may not be very co-operative at the time and may even resist their attempts to help you. Some people find it difficult to admit to their colleagues that they have diabetes. But if you keep it a secret you run the risk of causing a scare by having a bad hypo and being taken to hospital by ambulance for treatment. A needless trip to hospital should be avoided.

21 *My husband's hours of work can be very erratic. Sometimes he only gets 3 or 4 hours sleep instead of his normal 8 hours. Can you tell me what effect lack of sleep has on diabetes?*

Lack of sleep in itself will not affect diabetes although if your husband is under great pressure and the adrenaline is running very high, his blood glucose may be affected. The real problem with working under a strain is the tendency to ignore diabetes completely and assume that it will look after itself. Unfortunately a few minutes of each day has to be spent checking blood glucose, eating a snack or giving insulin. These minutes are well spent.

22 *I became diabetic 5 months ago, 1 week after I had started a new job. I am coming to the end of my 6 month probation period and have been given 2 weeks' notice because of my diabetes. They said I could not do shift work because of my diabetes. Could you help?*

This is a sad story and a good example of ignorant prejudice against diabetics. Of course, there are many diabetics on shift work who maintain good control – although it does require a bit of extra thought. There is no way you can force your employer to keep you on, but you should ask your clinic doctor to get in touch with him, on your behalf. The BDA will also be prepared to write in your support.

23 I am a public house manager and a diabetic for the past 19 years but my employers are now making me redundant. Apparently, their insurers cannot accept me for a permanent position owing to my diabetes. Who can help strengthen my case?

We know of several publicans with diabetes who run good pubs and still keep their diabetes under good control. However, people who work in licensed premises are at greater risk of drinking more alcohol than average and heavy drinkers are in danger from hypos (p. 129). We wonder if you have been having a large number of hypos which has made it difficult to continue in your present occupation. Ask your clinic doctor and the BDA to lobby on your behalf.

24 I have been refused a job with a large company because of my diabetes. Have I sufficient grounds to take proceedings against them for discrimination?

Unfortunately there is no legislation to prevent prejudice against diabetics, so we do not think you would get anywhere by taking the company to court. We know this sort of discrimination does sometimes happen, especially in large organisations, although, of course, it is very difficult to prove. It is hard to know how to overcome this sort of unspoken bias against diabetics.

It is the responsibility of diabetics who are at work to realise that they are, to some extent, on show. If they work well and have no time off for minor complaints, then the next diabetic who applies to the same firm will be looked on kindly and probably be taken on. On the other hand, someone who is constantly having hypos and missing work will give all diabetics a bad name.

The BDA have had discussions with medical officers responsible for the occupational health in large organisations such as London Transport, British Coal, British Rail, and many other organisations. These have resulted in an employment handbook which is circulated to diabetes clinics.

Other illnesses

*25 I have recently had a severe cough and cold and have
been given medication suitable for diabetics by the doctor.
Although I do not feel that my blood glucose is high,
my urine tests have been 2% or more. Could this be due
to the medication?*

This is a good example of the effect that any infection or
serious illness has on diabetes – it nearly always causes a
rise in blood glucose. Unfortunately diabetics often do not
start to feel unwell until the glucose reaches danger level.
Diabetics on insulin usually need more insulin when they
are ill and yet they are sometimes advised to stop insulin
completely if they do not feel like eating. This advice can
be fatal. The rules when you are ill are:

a test blood/urine frequently;
b if tests are high take extra doses of short-acting insulin;
c never stop insulin.

It is of course possible to get over a bad cold by carrying
on with your normal dose of insulin and accepting bad control
for a few days. However this means that your mouth and
nose will be slightly dehydrated and it will take a few extra
days before you feel back to normal. So you probably get
better more quickly if you adjust your insulin and try to
keep the blood glucose near normal.

Antibiotic syrup and cough linctus are often blamed for
making diabetes worse during an illness such as flu or chest
infection. In fact a dose of antibiotic syrup only contains
about 5 g of sugar and is not going to make any real
difference. It is the illness itself which unbalances the
diabetes. In general, medication from your doctor will not
upset your diabetes. One antibiotic (Keflex) may cause a
muddy colour of the urine which can be confusing.

*26 I have noticed that my son suffers from more colds since
becoming diabetic. Could this be due to his diabetes?*

Many parents make this observation but there is no real
reason why the common cold should be more common in
diabetes. However a relatively minor cold may upset the

diabetic control and lead to several days of illness (see previous answer). This may make it a more memorable event. To repeat the previous advice, *never* stop insulin.

27   *My daughter keeps getting infections and has been rushed to hospital on several occasions with high ketones requiring a drip. How can I prevent these infections? Will vitamins help?*

It sounds as though your daughter is a so-called 'brittle' diabetic and this must be very alarming for you. There are really two types of brittle diabetics. The first type are those who are really very well controlled and can prove this by frequent blood glucose measurements below 7 mmol/l and a normal HbA$_1$ but who quickly become very ill and 'sugary' at the first sniff of a cold or the beginning of an infection. The other sort are those who are normally poorly controlled with blood glucose results all over the place and who therefore have no leeway when they become ill. In the case of the first type it should be possible to increase the dose of insulin rapidly giving extra doses every few hours depending on the blood glucose. The second type are more of a problem as it is the overall control which needs to be improved and this can be very difficult (p. 104). Of course if an infection (e.g. cystitis) starts off the trouble then this must be treated immediately with antibiotics.

Provided your daughter has a reasonable diet, vitamins will not help.

28   *My 6-year-old daughter who is insulin dependent is troubled with frequent vomiting which occurs suddenly. She has ended up in hospital on several occasions as she becomes dehydrated. What can I do to avoid this?*

Vomiting in a young diabetic child has to be taken seriously and the hospital admissions are probably necessary to put fluid back into your daughter by means of a drip. She sounds like another brittle diabetic and the previous answer applies. As she gets older these attacks of sickness will improve.

29   *What is the best treatment for a diabetic suffering from hay fever? I understand that some products can cause*

drowsiness which could affect my balance and so be confused with a hypo.

Diabetics may receive the same treatment for hay fever as non-diabetics as this does not affect diabetic control. Antihistamines are often used and these may make people feel sleepy but this should be easy to distinguish from a hypo. Remember that people on antihistamines should take alcohol with great caution. Hay fever can also be alleviated by sniffing capsules which reduce the sensitivity of the membranes in the nose.

30   *I have just been in hospital with anaphylactic shock from a bee sting. I am a diabetic controlled with tablets and wondered if this had anything to do with the severity of my reaction?*

There is no connection between diabetes and allergy to bees.

31   *What is the effect of other illnesses on diabetes? Is my diabetic son likely to suffer more illness than other children of his age?*

Illnesses usually make diabetes worse in the sense that people on insulin need to increase the dose to keep blood glucose controlled. Diabetics on tablets or diet alone often find that a bad cold will upset diabetic control. In the case of a prolonged illness or one needing hospital admission a non-insulin dependent diabetic may need to have insulin injections for a time.

Diabetes itself does not necessarily make people prone to other illnesses. In fact a survey in a large American company reveals that diabetics had no more absences from work than non-diabetics. Most diabetic children grow up without any more illness than their non-diabetic friends.

32   *Since I was diagnosed diabetic I have been very depressed. Is there any link between these two conditions?*

People vary very greatly in their mental response to becoming diabetic. Some lucky ones take to their new condition easily, while others, like yourself, find the whole thing very depressing. The depression seems to take two forms – firstly, shock and even anger at the very onset coupled with fear of injections and of the unspoken fear of complications. A few weeks later comes the depressing realisation that diabetes is for life, and not just a temporary disease that can be 'cured'. This type of depression seems to affect young people who are worried and are feeling insecure about the future.

A few people with diabetes feel that, in some way, they are imperfect, especially if they have previously been fitness fanatics. The best way round this feeling of inadequacy is to throw yourself into sporting activities with extra enthusiasm. Exercise is good for us all and diabetics have managed to reach the top in most forms of sport from ocean racing to international football.

If you treat your diabetes in a positive way rather than letting the condition control you, the depression will gradually lift.

33 *How does stress and worry affect diabetes? I spend many hours studying and find that, if I study too long, I feel weak and my urine tests show negative. Are there any side effects to pressure which may affect my diabetes?*

In general, stress and worry tend to increase the blood sugar. A Scottish student told us that in the run up to her final examination, she had to *double* her insulin dose to keep perfect blood glucose control, even though she did not appear to be particularly anxious to her friends. Stress causes a release of adrenaline and other hormones which antagonise the effect of insulin.

During periods of stress it may be difficult to keep to strict meal times, so you could be going hypo. You need to check your blood sugar and if it is not below normal, then you are simply experiencing the tiredness we all feel after studying hard. Don't blame it on your diabetes but have an evening off from your studies.

Hospital operations

34 *Recently when I was in hospital to have my appendix removed, I was put on a 'sliding scale'. Please could you*

explain this, especially as it might save other people in a similar position from worrying?

We agree that the expression 'sliding scale' does sound rather alarming – but it is nothing to worry about. During and after an operation it can be difficult to predict exactly how much insulin a diabetic will need. The way round this is to use a 'sliding scale' so that more insulin is given if the glucose in the blood is high. In the past, a urine test would be done every 4 hours and a certain dose of insulin would then be given depending on the result of the test. Nowadays, during an operation, insulin is often given straight into a vein using a slow infusion pump. Many surgical wards have machines for measuring blood glucose and by doing this every hour the dose of insulin can be adjusted according to the result. In this way, diabetic control can be carefully regulated throughout the operation and until the patient is eating again. At this stage the insulin may be given by three or four injections a day, the dose given at each injection being determined from the blood glucose level according to the 'sliding scale'.

35   Are there any problems with surgery for the diabetic child?

Surgical operations on children usually involve a general anaesthetic and it is advisable to have nothing to eat or drink (nil by mouth) for 6 hours before the anaesthetic is given. Any difficulties caused by this period of fasting can be overcome by a glucose drip into the vein. The normal insulin injection is not given on the day of operation but small regular doses are either injected under the skin or pumped continuously into the vein. The dose of insulin is adjusted according to the blood glucose level.

In minor operations where the patient is expected to be eating an hour or so later, these elaborate procedures may not be necessary and insulin may simply be delayed until the next meal is due. If an emergency operation is necessary it is important that the doctors know that the patient is diabetic. This is another good reason for wearing an identification bracelet or necklace.

36 Must I tell my dentist I am a diabetic and will this affect my treatment in any way?

Being a diabetic will not affect your dental treatment at all. However, it is important to remove all possibility of a hypo while in the dentist's chair. If you are on insulin, warn your dentist that you cannot run over a snack or mealtime. It is less embarrassing to mention this before the start of a session than to have to munch Dextrosol while the dentist is trying to administer treatment.

Obviously you must warn the dentist if he plans to give you any form of heavy sedation. If a diabetic on insulin is to have dental treatment needing a general anaesthetic this is usually done in hospital.

37 Is a diabetic more likely to suffer from tooth decay or gum trouble?

There is an increased risk of infection in diabetics who are poorly controlled. The gums may become infected and this in turn may lead to tooth decay. However, a well controlled diabetic is not prone to any particular dental problem – in fact, there is a positive advantage to avoiding sweets which cause dental caries.

Driving

38 I drive a lot in my work and lunchtime varies from day to day. Does this matter? I am on two injections of insulin a day.

Yes, this can be a bit of a problem. The twice-daily insulin regimen is designed to provide a boost of insulin at midday to cope with the lunchtime intake of food. Once the early morning injection of insulin has been given, there is no way of delaying the midday surge. It is very common for people who are well controlled on two injections a day to feel a little hypo before lunch.

There are two solutions to your problem.
1 Eat some biscuits or fruit while you are driving – only do this in emergencies as you will not know how much

to have for lunch when you do get the chance to eat
properly.

2 Change your insulin regimen so that you have a small
   dose of short-acting insulin before each main meal and
   only have long-acting insulin in the evening to keep your
   diabetes under control during the night. You would still
   have to eat snacks between meals but the three- or
   four-injection method should make the timing of meals
   more flexible. With the new plastic syringes or insulin
   pens an extra injection is really no hardship.

*39 If I am taking insulin do I have to declare this when
     applying for a driving licence? If so am I likely to be
     required to provide evidence as to fitness to drive?*

Anyone with diabetes, whether needing insulin or not, must
declare this when applying for a driving licence. Having
declared that you are diabetic, the DVLC (Driving and Vehicle
Licensing Centre) will send you a form asking for details
about your diabetes and the names of any doctors you see
regularly. The DVLC also ask you to sign a declaration
allowing your doctors to disclose medical details about your
condition. There is usually no difficulty over a diabetic
obtaining a licence to drive. This will be valid for 3 years
only instead of up to the age of 70, which it is for most
people in the UK. It is, of course, the risk of sudden and
severe hypoglycaemia which makes diabetics liable to this
form of discrimination. In general the only people who have
difficulty in obtaining a 3 year licence are those on insulin
with very erratic control and a history of hypos causing
unconsciousness. Once the condition has been controlled and
severe hypos abolished, the diabetic may reapply for a licence
with confidence.

    The following statement (or a version of it) appears on
every driving licence: 'You are required by law to inform
the Drivers Medical Branch DVLC Swansea at once if you
have any disability (includes any physical or mental
condition), which is or may become likely to affect your
fitness as a driver, unless you do not expect it to last for
more than 3 months'. This includes diabetes or any change
in treatment, e.g. tablets to insulin. It is important to carry

out these instructions, as a diabetic who drives a car without informing the DVLC may find that his licence is invalid in the eyes of the law. Diabetics on insulin are not generally allowed to hold PSV or HGV licences.

40 As a new diabetic I have had to have a form signed by my doctor for my insurance company to insure my car. The doctor charged me £5 for this service and pocketed the fee without even giving me a receipt. Is this normal?

Motor insurance is another problem for the driver with diabetes. Failure to inform your insurance company of your diabetes may make your cover invalid in which case the consequences could be disastrous. The insurance company usually asks your doctor to complete a form. These forms vary but some of them are very long and ask a lot of irritating and irrelevant questions. Unfortunately there is a charge since doctors are not obliged to sign these forms and are therefore entitled to a fee, just as you are entitled to a receipt. You will probably find that doctors at the hospital clinic will fill in the form for nothing.

Unfortunately there may be financial penalties for being a diabetic and some insurance companies will load your premium. There is a wide variation from one company to another and it is worth shopping around for the best buy. The British Diabetic Association can also advise on insurance.

41 I have heard that a diabetic driver who had a motor accident while hypo was successfully prosecuted for driving under the influence of drugs and heavily fined. As a diabetic on insulin I was horrified to hear this verdict.

Several diabetics on insulin have been charged with this offence after a hypo at the wheel when the only 'drug' that they have used is insulin. It may seem very unfair but for any victim of the accident, it is no consolation that the person responsible was hypo rather than being blind drunk. These cases emphasise the importance of taking driving seriously. Remember the rules:

a always carry food/glucose in your car;

b if you feel at all hypo, stop your car and take some glucose;

c preferably check that your blood sugar is above 5 mmol/l
before driving again.

*42 I have been a bus driver for 15 years and was found
to have diabetes 5 years ago. Up till now I have been
on tablets but may need to go on to insulin. Does this
mean I will lose my job?*

As a bus driver you will hold a PSV (Public Service Vehicle)
licence. Diabetics on insulin are encouraged not to drive a
PSV. You are faced with a very difficult choice – either to
continue on tablets feeling unwell but holding down your
job, or else to start insulin and feel much better, but lose
your source of employment. We would have to advise you
to go on to insulin as you will probably come to this
eventually. Under certain circumstances the local authority
may allow people with stable control on insulin to hold a
PSV licence.

Any holder of an HGV (Heavy Goods Vehicle) licence may
also lose his licence and thus his livelihood if he has to
start insulin treatment. In certain circumstances he may be
able to regain it once his treatment has stabilised. Diabetic
HGV drivers who have already been on insulin for a number
of years *may* keep their licences provided they can prove
that their diabetic control is good and they are not subject
to hypos. The question of HGV licences is under review and
at present a number of cases are going through the courts.

*43 I recently read a newspaper article which implied that
diabetics who are breathalysed can produce a positive
reading even though they have not been drinking alcohol.
What does this mean?*

Diabetes has no effect on breathalyser tests for alcohol even
if acetone is present on the breath. However, the Lion
Alcolmeter widely used by the police does also measure
ketones, though this does not interfere with the alcohol
measurement. Anyone breathalysed by the police may also
be told that they have ketones and that they should consult
their own doctor. These ketones may be caused either by
diabetes which is out of control or by a long period of fasting.

Alcohol

*44   My husband likes a pint of beer in the evening. He has
    now been found to be diabetic and has to stick to a diet.
    Does this mean he will have to give up drinking beer?*

No. He can still drink beer but if he is trying to lose weight
he will need to reduce his overall calorie intake and
unfortunately all alcohol contains calories. There are about
180 calories in a pint of beer and this is equivalent to a
large bread roll. Special diabetic lager contains less
carbohydrate but more alcohol so in the end it contains the
same number of calories, with the drawback of being more
expensive and more potent. So your husband is probably
better off drinking ordinary beer, but if he is on the fat
side he will have to restrict the amount he drinks (p. 25).

*45   My teenage son has been diabetic since the age of seven.
    He is now beginning to show interest in going out with
    his friends in the evening. What advice can you give him
    about alcohol?*

Most diabetics drink alcohol and it is perfectly safe for them
to do so. However, if your son is on insulin he must be
aware of certain problems that alcohol can cause diabetics
– in particular alcohol can make hypos more serious. When
someone goes hypo a number of hormones are produced which
make the liver release glucose into the bloodstream. If that
person has drunk some alcohol, even as little as 2 pints of
beer, or a double gin, the liver will not be able to release
glucose and hypos will be more sudden and more severe. In
practice most alcoholic drinks also contain some carbohydrate
which tends to *increase* the glucose in the blood. So the
overall effect of a particular alcoholic drink depends on the
proportions of alcohol to carbohydrate. For instance lemonade
shandy (high carbohydrate/low alcohol) will have a different
effect on blood glucose from gin and slimline tonic (low
carbohydrate/high alcohol). Your son may notice that diabetic
lager is more likely than ordinary beer to cause a hypo
because it contains less carbohydrate but more alcohol.

   If he has been drinking in the evening his blood sugar
may drop in the early hours of the morning. To counteract

this it is sensible to eat a sandwich, a bowl of cereal or some similar long-acting carbohydrate before going to bed.

The best way for your son to discover how a certain alcoholic drink affects *him* is to do an experiment. He could stay at home one evening with a supply of his favourite drink and by measuring the blood glucose every hour would actually discover how different quantities of drink affected him. Someone else could also stay at home to do the blood tests for him. The experiment would provide useful information and could prevent an awkward experience later on. Diabetics are sometimes accused of being drunk when really they have become hypo after a modest amount of alcohol.

46 *I believe it is dangerous to drink alcohol when taking certain tablets. Does this apply to tablets used in diabetes?*

In general the answer is no. Some people on chlorpropamide (Diabenese) experience an odd flushing sensation when they drink alcohol but those patients can easily be changed to an equivalent tablet (e.g. glibenclamide) which does not cause this problem. The other consideration is that alcohol may alter the response to a hypo (see previous answer) and most tablets used for diabetes can cause hypos. If a patient on tablets is going to drink any alcohol he must be extra careful not to go hypo.

Drugs

47 *Is it true that diabetics taking vitamin C can get false results from Clinitest or Clinistix?*

Vitamin C is needed by the body in very small quantities and any excess is eliminated in the urine. Vitamin C may, in theory, react with Clinitest which is a test for reducing substances like glucose and Vitamin C. In practice, people can take large amounts of Vitamin C (up to 1 g a day) without affecting the Clinitest result. Clinistix is a specific test for glucose and will not be altered by vitamin C. The same applies to all blood testing strips.

48 Could the toxic affect of diazepam, Parstelin or Lentisol cause damage to the pancreas and, as a result, cause diabetes?

You mention examples from the three main groups of drugs used to treat depression and anxiety. None of these is known to have any affect on the pancreas or to be related in any way to diabetes.

49 My son was told that diabetics should not use Betnovate cream because it contains steroids. Is this true and why?

Most skin specialists avoid using powerful steroid creams such as Betnovate unless there is a serious skin condition. Very often a weak steroid preparation or some bland ointment is just as effective in clearing up mild patches of eczema and other rashes. Unfortunately, the very strong steroids are often used first, instead of as a last resort. The strong steroids can be absorbed into the body through the skin and lead to a number of unwanted side-effects. This advice applies to all people with skin problems and not just diabetics. One of the side-effects of steroids is to cause a rise in the blood glucose level. Thus, a non-diabetic may develop diabetes while taking steroids and a diabetic treated with diet may need to go onto tablets or insulin.

If there are good medical reasons for a diabetic to take steroids, in whatever form, he should be prepared to test his urine or blood for signs of poor control. If already taking insulin, the dose may need to be increased.

50 Can you tell me if any vaccinations including BCG are dangerous in a diabetic?

There is no reason why a diabetic child should not have full immunisation against the usual diseases. Sometimes the inoculation is followed by a mild flu-like illness which may lead to a slight upset of diabetic control. This is no reason to avoid protecting your child against measles, whooping cough and the rest. In some areas school children are given BCG as a protection against tuberculosis.

Diabetics should also have the normal immunisation procedures if they are travelling to exotic places.

*51   I understand that aspirin lowers the blood sugar. Should
      I avoid taking it?*

Large doses of aspirin given to diabetics not taking insulin
may have a small effect in lowering blood glucose but in
practice this does not cause any problem from hypoglycaemia.
It has no effect on the blood glucose of insulin-treated
patients. Aspirin can also cause indigestion and irritation of
the stomach lining but this is not a particular risk for
diabetics who may take aspirin and any other pain-killer in
the same way as non-diabetics.

*52   My wife suffers from bad indigestion. She is afraid to
      take indigestion tablets in case they upset her diabetes.
      Can you advise her what to do?*

Indigestion tablets and medicines do not upset diabetes.

53   Is it safe to take water tablets (diuretics) if one is diabetic?

Diuretics are given to people who are retaining too much
fluid in their body. This may happen in heart failure and
cause swelling of the ankles or shortness of breath. Diuretics
are usually very effective but, as a side-effect, they may
cause a slight increase in the blood glucose. This is especially
true of the milder diuretics such as Navidrex, which belong
to the thiazide group. The increase in sugar is only slight
but can sometimes mean that a patient controlled on diet
alone may need to take tablets. Diabetics already on insulin
are not affected by diuretics. The thiazide group of tablets
is also used in the treatment of raised blood pressure.

*54   Can you tell me if hormone replacement therapy is suitable
      for diabetics?*

Hormone replacement therapy is given to women who are
suffering unpleasant symptoms, usually hot flushes around
the time of the menopause. Hormone replacement therapy
is not usually given to people with certain conditions such
as strokes, thrombosis, high blood pressure, liver disease or
gall-stones. This form of treatment may have a slight
worsening effect on diabetes similar to the pill (p. 146 and
p. 150). Some doctors are reluctant to use these hormones

in any patient and may use diabetes as an excuse for not prescribing them. However, small doses of female hormones can cause dramatic relief of severe menopausal symptoms and there is no reason why diabetics should not benefit from them provided there is no history of strokes, thrombosis, etc.

55 Is there any special cough mixture for diabetics?

Yes. Various sugar-free cough mixtures (e.g. Dia-Tuss) which can be prescribed by your doctor. However, there are only a few grams of sugar in a dose of ordinary cough mixture and this amount is not going to have any appreciable effect on the level of blood glucose. So you can give ordinary cough mixtures in moderate amounts to a diabetic child.

56 I have been on insulin for diabetes for 7 years. I was recently found to have raised blood pressure and was given tablets, called beta-blockers, by my doctor. Since then I have had a bad hypo in which I collapsed without the normal warning signs of sweating, shaking, etc. Could the blood pressure tablets have caused this severe hypo?

Beta-blockers are widely used for the treatment of high blood pressure and certain heart conditions. They have an 'anti-adrenaline' effect which sometimes damps down the normal 'adrenaline' response to a hypo (p. 55). Thus, the low blood sugar may prevent someone thinking clearly without the normal sweating and shaking that warns of an impending hypo. Some beta-blockers have been designed to have their effect only in the heart without blocking the general adrenaline reaction of the body. These are theoretically much safer for diabetics taking insulin.

If you are already taking beta-blockers and having no unexpected problems from hypos, then you should carry on without worry. If you are taking beta-blockers for the first time, you should be warned by your doctor that your reaction to a hypo may be blunted. If this problem does occur, your doctor should either try a different beta-blocker or some other type of treatment for blood pressure.

57 *Please could you give me a list of tablets or medicines which may interfere with my diabetes?*

The important medicines which affect diabetics have been dealt with in this section. There are no medicines which must *never* be used but the following *may* increase the blood glucose and upset diabetic control:

a Steroids (e.g. prednisolone, Betnovate ointment). Steroid inhalers (e.g. Becotide) should not have any ill effect.
b Thiazide diuretics (eg Navidrex, Neo-Naclex).
c The contraceptive pill.
d Hormone replacement therapy (Harmogen, Prempac, Trisequens, Progynova).
e Certain bronchodilators (e.g. Ventolin) may have a slight effect on raising the blood glucose.
   Aspirin in large doses may lower blood glucose. Beta-blockers (eg Inderal, Tenormin) may prevent diabetics on insulin from recognising a hypo (p. 55).

Smoking

58 *I am a 16-year-old diabetic on insulin. I would like to know whether smoking low tar cigarettes could interfere with my diabetes? Would it cause any restriction in my diet?*

Smoking is unhealthy not only because it causes cancer of the lung but because it leads to hardening of the arteries – affecting chiefly the heart, brain and legs. The proper advice to all diabetics, especially teenagers, is *not* to smoke. Smoking will not directly affect diabetic control except, perhaps, by reducing your appetite.

59 *When my doctor diagnosed diabetes, he told me to stop smoking. Could you tell me if there is a particular health hazard associated with smoking as a diabetic? The problem is made worse for me by the fact that I have to lose weight and if I stop smoking I will do just the opposite.*

Smoking is a danger, not only to the lungs but because of the risk of increased arterial disease affecting any smoker.

The long-standing diabetic is also at risk of problems with poor blood circulation. It is foolish to double the diabetic risk by continuing to smoke. If the discovery that you are diabetic has come as an unpleasant surprise, this is a good time to turn over a new leaf and alter your lifestyle, by eating less and giving up cigarettes. It may be a lot to ask, but many people manage to carry out this 'double'. It will not kill you – on the contrary, you may live longer.

60   Since my husband, who has been diabetic for 23 years, has stopped smoking, he has not had a negative urine test. Why?

Your husband should be congratulated for giving up smoking. Most people who give up smoking do put on weight, on average 4 kg (9 lb). Presumably, this is because cigarettes suppress the appetite and people feel the need of another form of oral gratification when they stop smoking. If your husband has put on weight this explains why his diabetes has gone out of control. If so, then he must reduce weight and his diabetes should improve. If he is already thin and his blood sugars are high then he will have to take tablets or insulin to get things under control.

Miscellaneous

61   Is there any objection to my donating blood? I am on two injections of soluble insulin a day and my general health is fine.

There is no obvious reason why a fit diabetic should not be a blood donor. However, the blood transfusion authorities do not accept blood from a diabetic on insulin. They suggest that the antibodies to insulin found in all diabetics having injections may, in some mysterious way, harm the recipient of the blood.

62   My mother has been diabetic for 12 years and is subject to crashing hypos for no reason. She needs someone to be with her all the time. Would we be eligible for an attendance allowance as she needs watching 24 hours a day?

If you have to provide a continuous watch over your mother then you would be able to apply for an attendance allowance. Before admitting defeat, however, it would be better to try every means to prevent the hypos. Presumably you mother is having insulin, though you do not mention the dose or type of insulin she takes. At a guess, she is having a large dose of lente insulin every morning. This method of giving insulin sometimes leads to severe hypos at unexpected times of the day or night. Changing to more frequent but smaller doses of insulin might solve the problem. You may have to spend a lot of time and energy getting to grips with your mother's diabetes. It would do more for her self-confidence to abolish the hypos than to get an attendance allowance.

63 *Since becoming diabetic I have found that my food bills have risen alarmingly. Are there any special allowances I can claim to offset the very high cost of the food?*

Most diabetics are not entitled to any special allowance and, indeed, there is no real need for them to eat different food from others. Special diabetic products are not necessary and if eaten at all should be treated as luxuries. Now that diabetics are encouraged to eat food that is high rather than low in carbohydrate, they do not have to fall back on expensive protein as a source of calories.

64 *To what Social Security benefits am I now entitled now that I am diabetic?*

There are no special benefits given automatically to diabetics. If you are looking after someone with diabetes who is receiving attendance allowance you may be able to claim invalid care allowance. You must be of working age and the person you look after must need care for not less than 35 hours per week. You may claim attendance allowance if you have a diabetic child between the ages of 2 and 12, if you receive renal dialysis, or if you are insulin dependent and also visually handicapped. This is a discretionary award which depends on the decision of a delegated medical practitioner. If you are not working you can claim income support. If you are granted income support you may then claim other benefits.

65 *My local youth group is holding a sponsored fast over a weekend. I am an insulin dependent diabetic – can I take part?*

It would be very difficult and perhaps dangerous for you to go without food and, even more important, drink for 48 hours. The problem is that even in the fasting state you need small amounts of insulin to prevent the blood sugar rising. Having taken insulin, you would then need food to prevent an over-shoot leading to a hypo. Anyone who goes without food for long periods produces ketones and these could be an additional hazard in a diabetic.

66 *Is it true that a diabetic should not use an electric blanket?*

It is perfectly safe for a diabetic to use an electric blanket although underblankets should only be used to warm up the bed in advance. The manufacturers recommend that underblankets should be switched off before getting into bed – tempting though it is to lie there toasting yourself.

Hot water bottles are rather more dangerous as the temperature is not controlled. Diabetics with a slight degree of nerve damage can fail to realise that a bottle full of very hot water may be burning the skin of their feet. This is a common cause of foot ulcers in diabetics. It is better to be safe than sorry and avoid the comfort of a hot water bottle.

67 *My daughter is 10 and has had diabetes for 3 months. She has started to lose a lot of hair and now has a bald patch. Is this connected with her diabetes?*

Yes, it could be. There are three ways in which diabetes and hair loss may be connected.

a If your child was very ill with ketoacidosis at the time of the diagnosis, this could lead to a heavy loss of hair. If this is the case, the hair will regrow over the next few months.

b Alopecia areata is a skin condition which is slightly more common in people with diabetes. This is the likely diagnosis if your daughter has a well-defined bald patch with the rest of the hair remaining a normal thickness. If the patch is on the top of the head there is every chance that the hair will regrow over the next 6 months. There is no way of encouraging growth and steroid ointments may even cause permanent skin changes and make matters worse.

c Myxoedema or lack of thyroid hormones may occur with diabetes. If this is the cause of your daughter's hair loss you will notice other symptoms such as mental slowing, weight increase and an inability to keep warm. All these symptoms can be corrected by taking thyroid tablets.

Shortage of body iron may also cause hair loss although this is not connected with diabetes.

68 *I recently enquired about having electrolysis treatment for excess hair. I was told that, as a diabetic, I would need a letter from my doctor stating that my diabetes did not encourage hair growth. Could I use wax hair removers instead?*

There is no objection to diabetics having electrolysis. Diabetes does not cause excessive hair growth. It sounds as though the firm doing the electrolysis is keen to turn away customers.

Many women find wax hair removers useful for the less sensitive parts of the body. Make sure that it is not too hot.

69 *Is it safe for diabetics to use sunbeds and saunas?*

As safe as for non-diabetics. Exposure to ultraviolet radiation is known to increase the risk of skin cancer.

Make sure you can recognise a hypo when you are hot and sweaty. Keep some means of treating a hypo with you – not with your clothes in the changing room.

70 *I would dearly love to have my ears pierced but when I asked my doctor about this, he said there was a chance that my ears would swell. Please could you advise me if there is a great risk of this happening?*

Anyone who has their ears pierced runs a small risk of infection until the wound heals completely. The risk in a well controlled diabetic is no higher than normal. If the ear does become red, swollen and painful, you will need an antibiotic.

71 *Is there any connection between vertigo and diabetes? I have been diabetic for $2^1/_2$ years controlled on diet alone.*

Vertigo, in the strict medical sense, describes that awful feeling when the whole world seems to be spinning round. It is usually due to disease of the inner ear or of the part of the brain which controls balance. This is not connected with diabetes in any way. However, simple dizzy spells are a common problem with many possible causes which may be difficult to diagnose. If dizziness occurs when you move from sitting down to the standing position, it may be the result of a sudden fall in blood pressure. This can sometimes be due to a loss of reflexes from diabetic neuropathy (p. 187). There are no other connections between diabetes and vertigo.

72 *My husband's grandmother is 84 and a diabetic. Although she is fiercely independent, she cannot look after herself properly and will have to go into a home. Can you let me know of any homes which cater especially for diabetics?*

Because diabetes becomes increasingly common in the elderly, most homes for the elderly are well experienced in looking after diabetics. The staff of the home will probably be happy to do urine tests, ensure that diet is satisfactory and give the old lady her tablets and, if necessary, insulin injections. If your grandmother-in-law is too fit and independent to accept an old people's home, she may be a suitable candidate for a warden-controlled flat.

73 *My wife, who was diagnosed diabetic a few weeks ago, is about to return to work. I feel that she should wear some sort of identity disc or bracelet showing she is diabetic but she is reluctant to wear anything too eye-catching. Have you any suggestions?*

It is very important that all diabetics, especially those on insulin, should wear some form of identification. Accidents can and do happen and it may be vital that any medical emergency team knows that your wife is diabetic.

Medic-Alert provide alloy bracelets or necklets which are functional if not very beautiful.

SOS/Talisman produce a medallion which can be unscrewed to reveal identification and medical details. These can be bought in most jewellers and come in a wide range of styles and prices, including those in 9 carat gold. Alternatively, your wife might prefer a do-it-yourself disc or bracelet inscribed DIABETIC ON INSULIN. This could be effective without being too eye-catching.

74   Could you tell me what ointment to use for diabetic skin irritation?

The most common cause of skin irritation in diabetics is itching around the genital region (pruritus vulvae). The most important treatment is to eliminate glucose from the urine by controlling diabetes. However, the itching can be relieved temporarily by cream containing a fungicide (e.g. Nystatin).

75   I believe that diabetics are entitled to free prescriptions. Please could you tell me how to apply?

One of the few definite advantages of being diabetic is exemption from payment on all prescription charges – even for treatment which is not connected to the diabetes itself. This does not apply to people who are treated on diet alone who are not exempt from prescription charges.

You must obtain a form entitled *NHS Prescriptions – How to get them free* from a chemist, hospital pharmacy or a Post Office. Having filled in the form yourself, it must be signed by your family doctor or clinic doctor and sent to the local Family Practitioner Committee. The chemist should be able to give you the address. You will, in due course, receive an exemption certificate. Please remember to carry this certificate wherever you are likely to need a prescription, for instance, when coming to the diabetic clinic or going on holiday in the UK.

5

Sex and contraception

FAMILY PLANNING CLINIC

Introduction

Although modern society has removed many of the taboos
and inhibitions about sex and contraception, many people
still find it a difficult subject to ask personal questions about.
There are very many old wives' tales about diabetes and
sex and most of these are rubbish. Basically, diabetics are
no different from non-diabetics in any aspect of sex, sexuality,
fertility, infertility and contraception. There are however a
few exceptions such as the undoubted risk of impotence in
male diabetics who have had diabetes for many years with
evidence of extensive neuropathy. Even this has to be
considered in relationship to the fact that impotence is a
common problem in non-diabetics and there is good evidence
to show that diabetics do in fact have no more problems

than a carefully matched group of non-diabetics. There is certainly good evidence that the female diabetic is totally without risk of developing any problem analogous to impotence. Frigidity, on the other hand, is not uncommon in both diabetic and non-diabetic women just as impotence is not uncommon in diabetic and non-diabetic men.

Various contraceptive devices have at times been claimed to be less effective in diabetics – the evidence to support this is poor and, in the opinion of the authors, diabetics should consider themselves entirely normal as far as contraceptive practice is concerned.

There was, in the 1960s and 70s, much emphasis on the potential risk of precipitating diabetes in non-diabetics taking oral contraceptives. It is now felt that the risks were grossly exaggerated in the press.

Impotence

1   Does diabetes affect the sex life (especially in males)?

No. The vast majority of diabetics, both male and female, are able to lead completely full and normal sex lives. This does not mean that problems do not occur but that most of these problems have nothing to do with diabetes. If, for any reason, diabetic control is lost with severe hyperglycaemia then this can affect sex life. In a minority of diabetics who have either bad neuropathy or arterial disease a loss of sexual potency can be directly attributed to diabetes but this is uncommon. The majority of diabetics, both male and female, can look forward to a completely normal sex life.

2   Is it normal for diabetics to suddenly find themselves totally uninterested in sexual intercourse?

No more so than in non-diabetics. The feeling you describe is more common in females than males but no more common in diabetics than non-diabetics.

3   Does a low blood sugar affect the ability to achieve or maintain an erection and more importantly, the ability to ejaculate?

No, unless the blood sugar is very low (less than 2 mmol/l) in which case many aspects of nerve function are impaired and this can affect both potency and ejaculation. These return to normal when the blood sugar is back to normal.

4   *Is there some drug or hormone which will help cure impotence?*

It is extremely rare that impotence is due to a hormonal abnormality. Most cases of impotence are due to psychological causes and often respond to appropriate advice and occasionally drug treatment. If there is a hormonal defect, hormone replacement treatment will cure that particular form of impotence. It is essential to get a correct diagnosis in order to ensure appropriate therapy. Recently it has been shown that the injection of a drug called papaverine directly into the penis can sometimes be helpful. It leads to an erection which may be good enough for satisfactory intercourse. In people who have been impotent for some time and who are disturbed by their inability to obtain an erection, the benefits are often sufficiently great to make this an acceptable and effective form of therapy.

5   *The problem of impotence worries me. It must be causing many diabetics similar worries.*

From your question we understand that it is the possibility of becoming impotent that causes you most worry. There is no doubt that many diabetics worry about possible complications which may lie ahead of them at some stage in the future, and many male diabetics have loss of potency at the top of their worry list. Our advice is to worry more about keeping your diabetes under control and balanced and less about what skeletons there could be in the cupboard. By ensuring that you have good diabetic control you are doing everything that you possibly can to avoid trouble in the future and the chances are that you will steer clear of trouble throughout your life.

6   *My wife left me because I was impotent and the doctors say that there is nothing they can do for me – why was I not told about this?*

Are you sure impotence is the only reason your wife left? I am surprised that the doctors said that there is nothing they can do for you, because even for those who are completely impotent there are now several treatments that can be tried. Perhaps your impotence became a flashpoint for domestic rows? In our experience, most wives are sympathetic and understanding about impotence (whatever the cause) provided both partners can talk about the matter in an open manner. We have known frank discussions lead to an increase of affection within marriage. Keeping things bottled up leads to the aggression and resentment that emerges from your question.

7   *I have had trouble keeping an erection for the last few months – has this anything to do with my diabetes? I also had a vasectomy a few years ago.*

This is difficult to answer without knowing more about your medical history. Certainly it is unlikely that the vasectomy had anything to do with your current problem. Failure to maintain an adequate erection may occasionally be an early symptom of diabetic neuropathy. However, and at least as commonly, it is a symptom of growing older and we would need to do detailed tests on you to be quite sure what exactly is the cause.

8   *I suffered a stroke affecting the right side of my body 12 months ago at the age of 40 and now suffer from partial impotence. The onset seemed to coincide not with the stroke but with taking anticoagulants. Are these known to cause impotence? I have heard that blood pressure tablets can cause impotence and I have been taking these for 3 months and wonder whether this is a factor?*

A severe stroke can sometimes be associated with impotence. A stroke is often due to narrowing of the arteries inside the head; the arteries elsewhere may also be narrowed and if the ones supplying blood to the genital organs are affected then it could contribute to your impotence. You are also quite right about the question of drugs. Some blood pressure lowering drugs may cause impotence and can interfere with ejaculation. It may be possible to try other drugs which may help the problem. It would be unwise to stop taking the drugs since this would lead to loss of control of your blood pressure. We suggest you ask your doctor to try different tablets for your high blood pressure.

9 *My husband, who is a middle-aged insulin dependent diabetic, has been impotent for the past 2 years. Please will you explain his condition as I am worried that my teenage son, who is also diabetic, may also discover that he is impotent. It is difficult to discuss this with the doctor as he is unsympathetic.*

We are sorry that you find it is difficult to discuss this with your own doctor. This is a subject some people find embarrassing but it is a very important question that is always being raised by diabetics. Impotence (or the fear of it) worries and upsets many people and is certainly not so rare that we can ignore it. It has been claimed that as many as 20% of diabetic men (though the figure is probably not as high as this) may at some stage become impotent. Most impotent men are not suffering from diabetes: anxiety, overwork, tiredness, stress, guilt, alcohol excess and grief can contribute to impotence. Any man may find that he is temporarily impotent and there is no reason why diabetic men should not also experience this. Fear of failure can perpetuate the condition. Overwork or worry is frequently the cause of lack of interest in sex and even of impotence. Excess alcohol can cause prolonged lack of potency.

Some diabetics do become impotent, due to problems with the blood supply or the nerve supply to the penis. This usually develops slowly and in the younger insulin dependent diabetic we believe it can be prevented by strict blood sugar control. In the older patient (who does not require insulin) the condition does not respond well to treatment probably because the blood sugar has been high for a long time before the diabetes was diagnosed. In this age group impotence is more commonly due to other factors and not to diabetes. We hope you will be encouraged to discuss the matter further with your own doctor or with the doctor in the diabetic clinic which your husband and son attend.

10   Is there any treatment for impotence?

Yes. Depending on the cause, there are several effective forms of therapy. Counselling by a therapist trained in this subject can be helpful, particularly in cases where the stresses and conflicts of life are the root-cause. Testosterone is effective in those with a hormone deficiency. Vacuum therapy, with a device that looks like a rigid condom, is also a harmless (if expensive) form of therapy which has been useful in many cases. Injections of papaverine into the penis, and penile implants (which require an operation) are more invasive but effective. The best choice for an individual requires a considerable amount of thought and discussion with your doctor.

11   After sexual intercourse I recently suffered quite a bad hypo. Is this likely to happen again and if so, what can be done to prevent it?

This form of physical activity can, like any other, lower the blood sugar level of insulin-treated diabetics and lead to hypoglycaemia. When this happens, and it is not at all uncommon, then the usual remedies need to be taken – more food or sugar beforehand or immediately afterwards.

The pill, IUD and vasectomy

12   Are there any extra risks that diabetic women run in using the contraceptive pill?

Use of the oral contraceptive pill is the same in both diabetics and non-diabetics. It is now well known that the pill carries with it small risks, although these are obviously less than the risks of pregnancy itself. This is why all women are examined and questioned before starting the pill because there are a few conditions in which it is best avoided and other methods of contraception used. The same arguments apply equally to diabetics and non-diabetics. Healthy diabetic women who have been checked the same way as non-diabetics may certainly use the pill and there are no additional risks. When diabetics start using the pill there is sometimes a slight deterioration of control. This is rarely a problem and is usually easily dealt with by a small increase in treatment, which in those taking insulin may mean a small increase in insulin dose. It is a simple matter to monitor the blood or urine level and make appropriate adjustments.

There is nothing to suggest that the pill causes diabetes when taken by non-diabetics. It is all right for the non-diabetic relatives of diabetics to use the pill but of course they, like others, should attend for regular checks by their general practitioner or family planning clinic.

13 *I have just started the menopause and wondered if diabetics have to wait 2 years after the last period before doing away with contraception?*

Although the periods may become irregular and infrequent at the start of the menopause it is still possible to be fertile and this advice is a precaution against unwanted pregnancy. It applies equally to diabetics and non-diabetics.

14 *My doctor prescribed the pill for me but on the packet it states that they are unsuitable for diabetics. As my doctor knows that I am a diabetic is it safe enough for me?*

Yes. There used to be some confusion about whether the pill was suitable for diabetics but there is now general agreement that diabetics may use the pill for contraceptive purposes without any increased risks compared with non-diabetics.

15 *I am a diabetic and I am marrying another diabetic in 8 weeks' time. Please could you advise me on how to stop becoming pregnant?*

We are not quite clear from your letter whether you wish to be sterilised and not have children or whether you are just seeking contraceptive advice. If it is that you and your fiancé have decided that you do not want to have the anxiety of your children inheriting diabetes and that you have made a clear decision not to have children, then you have the option of your fiancé having a vasectomy or being sterilised yourself.

These are both very fundamental decisions and will require careful thought because they are probably best considered as irreversible procedures. If you are quite certain about this plan then they are probably the best procedures to consider. We would advise you both to discuss this with your GP and seek referral either to a surgeon for vasectomy for your fiancé or to a gynaecologist for sterilisation. Whichever referral you get, you must both attend since no surgeon is going to undertake this procedure unless he is absolutely clear that you have thought about it carefully and have come to a clear, informed decision. If our interpretation of your question has not been right and you are merely looking for contraceptive advice then the best source of this is either your GP or the local family planning clinic.

16 Can you please give me any information regarding vasectomy and any side-effects it may have for diabetics?

Vasectomy is a relatively minor surgical procedure which involves cutting and tying off the vas deferens which is the tube that conveys the sperm from the testicle to the penis. Vasectomy may be carried out under either local or general anaesthesia usually, but not always, as a day case. As a diabetic you may be advised that it would be simpler to have it under local anaesthesia since in this way your eating should not be affected and the balance of your diabetes not disturbed. The side-effects of the operation are primarily discomfort although infections and complications do rarely occur.

There are a few medical reasons for avoiding this operation but they apply equally to non-diabetics as they do to diabetics.

17 Is the 'progesterone only' pill suitable for diabetics?

Yes, although recently these have become less popular both for diabetics and non-diabetics.

18 I have been warned that IUDs are more unreliable in diabetics than non-diabetics. Is this really true?

IUDs (intra uterine contraceptive devices) are generally regarded as slightly less reliable contraceptives than the pill and there has been one report suggesting they may be even less reliable when used by diabetics. Not all experts agree about this, as there are no other reports containing this observation. There has also been a report suggesting that diabetics may be slightly more susceptible to pelvic infections when using an IUD. On balance, our recommendation is that IUDs should be considered as effective and useful in diabetics as in non-diabetics.

Thrush

19   I keep getting recurrence of vaginal thrush and my doctor says that as a diabetic there is nothing that I can do about this – is this correct?

Thrush is due to an infection with a yeast that thrives in the presence of a lot of sugar. If your diabetes is badly controlled and you are passing a lot of sugar in the urine then you will be very susceptible to thrush and however much ointment and cream you use it is likely to recur. The best line of treatment is to control your diabetes so well that there is no sugar in the urine and then the thrush will disappear, probably without the need for any antifungal treatments although these will speed the healing process. As long as you keep your urine free from sugar you should be free from any recurrence of the thrush.

20   I am a diabetic with thrush. I have been well controlled for 10 years now. I do regular blood tests and most of them are less than 10 mmol/l and when ever I check a urine test it is always negative. I have been taking the oral contraceptive pill for 3 years and I understand both diabetes and the pill predispose one to thrush. Can you advise me what to do?

Since your diabetes is well controlled and your urine consistently free from sugar, diabetes can probably be excluded as a cause of the thrush. One has to presume that in your case it is a relatively rare side-effect of the pill and you would be best advised to seek alternative forms of contraception.

Hormone replacement therapy

21 *During the past 5 years I have had trouble with my*
    periods being very heavy and on several occasions I have
    become very anaemic. I have tried hormone replacement
    therapy (HRT) which interferes with my diabetic control
    and it has been suggested that I have a hysterectomy. I
    have heard that depression is common after this operation
    and that HRT is often given to alleviate this feeling but
    if this treatment makes diabetic control more difficult,
    how will I cope? I realise that I should ask both my
    diabetic and gynaecological consultants these question but
    I never seem to ask the right questions at the clinic.

Many people do have the impression that depression is
common following hysterectomy. There is no reason for this.
Anyone might get a little bit depressed after an operation
in the same way that they would after any illness. A few
women may feel that if they have their womb removed they
have lost some of their femininity and therefore will become
depressed. However, the womb is merely a muscle and has
no effect at all on feminine characteristics apart from its
relationship with menstruation. Unless the ovaries are taken
out at the same time there is no reason why you should
require HRT. If the ovaries are removed then HRT should
not upset your diabetes unless of course you take more
hormones than you were producing yourself before the
operation. This could easily be put right by reducing the
dosage or altering the preparation used. The best person to
discuss this with is your consultant. Make a list of the
questions you want to discuss with him before you see him.
Many patients find that what they wanted to discuss goes
straight out of their mind as soon as they walk through the
consulting room door. He will not be at all put off if you
arrive with a list of questions.

22 *I have read in a magazine that the pill can now be*
    taken by diabetics. My question is whether following this
    significant advance it can be hoped that hormone
    replacement therapy, which is widely available to

non-diabetics during the menopause, may also become available to diabetics?

Hormone replacement therapy for the menopause consists of small doses of oestrogens which are given to replace the oestrogens normally produced by the ovaries. Oestrogen levels in the blood at this time begin to decline, and if they decline rapidly can cause unpleasant symptoms. Replacement therapy is thus designed to allow a more gradual decline in circulating oestrogens. There is no reason why diabetics should not use this sort of hormone replacement therapy if the symptoms warrant it. Like the pill, which also contains oestrogen, this sort of hormone therapy does often impose a slight increase in demand for insulin. A diabetic on diet alone or on diet and tablets might possibly find that she cannot meet the increased demand for insulin without having supplementary insulin by injection. However, this would be very unlikely. Similarly a diabetic already on insulin may need to increase the dose. On balance, therefore, if the menopausal symptoms are sufficient to warrant hormone replacement therapy, which would anyway only be required for a limited period, then the risk of causing a need for insulin injections in the diabetic who is not already on insulin would be small. This would not be of any importance if the diabetic was already on insulin.

Termination

23   Is diabetes grounds for termination of pregnancy?

Not unless your doctor considers that pregnancy would be detrimental to your health which may occasionally be the case. All the reasons for termination of pregnancy apply equally to diabetics as they do to non-diabetics.

24   Is it safe for a diabetic to have an abortion?

There is no added hazard to diabetics undergoing termination of pregnancy and care of the diabetes during this operation does not raise any special difficulties.

Infertility

25   Are diabetics more likely to be infertile than non-diabetics?

There is nothing to suggest that diabetic men are any less fertile than non-diabetic men and this is generally true for diabetic women. In the case of women however, extremely poor diabetic control with consistently high blood sugar readings is associated with reduced fertility. This is probably just as well as there is good evidence to show that the outcome of pregnancy is much worse in those who conceive when diabetic control is poor.

26   Can diabetics expect the same treatment for infertility as non-diabetics?

Yes. As mentioned above diabetes is rarely the cause of infertility. If control is anything other than excellent, then improving control should be the first goal. If that is not successful than expert opinion on management from a specialist is the next step.

6
Pregnancy

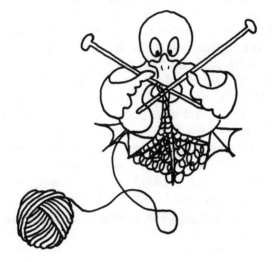

Introduction

Pregnancy was the first aspect of diabetic life where it was shown without any doubt that poor blood glucose control is associated with many complications for both mother and child and that these complications are preventable by strict control. The outcome for diabetics who are pregnant and for the babies that they carry is directly related to how successful they are in controlling blood sugar concentration. If control is perfect from the moment of conception to delivery, then the risks of pregnancy to mother and baby are no greater than in non-diabetics.

We now know that poor control at the time the egg is fertilised (conception) can effect the way in which the egg divides and changes into the foetus (in which all organs and

limbs are present but very small) in such a way as to cause
congenital abnormalities (such as hare-lip, contracture of the
spine and holes in the heart). The risk of this happening
can be reduced to a minimum, and possibly even eliminated,
by ensuring perfect diabetic control (normal HbA₁) before
getting pregnant.

For those who become pregnant when control is poor, there
will be an increased risk of congenital abnormalities – some
of which may be detectable by ultrasound very early in
pregnancy when termination is possible if a major defect is
detected. When no defect is detected the outcome of the
pregnancy will still be dictated by the degree of control
during the 40 weeks of pregnancy and during labour and
delivery. Modern antenatal care is usually shared between
the diabetic specialist and the obstetrician, often at a joint
antenatal clinic. So long as control remains perfect (normal
HbA₁) and pregnancy progresses normally, there is no need
for hospital admission. With the excellent control that is
now possible, the baby will develop normally and we believe
that the pregnancy can be allowed to go to its natural term
(40 weeks). If spontaneous labour begins the procedure is
no different from non-diabetics other than the continued need
to keep the mother's blood sugar normal to prevent
hypoglycaemia in the infant shortly after birth.

Diabetics are not immune to obstetric and antenatal
complications and these will be treated in the same way as
they would be in non-diabetics. When satisfactory diabetic
control is not achieved at home, then admission to hospital
becomes essential but there are very few mothers who cannot
achieve and maintain normal blood sugar values as an
out-patient, at least while they are pregnant. It is a
remarkable example of the importance of motivation in the
struggle for good diabetic control. The single-mindedness of
the pregnant mother is able to cope with almost anything
to protect the growing baby from harm. Sadly this motivation
is often lost once the pregnancy is over and control slips
back to where it was before.

There is no inherent reason why control is easier during
pregnancy. The evidence suggests that this success is due
to motivation, one has to realise that it should be possible

to achieve this level of motivation in non-pregnant females (and even males!) since the rewards are just as immediate and tangible – good health and confidence in the future.

A very comprehensive pregnancy information pack is available from the BDA.

Genetics

1   *If diabetes is known to be in the family can other members of the family take any preventive action?*

The inheritance of diabetes is a complicated subject – indeed different sorts of diabetes appear to be inherited in different ways. For instance a tendency for one sort of diabetes (insulin dependent or juvenile onset) can be inherited, but only a small proportion of these people will go on to develop diabetes. One can now tell if these people at risk have inherited the relevant genes but even if they have, there is no way, as yet, of predicting their chances of developing diabetes. The more common non-insulin dependent (or maturity onset) diabetes often treated by diet or by diet and tablets is not associated with any known single gene abnormality but is thought to be strongly inherited. Indeed when we have learnt more about it, it may well prove that there are several different sub-types which cannot be distinguished from one another – all inherited in different ways. We do know that many of these patients are overweight and that obesity not only makes diabetes worse but it may even lead to its appearance in susceptible people.

There is no really effective action other family members can take except to follow the usual health advice to keep physically active, eat a balanced diet and avoid obesity. It is worth bearing in mind the slight possibility that someone else in the family may become diabetic – especially if he ignores this advice – and test his urine as soon as he develops any symptoms which you may think relevant so that the diabetes can be detected and treated early on.

2   *The man I am going to marry is a diabetic. Will there be any risk in having children?*

If you are not a diabetic yourself and there is no diabetes in your family then the risk of your children developing diabetes in childhood or adolescence, if the father is diabetic, is probably about 1 in 20. Provided you are both in good health it is certainly all right to have a family. If you were diabetic and your fiancé were an insulin dependent diabetic, then there would be an increased risk of your children developing diabetes.

There is a rare form of non-insulin dependent diabetes in which there is a strong hereditary tendency. This is called maturity onset diabetes of the young, commonly known as MODY. The risk of your children getting diabetes of this unusual kind would then be rather high but it is often a relatively mild form of diabetes and runs true to type throughout the generations.

The study of inheritance of diabetes is a complicated subject and you would be well advised to discuss this further with your specialist or a professional genetic counsellor.

Pre-pregnancy

3   *I am a diabetic on tablets which I chose rather than insulin and I am pregnant again. As I have had a previous miscarriage I am worried about the chance of this recurring; both my husband and I smoke a lot. How can I make sure that this pregnancy is successful?*

Diabetic control certainly affects the outcome of pregnancy – better control leads to more successful pregnancies.

Good control should be established before conception if the pregnancy is planned, and is probably best maintained by either diet alone or if this fails, by diet with insulin. We do not advise patients to take tablets throughout pregnancy although they do not harm the baby if they are taken inadvertently in the early part of pregnancy. The major hazards relate to the immediate period after birth. The tablets can cross into the baby's circulation and stimulate insulin secretion from the pancreas causing hypoglycaemia in the baby.

It should also be said here that most diabetics of childbearing age are already being treated with insulin, so that they are not normally faced with your decisions.

You obviously know already that smoking affects the baby and that heavy smoking is associated with more miscarriages and smaller babies. In asking the question we suspect that you already know the correct answer – take insulin and give up smoking.

There is also more recent evidence to link even modest regular alcohol intake in pregnancy with unfavourable outcome as far as the baby is concerned. You should stop drinking alcohol until the pregnancy is over.

4   Why must I ensure that my diabetic control is perfect during pregnancy?

To ensure that you reduce the risks to yourself and your baby to an absolute minimum. If you are able to achieve this degree of control from before the time of conception through to the time of delivery you can reduce the risks to your baby to those which are virtually indistinguishable from those of non-diabetics. On the other hand, if you do not control your diabetes properly and pay no attention to it then the risk to the baby increases dramatically.

Management

5   I am 25 years old and an insulin dependent diabetic. My husband and I plan to start a family but first I would like to complete a 3 year degree course at university. By the time this course finishes I will be 29. Can you tell me if this will be too old to have a baby?

You pose a difficult question as to the ideal age a diabetic should have a baby. The age of 29 is not too old to start a family but there are certain advantages in starting younger, particularly if you are a diabetic and if you plan more than one pregnancy. Starting a family may be hard work whether you are a diabetic or not. If you add increasing age to the difficulties, we are sure you will understand why one normally recommends starting earlier rather than later.

It is of course difficult to give exact advice to individual people without knowing them personally and the right person to talk to is your clinic doctor who knows both you and your diabetes.

6   *I am worried that if I become pregnant whilst my husband's diabetes is uncontrolled the child will suffer – am I right?*

No. There is no known way in which poor control of your husband's diabetes can affect the development of a child that you will carry.

7   *When 7 months pregnant I developed diabetes. I had 8 units of insulin a day. After my baby was born, the tests were normal so I stopped taking insulin. I would now like another baby. My GP says I could become permanently diabetic. Another doctor, however, says this is very unlikely – please could you advise me?*

You have had what we call gestational diabetes (i.e. diabetes that occurs during pregnancy and then goes away again when you are not pregnant). The chances are that this will recur in every subsequent pregnancy. You may well find that at some stage it does not get better at the end of the pregnancy and that you are then permanently diabetic. Even if you do not have further pregnancies, you are a 'high risk' (greater than 1 in 2) case for developing diabetes at some stage in the future. Your pancreas produces enough insulin to cope with everyday life but the extra demands of pregnancy are more than it can manage, hence the need for extra insulin. You should pay particular attention to your diet and fitness, and keep your weight at even slightly below your ideal weight for your height. The decision about further pregnancies with the greater risk of developing permanent diabetes is one that you and your husband must take after you understand the facts.

8   *When I had my first baby, I was in hospital for the last 2 months and I was given a caesarian section after 36 weeks of pregnancy. My baby weighed 3.7 kg (8 lb 4 oz) even though it was 4 weeks early. During my most recent*

pregnancy I was allowed to go into labour which occurred at 39 weeks and the baby weighed 3.2 kg (7 lb) and I spent absolutely no time at all in hospital other than going into hospital as I went into labour. My first child is 5 years old now and is very well and my new baby seems to be progressing very well. Why has there been such a big change in treatment?

The last 10 years have seen a dramatic change in our attitudes to the care of pregnancy in diabetics. Good blood sugar control is the most important goal during pregnancy and with home blood glucose monitoring this can be achieved in the majority of diabetics without the need for admission to hospital at any stage. It sounds as if your control was worse during the first pregnancy than the second. Early delivery by caesarian section was decided because the baby had already grown to 3.7 kg by 36 weeks and they were worried that it would become even bigger if left to 38 or 39 weeks. The heavier baby in the first pregnancy is because the high blood sugar you were running resulted in more fat being laid down on the baby to increase its weight. However, during your second pregnancy, when your diabetic control was clearly a good deal better, the baby grew at a more normal rate so that it was at the correct weight when you went into labour at the end of pregnancy.

9   *During my last labour I was given a drip and had an insulin pump up all day. Why was this necessary?*

Strict blood sugar control during labour is very important to ensure that you do not put your baby at risk from hypoglycaemia in the first few hours of life. If there is any possibility that your labour may end up with an anaesthetic (e.g. for forceps delivery or possible caesarian section) then the simplest way to keep diabetes well controlled is with glucose being run into your circulation and matched with an appropriate dose of insulin. With the pump this means that – should an emergency arise – you will be immediately ready.

10   *During my pregnancy I found attending the antenatal clinic a nuisance and I did not like to keep my diabetes*

too well controlled because if I did I had many hypos. Labour and delivery seemed to go quite normally but my baby was rather heavy. He was 4.2 kg (9 lb 4 oz), and had to spend a long time in the Special Care Baby Unit because they said he was hypoglycaemic – how do I avoid all this trouble in my next pregnancy?

If you want to go ahead and have further babies then it is essential that you change your attitude to the antenatal clinic and of controlling your diabetes throughout the pregnancy. The trouble your baby had from hypoglycaemia was a reflection on the fact that the baby had been exposed to a very high glucose concentration throughout pregnancy and had to produce a lot of insulin from its own pancreas to cope with this extra load of sugar from you. Immediately after birth it no longer had the glucose coming from you but still had too much insulin of its own, hence the hypoglycaemia. You can prevent this risk in subsequent pregnancies by ensuring that your control is immaculate. This will require you to attend the antenatal clinic on a regular basis and to do frequent blood glucose monitoring and to ensure that your control is excellent. If you can do this you should be able to eliminate any risk of hypoglycaemia in your baby.

11 Is it all right for me to breast-feed my baby if my blood sugars are too high?

Breast-feeding is generally encouraged these days in both non-diabetics and diabetics. There are no special difficulties in the diabetic and the presence of a slightly raised blood sugar need not worry you too much provided that your diabetic control is not too bad. For the best results with breast-feeding, a diet fairly high in calories is needed and you should keep a watchful eye on the diabetes, making appropriate adjustments to the insulin dose if necessary. If you find this all too much, it is perfectly all right to bottle-feed.

12 I am married to a diabetic who takes insulin to control his diabetes. I have just fallen pregnant, so what special things do I need to do during pregnancy to ensure that it goes smoothly and without complications?

You need take no special precautions other than those taken by non-diabetics as the fact that your husband is a diabetic does not put your pregnancy at any particular risk. It is only when the mother is diabetic that the strict control and careful monitoring of control of blood glucose become essential

13 I have been told that I must keep my blood sugars as low as possible during pregnancy. Please can you tell me what they should be?

Your blood sugars before meals should be 3-6 mmol/l and 2 hours after meals no higher than 10 mmol/l.

14 I am frightened of having hypoglycaemic attacks especially as I have been told to keep my blood sugars much lower. What should I do?

There is no reason why you should have any hypoglycaemic attacks whilst pregnant, but all diabetics should be prepared for a hypo. Carry glucose or dextrose or something like a mini Mars bar on you at *all* times. Most convenient are Dextrosol tablets – one of these raises the blood glucose by about 0.5 mmol/l, so you should take 2-4 for a hypo.

15 Do hypoglycaemic attacks during pregnancy harm the baby?

No. There is no evidence to suggest that a very low blood sugar in the mother can harm the baby.

Complications

16 My second son was born with multiple defects and has subsequently died. I have been an insulin dependent diabetic for 14 years (since the age of 10). Are diabetics more likely to have an abnormal baby?

The secret to a successful pregnancy in a diabetic is perfect blood sugar control starting before conception and lasting throughout pregnancy. There is good scientific evidence to suggest that multiple developmental defects are caused by poor control in the first few weeks of pregnancy and that the risk of this can be avoided by ensuring immaculate control at the time that the baby is conceived. The risks in terms of multiple congenital defects seem to be confined to the very early stages of the pregnancy. This is hardly surprising because this is the stage when the various components of the baby's body are beginning to develop and is the stage where other illnesses such as German measles (rubella) also affect development.

Good control is also needed for the rest of the pregnancy because the gradual maturation and growth of the baby can be disturbed by poor control. In particular with poor control the baby grows rather faster than normal and is large in size although the development of the organs remains relatively immature in terms of their function. This does not happen with well controlled diabetes. Because the baby is large the mother has to be delivered early and because the baby is immature it is susceptible to a number of added risks immediately after birth.

17 *I had three hypoglycaemic comas when expecting my son 11^1/$_2$ years ago and I wondered whether this could have caused brain damage? As although he is bright and is in the A stream at school he doesn't seem to be able to keep his work reasonable and presentable.*

We are sure that we can reassure you that your son has not got brain damage. This rarely happens even to the diabetics themselves and if you have managed to survive the comas without brain damage then there was no risk to your child.

18 *I have read that the babies of diabetic mothers tend to be fat and have lung trouble shortly after birth and also be susceptible to hypoglycaemia (low blood sugar) shortly after birth. Is this true, and if so why does it happen?*

We now know that if the mother runs a high blood sugar throughout pregnancy, sugar gets across the placenta into the baby's circulation and causes it to become fat. This is because the baby's pancreas is still capable of producing insulin even though the mother's cannot. As a result of this the baby grows bigger during pregnancy and delivery has to be carried out earlier to avoid obstruction of labour by the large baby. This used to be carried out most commonly by caesarian section at about 36 weeks of pregnancy. One of the complications of this method of delivery was lung trouble in these babies, known as the Respiratory Distress Syndrome (RDS), caused by the fact that the babies were born before the lungs were properly developed. We now know that if the mother's blood sugars are kept strictly within normal limits during pregnancy, babies do not grow faster than they should and pregnancy can be allowed to continue for the normal period of 40 weeks. This avoids the risk of caesarian section in the majority of patients and RDS is rarely seen because the babies are fully mature when they are born. The low blood sugar during the first few hours after birth was a result of the fact that the baby's pancreas had been producing a lot of insulin during the pregnancy to cover the high blood sugar of the mother which was passed across the placenta to the baby. If the blood sugar is strictly controlled during pregnancy and delivery, hypoglycaemia is seldom a problem.

19 Are babies of diabetic mothers more likely to have jaundice?

Babies born to diabetic mothers are likely to be jaundiced. This is partly because they tend to be born early. We do not know the other reasons why the mature babies are jaundiced. The jaundice is usually mild and clears without treatment.

20 I developed toxaemia during my last pregnancy and had to spend several weeks in hospital even though my diabetic control was immaculate. Luckily everything turned out all right and I now have a beautiful healthy son. Was the toxaemia related to me being a diabetic? And is it likely to recur in future pregnancies?

There is some doubt as to whether or not diabetics are more prone to toxaemia. On balance most experts believe that they are not more likely to develop it. Regarding your second question, you are not more likely to get toxaemia in your future pregnancies – indeed the risk is less.

21 *During my last pregnancy I had hydramnios and my obstetrician said that this was because I was a diabetic. Is this true? And is there anything that I can do to avoid it happening in future pregnancies?*

Hydramnios, which is an excessive amount of fluid surrounding the foetus, is, unfortunately, more common with diabetic mothers and does appear to be related to how strictly you control the diabetes throughout pregnancy. Our advice to you is that on future occasions you can reduce the risk to an absolute minimum by ensuring that your HbA$_1$ and blood sugars are completely normal from the day of conception.

22 *During the recent delivery of my fourth child which went quite smoothly I had an insulin pump into a vein during labour. I had not had this in my previous three pregnancies, although I had been diabetic in all of them. Why did I need the pump this time?*

We now know that it is very important to keep the blood sugar within normal limits during labour to minimise the risk of the baby developing a low blood sugar (hypoglycaemia) in the first few hours after birth. This is most effectively and easily produced by the use of an intravenous insulin infusion combined with some glucose given as an intravenous drip. This means that the blood sugar can be kept strictly regulated at the normal level until delivery has been achieved and ensures that, should complications arise and something like a caesarian section be required, you are all ready immediately for an anaesthetic and operation.

23 *I have had a previous child that was delivered by caesarian section. Do I have to have a caesarian section with my next pregnancy ?*

It all depends on why you had the caesarian section. If it was performed for an obstetric reason which is likely to be present in this pregnancy, then the answer is yes. If it was performed because the first baby was large or just because you are a diabetic, the answer could be no.

Some doctors do consider it safer to deliver women by caesarian section once the mother has had one. Others would allow you a 'trial of labour'. In other words, you would be allowed to start labour and, if satisfactory, you may be able to deliver your baby vaginally.

24 My doctor tells me that I will have to have a caesarian section because my baby is in a bad position and a little large. What sort of anaesthetic is best?

Nowadays approximately 50% of women have caesarian sections under epidural anaesthetic rather than under general anaesthetic. If you have an epidural anaesthetic your legs and abdomen are made completely numb. This is done by injecting local anaesthetic solution through a needle into the spinal canal. You remain awake for the birth of your baby and therefore remember this event. In most cases this kind of anaesthetic is better because your baby receives no anaesthetic and therefore is not sleepy.

If you are interested in having your baby this way, you must discuss it with your obstetrician.

25 My baby had difficulty in breathing in his first few days in the Special Care Unit. They said this was because of my poor diabetic control – why was this?

It sounds as if your baby had what is called the Respiratory Distress Syndrome (RDS) which occurs most commonly in premature babies. It occurs in babies of diabetic mothers where the baby has grown too quickly because of poor blood glucose control and is born before it has become fully mature. It used to be a relatively common cause of death in the babies of diabetic mothers but now, because of stricter control and supervision, the mother does not have to be delivered early. It is now uncommon and indeed can probably be completely prevented if patients control their blood glucose throughout pregnancy, thus allowing the pregnancy to proceed for the normal 40 weeks.

7
Diabetes in the young

Introduction

This chapter about diabetes in young people divides naturally into three main age groups: babies, children and adolescents. The sections on babies and children consists of questions asked by parents and the answers are naturally directed at them. The section on adolescents is for both young people and their parents.

Apart from the experience of BDA camps, none of the authors has actually lived with the daily problems of bringing up a child with diabetes. However, we have listened to hundreds of parents who have felt the despair of finding that their child is diabetic and then overcome their fears to allow their child to develop to the full. Mothers and fathers usually end up by being especially proud of children who are diabetic. We hope to pass on some of this experience to those parents who are still at the frightened stage.

The baby with diabetes

1   My baby developed diabetes when she was 4 weeks old. She is now 6 weeks and looks very healthy but I would like emergency advice in order to protect her life. What food and treatment should I give?

You must be relieved that your baby is better now she has started treatment, but worried about the difficulties of bringing up a diabetic from infancy. Under the age of 1 year, diabetes is very rare so you will not find many doctors with experience of this condition. However, the general principles are the same and there is no reason why she should not grow into a healthy young woman. The British Diabetic Association has produced a special youth pack for children under 5 years. This contains many useful documents including a booklet about babies with diabetes. The BDA might also be able to put you in touch with other people who have had the same problem. Practical advice and reassurance from these people would be more use than any theoretical advice.

Like all babies, your daughter will be fed on breast or bottle milk. For the first 4 months frequent feeds are best – 3 hourly by day and 4 hourly by night. Bottle-fed babies usually need $2^{1}/_{2}$ ounces of milk per pound body weight each day (168 g per kg). Some babies grow very rapidly and need more milk than this while others may need solids earlier than 4 months. This may be a help in diabetic babies as the solids will slow down the absorption of milk. It is important to wake young diabetic babies for a night feed to avoid night-time insulin reactions. If there is any doubt about this, do a blood glucose check while the baby is asleep. If the blood glucose is low an additional 5-10 g carbohydrate should be given.

2   My little boy is nearly 1 year old and has been ill for a month, losing weight and always crying. Diabetes has just been diagnosed. Does this mean injections for life?

Yes. We are afraid it does literally mean 'injections for life'. The thought of having to stick needles into a young child quite naturally horrifies parents. But with loving care, explanations and playing games like injecting yourself (without insulin) and a teddy bear (using a different needle) and perhaps some bribery, most children accept injections as part of their normal day. Young children grow up knowing no other way of life and they often accept this treatment better than their parents. Encourage the child to help at injection time by getting the equipment ready or perhaps by pushing in the plunger and pulling out the needle.

3   *How can I collect urine for testing from my 18-month old diabetic son? I have been given lots of different suggestions but none of them seem to work.*

It is not easy to get clean samples of urine from babies in nappies. Many infants will produce a specimen by reflex into a small potty when undressed. You can also squeeze a wet nappy directly onto a urine testing stick. But be warned – washing powders or fabric softeners in the nappies alter the urine test result.

Diastix or Diabur-Test 5000 can be used for testing for glucose, whilst Ketostix or Ketur Test are used to test for ketones. Keto-Diastix tests for glucose and ketones. Infants are much more likely than older people to have ketones in the urine. This is because they rapidly switch to burning up fat stores in the fasting state. It is important to check on ketones and try to keep the urine ketone-free, although you should not worry if ketones appear for a short time.

You will also have to do blood tests on your child. Parents expect these to be very painful to children but finger prick blood tests are surprisingly well accepted by young people. They enable you to check accurately what is happening if your child feels unwell or looks ill. Urine tests only provide a guide about the diabetic state since the last urine specimen. The blood test confirms what is happening at that very instant. It is the only reliable way of deciding whether your child is hypo or just tired and hungry. Blood sugars are also necessary to check the overall diabetic control and to help you decide on the dose of insulin if the blood sugar rises during an illness. Blood samples should be obtained with an automatic finger pricker – the Autolet (Owen Mumford Medical Shop) has a special platform for children, but the Soft Touch (Boehringer), the Ames Glucolet (Bayer Diagnostics) and the Monoject (Mariner Medical) are all suitable.

4 *My 2-year-old diabetic daughter makes an awful fuss about food. Meals are turning into a regular struggle. Have you any suggestions?*

Food is of great emotional significance to all children. If meals are eaten without complaint, then both mother and child will be satisfied. All children go through phases of food refusal because of a need to show their growing independence, their ability to provoke worry or anger in parents and their attempts to manipulate the situation. Food leads to the well-known breakfast battleground which occurs in all families at some stage. The only way for the parent to win is to remain in control of the weapon. Usually when young children begin their negative phase (10-18 months), they dislike being told to leave the table and go away. They often return and accept food rather than remain alone and hungry.

The battle is even more difficult for the parents if the child is diabetic – the child has some explosive weapons! However, the parents must stay in control: try distracting attention away from food by toys, music, talk or your own relaxed approach to eating. You may have to send your daughter away from the table if she is refusing to eat properly. Hypoglycaemia often provokes hunger and, anyway, a couple of mild hypos due to food refusal is a small price to pay for better behaviour next time. Be prepared to modify the type of carbohydrate within reason if she consistently refuses the diet recommended by the hospital. Bread, potatoes, biscuits, fruit juices and even ice-cream can be offered as alternatives.

5 *My 5-year old son has been a diabetic since he was 18 months and he is only 3' 2" (96 cm) tall. I have been*

*told that he is very short for his age. The doctor says
that poorly controlled diabetes could be slowing his
growth. Is this true?*

The average height for a five year old boy is 3' 6" (108
cm), so your son is certainly short for his age. Having high
sugar levels for several years could be the cause of this. If
you now keep his diabetes under control and make sure
that he has plenty to eat, he should grow rapidly and may
even catch up with his normal height. However, his short
stature may be due to a growth disorder and may need
further investigation.

6   *My daughter is now 6 years old and has been diabetic
for 4 years. She is on 12 units of Monotard insulin, once
a day. Her urine test in the morning is always 2% and
the teatime test ¹/₄%. My own doctor is satisfied with
her tests and says that negative tests in a child of this
age means a risk of hypos. However, the school doctor
says her diabetes is out of control and she should have
two injections a day. What do you advise?*

Until a few years ago most doctors did not try to achieve
close diabetic control in children. It was considered good
enough if the child felt well and was not having a lot of
hypos. The feeling nowadays is that good control *is* important
to allow normal growth and prevent long-term complications.
In the first place, you should start measuring your daughter's
blood glucose. This will tell you how serious is the early
morning high sugar and also whether she is running the
risk of a hypo at any other time of the day. It is likely
that she will need an evening injection to control the morning
blood sugar. It is true that keeping the blood sugar down
towards normal may make a hypo more likely. Mild hypos
do not cause any harm and even severe reactions do no
damage, except to the parent's confidence! You must not
worry about a few days or weeks of poor control and you
will never achieve perfection in a little girl whose activities
and lifestyle is changing from day to day.

The child with diabetes

7   *I have been told not to expect my daughter to be as tall as she would have been if she had not been diabetic. Is this true? If so, what can I do to help her reach her maximum height?*

Unless your daughter's diabetic control has been very poor, there is no reason why she should not reach her proper height without any special encouragement. We know of one 16-year-old boy who is 6′ 2″ (165.8 cm) tall and has been diabetic for 15 years. Diabetes does not have to stunt your growth.

8   *My 18-year old-son is only 5′ 2″ (157 cm) and very immature. I have heard that diabetics reach puberty a year or two later than anyone else. Will he grow later?*

If your son is sexually underdeveloped then he will certainly have a growth spurt when he goes into puberty. However, 5′ 2″ (157 cm) is very undersized for a boy of eighteen. It *could* be poor diabetic control that has stunted his growth but there are other possible factors including the physical stature of his father and yourself. If you are both a normal height, there could be some other medical reason for your son's short size. It would be worth consulting your GP or clinic doctor rather than blaming it automatically on diabetes.

9   *My son, aged 10, started insulin last year and his dose of insulin has gradually dropped until recently he has come off insulin completely and is on diet alone. Will he now be off insulin permanently?*

No. There is a 99.9% chance that he will have to go back on insulin. This so-called 'honeymoon period' (p. 47) can be very trying as it raises hopes that the diabetes has cleared up. Unfortunately, this never happens in young people.

10   *Are there any special schools for diabetic children?*

There are no special schools for diabetics and they would not be a good idea. It is most important that a young diabetic grows up in normal surroundings and is not encouraged to

regard himself as 'different'. So he should go to a normal
school and grow up in a normal family atmosphere.

11 *I think my newly diagnosed diabetic son is using his
    insulin injections as a way of avoiding school. I can't
    send him to school unless he has his insulin but it
    sometimes takes ages before I can get him to have his
    injection. I have two younger children and a husband
    whom I also have to help to get to school and work.
    How should I cope with my temperamental son?*

You raise several related points. Firstly, you assume that
he is using his insulin injections to avoid school. You may
be right if he resisted going to school before becoming diabetic.
In this case you should try the same tactics you used before.
Alternatively, his dislike of school could be related to the
diabetes, for example, an overprotective attitude by sports
instructors, frequent hypos or embarrassment about eating
snacks between meals. If you suspect such difficulties, a
talk to your son and his form teacher might clear the air.

He may be happy about school but actually fears his insulin
injections so that things get off to a slow start in the morning.
Problems with injections have been reduced with the
introduction of plastic syringes with short, sharp needles,
but some children focus their dislike for diabetes as a whole
on the unnatural process of injecting themselves.

The BDA has produced a School Pack to help parents
communicate with the school. It contains a number of leaflets
to be given to teachers and those responsible for diabetic
school children. You should apply to the BDA for a copy of
this publication.

12 *When my son starts school, would it be better for him
    to return home for lunch or let him eat school dinners?*

It depends largely on your son's temperament and attitude
to school. Some 4-year-olds skip happily off to their first
day at school without a backward glance (much to their
mother's chagrin), while other perfectly normal children make
a fuss and have tummy aches at the start of school. Diabetes
will tend to add to these problems. You will have to talk
to the teachers and it would be worth asking their advice

and making sure that someone will take the responsibility of choosing suitable food for your son – you can't leave that to a 4- or 5-year old child.

13 *My 10-year-old son has recently been diagnosed diabetic. What is the best age for him to start doing his own injections?*

The fear of injections loom large in a child's view of his own diabetes. Many children actually make less fuss if they do their own injections and most diabetic specialist nurses would encourage a 10-year-old to do his own injections right from day one. We know a little girl who became diabetic at the age of 6 and who gave herself her own first injection without any fuss – and has been doing so ever since. Plastic syringes which can be reused take a lot of the horror out of injections.

If you do have an injection problem or if you want your son to have a good summer holiday, send him on a BDA holiday – you will find details in *Balance*.

14 *When I heard that I was to have a diabetic child in my class (I am a junior school teacher), I read up all I could about diabetes. Most of my questions were answered but I cannot discover what to do if the child eats too much sugar. Will he go into a coma? If so, what do I do then?*

Eating sugar or sweets may make his blood sugar rise in which case he may feel thirsty and generally off-colour. Coma from a high blood sugar takes some time to develop and there is only cause for concern if he becomes very drowsy or starts vomiting. If this does happen, you should contact his parents. A child who is vomiting with poor diabetic control may need to go to hospital.

The most common sort of coma, which may occur over a matter of 10 minutes, is due to a hypo. In this case the blood sugar level is too low and he needs to be given sugar at once. The causes of hypo are delayed meals, missed snacks or extra exercise.

15 Can I apply for an attendance allowance to look after my son who has frequent hypos and needs a lot of extra care?

Yes, as the parent of a child with unstable diabetes you can apply for attendance allowance. Many people in your position have successfully applied and feel that it provides some recognition of the burden of being responsible for a child with diabetes, especially if hypos are a major problem.

There is an opposing view that diabetes should not be regarded as a disability and that applying for an allowance fosters a feeling that the child is an invalid.

16 My little boy is diabetic and is always having coughs and colds. These make him very ill and he always becomes very sugary during each illness despite antibiotics from my doctor. Could you please give me some guidelines for coping with his diabetes during these infections?

Here are some guidelines:

1 *Insulin.* Never stop the insulin even if the child is vomiting. During feverish illnesses the body often needs *more* insulin, not less. During an illness it may be useful to use only clear (short-acting) insulin. You may have to give three or four injections a day as this is much more flexible and you can respond more quickly to changes in the situation. Give one third of the total daily insulin dose in the morning, as clear insulin only.
2 *Food.* Stop solid food but give sugary drinks e.g. Lucozade 60 ml (10 g) or orange squash with two teaspoons of sugar (10 g). Milk drinks and yogurt are an acceptable alternative for ill children. Aim to give 10-20 g of carbohydrate every hour.
3 *Blood tests.* At midday, check the blood sugar and if it is 13 mmol/l or more, give the same dose of clear insulin plus an extra 2 units. Repeat this process every 4-6 hours, increasing the dose of insulin if the blood sugar remains high. Once he is better, cut the insulin back to the original dose.

4 *Ketones.* Check the urine for ketones twice daily. If these are +++, either your son needs more food or his diabetes is going badly out of control.

5 *Vomiting.* Young diabetic children who vomit more than two or three times should *always* be seen by a doctor or specialist nurse to help supervise the illness. They can become dehydrated in the space of a few hours and if vomiting continues they will need fluid dripped into a vein. Unfortunately this means a hospital admission.

17 *I am headmaster of a school for deaf children and one of my pupils developed diabetes 2 years ago. Since then his learning ability has deteriorated and I wondered if this had any connection with his diabetes?*

No. Diabetes in itself has no effect on learning ability and there are plenty of diabetic children who excel academically. Poorly controlled diabetes with a very high blood sugar could reduce his powers of concentration. Hypoglycaemic attacks are usually short lasting but he could be missing a few key items while his blood glucose is low and be unable to catch up. At a psychological level, the double handicap of deafness and diabetes could be affecting his morale and self-confidence. Perhaps he would be helped by meeting other diabetic boys of his age. This often helps children to realise that diabetes is compatible with normal life and activities.

18 *My son was recently awarded a scholarship to a well-known public school but when they found he was diabetic, he was refused admission on medical grounds. They can give no positive reason for this and our consultant has tried very hard to make them change their minds. Why should he be so penalised?*

This was a disgraceful decision based on old-fashioned prejudice. It looks as if nothing will make the school change its mind but I wonder if you told the British Diabetic Association about this matter. They might have brought more pressure to bear to make the school reconsider this extraordinary decision.

19 *How does my son tell his school friends about his diabetes?*

It is very important that your son tells his close friends that he is diabetic. He should explain about hypos and tell them that if he does behave in an odd way they should make him take sugar and he should show them where he keeps his supplies. If your son shows his friends how he measures his blood glucose they will almost certainly be interested in diabetes and be keen to help him with it. As he becomes older and spends more time away from home he will come to depend more on his friends.

20 *My 10-year-old son moves on to a large comprehensive school in a few months time. Up till now he has been in a small junior school where all the staff know about his diabetes. I worry that he will be swamped in the 'big' school where he will come across lots of different teachers who know nothing about his condition. Have you any advice on this problem?*

Moving up to a big comprehensive school is always a daunting experience and is bound to cause the parents of a diabetic child extra worry. The important thing is to go and talk to your son's form teacher, preferably before the first day of term when he will have hundreds of new problems to cope with. Assume that the teacher knows nothing about diabetes and try to get across the following points:

a My child needs daily insulin injections.

b He may need to eat at certain unusual times.

c Describe how your son behaves when hypo and emphasise the importance of giving him sugar. If he is hypo do not send him to the school office alone.

d Staggered lunch hours may be a problem as he may need to eat at a fixed time each day.

e Please let us know if he is going to be kept in late (e.g. for detention) as parents of diabetics tend to worry if their children fail to show up.

f Make sure all his teachers know these facts.

The BDA supplies a School Pack which should help explain diabetes to his teachers and it is especially important to speak personally to his sports and swimming instructors. If there are problems with the school over such things as sports, outings or school meals, your diabetic clinic may have a specialist nurse or health visitor who could go to the school and explain things. You will probably have to repeat this exercise at the beginning of every school year.

21 *What arrangements can I make with school about my 9-year-old daughter's special requirements for school dinners?*

It is important to go and see the head teacher and preferably the caterer to explain that your daughter must have her dinner on time. Explain that she needs a certain amount of carbohydrate in a form which she will eat and that she should avoid puddings containing sugar. If the diabetic clinic has a specialist nurse or health visitor, she may be able to go to the school and give advice.

Most parents of diabetic children get round the whole problem by providing a packed lunch. This means that you have more control over what your daughter eats and you can supply the sort of food she likes and that is good for her. When she goes on to secondary school she may be faced with a cafeteria system. This should allow her to choose suitable food but she may also choose unsuitable items (e.g. jam doughnuts).

22 *My son is diabetic. Can I allow him to go on school trips?*

In general the answer is yes, but for your own peace of mind you would want to be satisfied that one of the staff on the trip was prepared to take responsibility for your son. Day trips should be no problem as long as someone can be sure that he eats on time and has his second injection if necessary. At junior school level long trips away from home, especially on the continent, could be more difficult and it really depends on you finding a member of staff that you can trust. They will need to keep an eye on your son and to know how to cope sensibly with problems like a bad hypo. Once in secondary school most diabetic children manage to go away on trips with the school, scouts or a youth group. Of course one of the adults in the party should be responsible, but as your son gets older he will be better able to look after himself. The British Diabetic Association has the following check list for school trips and holidays:

a Identification necklace or bracelet
b Glucose
c Insulin, syringe, needles
d Testing equipment for blood/urine
e Food to cover journeys with extra for unexpected delays
   This is part of the School Pack which is available from the BDA.

23 My 10-year-old child has heard about BDA camps from the clinic. I am a bit worried about letting him go off on his own for 2 weeks. Do you not think that I should wait a few years before sending him to a camp?

The BDA has been organising holidays for children since the 1930s and it has become an enormous enterprise. Nearly 1000 children take part in these holidays each year, so in one sense your son will not be on his own. Young children love going on group holidays, and the fact of being with other diabetics gives them a great sense of confidence – for once the diabetics are not the odd ones out. The children learn a great deal from each other and from the staff. Your son will have an exciting holiday and you will have a few weeks off from worrying about his diabetes.

24 Is it safe to let my little girl go on a BDA camp?

The Youth Department of the BDA has had years of experience in running holidays for children. The average camp consists of 30-35 children who are supervised by the following staff:

Warden, responsible for planning;
Senior Medical Officer, who is experienced in diabetes;
Junior Medical Officer;
2-4 Nurses, usually with a special interest in diabetes and/or children;
3 Dietitians;
1-2 Deputy Wardens;

8 Junior Leaders, young adults with diabetes themselves, who give up 2 weeks to help.

The staff/child ratio is about 1:2 and there is always close supervision on outings and all sports, especially swimming.

Diabetes and the adolescent

25 *My daughter and I are getting extremely anxious although our GP tells us there is nothing to worry about. She became diabetic when she was 14, 1 year after her periods had started. They stopped completely with the diabetes and have never started again, although we have now waited for two years. Is our GP right to be calm and patient, or are we right to be worried?*

A major upset to the system such as diabetes may cause periods to stop in a young girl. It is a little unusual for them not to reappear within 2 years and we would like to be certain that your daughter's diabetes is well controlled *and* that she is not underweight. Your doctor will be able to answer these two questions. If her diabetic control is good and she is normal weight, then it would be reasonable to await another year or two before embarking on further investigations. There is a very good chance that her periods will return spontaneously. If they do not return, nothing will be lost by waiting for another 2 years.

26 *I am nearly 16 and have not started menstruating yet. Is this because I am a diabetic? Since I was diagnosed, I have put on a lot of weight.*

On average, girls with diabetes do tend to start their periods at an older age. We assume from your question that you are now overweight and this may be another cause for delay in menstruation. Presumably you have begun to notice other signs of puberty such as breast development and the growth of pubic hair. If so, you should make a determined effort to lose weight and control your diabetes carefully. This will involve a reduction in your food intake and probably an adjustment on your dose of insulin. If, after another year,

you have still not seen a period then you should discuss
the matter with your doctor.

27 *My son has just heard that he will be going to university
next year. While we are all delighted and proud of him,
I worry because he will be living away from home for
the first time. For the 7 years of him being diabetic I
have accepted most of the anxiety and practical
arrangement of his meals and he has done his best to
ignore his diabetes. How is he now going to face it alone?*

If your son is bright enough to get into university, he should
be quite capable of looking after his diabetes. However, you
are right to point out that your son's attitude towards his
diabetes is also important. All mothers worry when their
children leave home for the first time and it is natural for
a diabetic child to cause extra worry. You can be sure,
however, that the training you have given him over the
years will bear fruit. Most children like to spread their wings
when first leaving home and you can expect a period of
adjustment to his new responsibilities. Provided he realises
why you regard good diabetic control as important, he will
probably become a model diabetic in good time. It would
also be sensible for your son to contact the diabetic clinic
in his university town, so that they can give support if
necessary.

28 *How does diabetes affect my prospects for marriage?*

We have never heard a diabetic girl or boy complain that
diabetes has put off potential marriage partners, although
we suppose it could be used as an excuse if someone was
looking for a convenient way out of a relationship.

If your diabetes has affected your own self-confidence and
made you feel a second-class citizen, then you may sell
yourself short and lose out in that way. You can be assured
that diabetics make excellent husbands and wives.

29 *I am an insulin dependent diabetic and have recently
made friends with a super boy but am frightened that
he will be put off if I tell him I am a diabetic. What
should I do?*

The standard answer is that you must tell your new boyfriend at the beginning. However, you have obviously found this a problem or you would not be asking the question. There is no need to broadcast the fact that you have diabetes. It would be possible to conceal diabetes completely from a close companion, although sooner or later he will inevitably discover the truth.

Once you get to know him better your best plan would be to drop a few hints about diabetes without making a song and dance about it. If the relationship grows, you will want to share each other's problems – including diabetes. We have never known a serious relationship break up because of diabetes.

30 My 15-year-old son developed diabetes at the age of 12. Initially he was very sensible about his diabetes but recently he has become resentful saying that he is different from everyone else and blaming us for his disease. What do you suggest?

You must first realise that most diabetics of all ages (and their parents) feel resentful about this disease which causes so much inconvenience in a person's life. Many 12-year-old children conform with their parent's wishes and generally do as they are told. However, by the age of 15 other important pressures are beginning to bear on a developing young person. In the case of a boy, the most important factors in life are (1) his friends and (2) girls. While you as parents are prepared to make allowances and provide special meals etc, most young lads want to join the gang and do not wish to appear 'different'.

At a Firbush camp (which was restricted to hand-picked, well adjusted young adults with diabetes), the organisers were horrified to discover how angry the young people felt about their condition. Of course this anger will often be directed at the parents. We can only give advice in general terms which apply to most adolescent problems:

a Keep lines of communication open.
b Boost his self-esteem by giving praise where praise is due even if your own self-esteem is taking a hammering.

c Allow your son to make his own decisions about diabetes. If you force him to comply, he will simply avoid confrontation by deceiving you.

d Remember that difficult adolescents turn into successful adults.

31 Our 15-year-old daughter has had diabetes for 4 years and until recently has always been well controlled. Now it is very difficult to get her to take an interest in her diabetes and she has stopped doing blood tests. At the last clinic visit, the doctor said that her HbA₁ was very high and he thought she was probably missing some of her injections. I really do not know what to do.

This is a very upsetting situation for all concerned and unfortunately it is not uncommon. Diabetes is difficult because it places great demands and restrictions on people but in the short term they have nothing to show for their efforts. Like most girls of her age, your daughter probably wants to lose weight and she may have discovered that allowing her sugars to float up is a very effective way of quickly losing a few pounds in weight. Thus there may be positive gain to your daughter in missing a few insulin injections.

There is no easy solution to this problem especially as many girls in this situation brightly turn up at the clinic and announce that 'everything is fine'. Simply challenging your daughter and threatening her with long-term complications of diabetes is unlikely to do much good. It is better to try and get her to realise that you understand that living with diabetes is not easy and allowing her to express her own feelings about it. Of course she may be at a stage of feeling that parents are light-years away from her own experience in which case she is more likely to unburden herself to a close friend, especially someone else with diabetes.

8
Long term complications

Introduction

Before insulin was discovered diabetics did not survive long
enough to develop diabetic complications as we know them
today. In the early days after the great discovery, it was
commonly believed that insulin cured diabetes. We are now
in a better position to realise that although insulin produced
nothing short of miraculous recovery in those on the verge
of death from diabetic coma and allowed them to return to
a full, active and enjoyable life, it is no cure for the condition.
But used properly insulin results in full health and activity
and a long life.

The life expectancy of diabetics has increased progressively
since insulin was first used in 1922 and there are now many
hundreds (and probably many thousands) of patients who

have successfully completed more than 50 years of insulin treatment. Increased longevity has brought with it a number of the so-called 'long-term complications', some of which (such as heart disease and gangrene of the legs) occur not uncommonly in non-diabetics and are generally considered to be inevitable consequences of the ageing process (we have to die sometime!). Others are not seen in non-diabetics. These conditions are therefore considered the long-term complications specific to diabetes; the three most important are eye damage (retinopathy), nerve damage (neuropathy) and kidney damage (nephropathy).

Diabetic retinopathy can lead to loss of vision and indeed is now the commonest cause of blindness registration in people under 65 in the United Kingdom. Fortunately it only leads to visual loss in a small proportion of diabetics. Diabetic neuropathy, by leading to loss of feeling, particularly in the feet, makes affected patients very susceptible to infections and occasionally gangrene with the subsequent need for an amputation. It can also cause impotence. Diabetic nephropathy can cause kidney failure and is now the commonest reason for referral for renal dialysis and transplantation in the United Kingdom and Europe in young people, although again it only occurs in a very small number of diabetics.

It is not surprising that diabetics dread the thought of diabetic complications. In the past they worried about them but never enquired about them as they were a taboo subject. This meant that they were only for discussion between doctors and not between doctor and patient.

The world has changed and today patients rightly demand to know more about their condition ('whose life is it anyway?') and the majority now find out about the dreaded 'complications' very soon after they are diagnosed as diabetic. There are so many old wives' tales circulating about diabetic complications and it is perhaps *the* most important area in diabetic counselling where the *facts* rather than opinions must be stated.

Although medical science has made impressive progress since the discovery of insulin there is still a long way to go. The absolute proof that good blood sugar control in diabetic patients will prevent the complications developing has not yet been made. The scientific evidence from studies of experimental diabetes in animals is very strongly in favour of this however, and all the evidence from humans is in keeping with this. We believe that the specific diabetic complications are a direct result of a raised blood sugar level over many years and that they are all preventable by maintenance of normal blood glucose values, HbA_1, or fructosamine values.

Some of the questions in this chapter relating to eyes and feet are not strictly questions about complications, but as they do not easily fit in anywhere else in the book they have been included in this chapter under their specific headings.

General questions

1   *Can a diabetic who is controlled only by diet suffer from diabetic complications?*

Complications may occur in any type of diabetic. The cause of diabetic complications is not well understood although bad control of diabetes is the most important predisposing factor. The duration of diabetes is also important – complications are rare in the first few years of the disorder and occur more commonly after many years.

Diabetics treated with diet alone are usually diagnosed in middle or late life. At the time their diagnosis is made, the disease may have been present for a long time, often many years, without the person having any knowledge of it, and therefore without any attempt being made to control it. Thus it is not surprising that complications can occur in some diabetics even when they are treated with diet alone. Good control in these patients is clearly just as important as in insulin dependent diabetics.

2   *My child has been diabetic for 3 years and I am trying to find out more about the disease. I recently read a book which said that some diabetics may suffer coronaries or go blind. I don't know if this is true and find it very*

upsetting. Surely they shouldn't be allowed to write such things in books that diabetics might read?

You raise a very important matter. Diabetes was almost always fatal within 1 or 2 years of diagnosis until the outlook was revolutionised by the discovery of insulin. None the less, it still required a lot of work and experimental development in the manufacture of insulin before a diabetic was able to lead an almost normal life, with the aid of one or two insulin injections a day.

After several years it became obvious to doctors that some diabetics were developing what we now call 'chronic complications'. It was clear that these took many years to develop. This became the object of a massive research drive, requiring the investment of much effort and entailing many years of work by doctors and other scientists. We now understand how some of these complications occur, and we know how to treat them if they occur. We realise that strict diabetic control is important in their prevention. For this reason, all doctors and other medical personnel treating diabetics spend much of their time and effort trying to help patients improve their control and keep their blood sugars as near normal as possible. These complications do not occur in all diabetics by any means, although nowadays, when diabetics are living longer than ever before, the complications are becoming more important.

You ask whether facts like these should be made available to diabetics. The majority of patients like to be correctly informed about their condition, its management and its complications. Modern treatment involves increasing frankness between doctors and patients in discussing all aspects of the condition. A recent survey among our own diabetic patients showed the majority demanded to be told the facts about complications.

3   *What are the complications and what should I keep a lookout for to ensure that they are picked up as soon as possible?*

The complications specific to diabetes are known as diabetic retinopathy, neuropathy and nephropathy. Retinopathy means damage to the retina at the back of the eye. Neuropathy means damage to the nerves which can affect nerves supplying any part of the body but generally referred to as either 'peripheral' when affecting nerves supplying muscles and skin, or 'autonomic' when affecting nerves supplying organs such as the bladder, the bowel and the heart. Nephropathy is damage affecting the kidney, which in the first instance makes them more leaky so that albumin appears in the urine; at a later stage it may affect the function of the kidneys and in severe cases lead to kidney failure.

The best way of detecting them early is to visit your doctor or clinic for regular review. Regular attendance at the diabetic clinic is important so that any complications can be picked up at an early stage and treatment instigated where appropriate.

Prevention is, however, clearly better than treatment and we believe that if you can control your diabetes properly you will not be likely to suffer these complications.

4 *Is it possible to avoid complications in later life? If so, how?*

Yes. We believe that all diabetics could avoid complications if they were able to control their diabetes perfectly from the day they were diagnosed as diabetics. There are now many people on record who have gone 50 years or more with insulin dependent diabetes who are completely free from any sign of complication. The best advice to give you on how to avoid them is to take the control of your blood sugar and diabetes seriously from the outset and to attend regularly for review and supervision with somebody experienced in the management of patients with diabetes. Focus on learning how to look after yourself in such a way that you can achieve and maintain a normal HbA$_1$ or fructosamine level (p. 96). If you can do that and keep the HbA$_1$ normal you can look forward to a life free from the risk of diabetic complications.

5 *To what extent are the complications of diabetes genetically determined?*

This is a very difficult question. Most specialists believe that there is a hereditary factor which predisposes some patients to develop complications and makes others relatively immune from them but so far scientific evidence to prove this is not very strong.

6   *What is the expected lifespan of someone with insulin dependent diabetes and why?*

The lifespan depends to a very great extent on how old the patient is when the diagnosis is made. The older the patient at the time of diagnosis the closer the lifespan is to that of non-diabetics. Looking back to the past we know that when diabetes was diagnosed in early childhood then the lifespan in insulin dependent diabetics was generally reduced, mainly because of premature deaths from coronary attacks and kidney failure. We know, however, that the lifespan of diabetics has improved with better medical care. We believe that the life expectancy of a child diagnosed as a diabetic in the 1990s is longer than ever previously possible and may be nearly as good as an equivalent non-diabetic child. We know that longevity is greatest in diabetics who make regular visits to their clinic and who keep themselves under strict control. Those who die prematurely are more likely to be those who do not attend clinic regularly, are not being supervised adequately and do not control themselves well.

7   *My diabetic specialist has said that it does not follow that unstable diabetics get all the side-effects and ill health in their later life, often evidently well controlled diabetics became ill and unbalanced diabetics remained reasonably healthy. Is this really true?*

There is an element of truth in the statement that you report but the word 'often' should be replaced by 'very occasionally' and the statement should read 'well controlled diabetics rarely become ill and develop side-effects whereas unstable and unbalanced diabetics often develop ill health and side-effects in later life'.

8   *For the last 2 years my cheeks have become increasingly
     hollow although my weight is static – is this due to
     diabetes?*

Quite a lot of middle-aged and elderly people become slim
up top and pear shaped below, whether or not they have
diabetes.

However, there is a rare form of diabetes, called
lipoatrophic diabetes and this could possibly be the
explanation for the hollowing of your cheek. This is not a
recognised complication of diabetes but a rare form of the
condition.

9   *I have had diabetes for the past 10 years and have
     recently developed an unsightly skin condition on my
     shins. I was referred to a skin specialist who told me it
     was related to my diabetes and would be very difficult
     to cure. What is it and why does it occur?*

Necrobiosis lipoidica diabeticorum (otherwise known as
necrobiosis) is a strange non-infective but often unsightly
condition that most commonly appears on the shins although
it may occasionally appear elsewhere. It may occur in people
years before they develop diabetes or at any time thereafter.
Nobody knows much about it and treatment is not very
satisfactory. Local steroid injections or freezing with liquid
nitrogen (cryotherapy) can improve the cosmetic appearance
by changing it from an active red patch to an inactive pale
scar.

Eyes

10   *I had a tendency towards short-sightedness before being
     diagnosed as a diabetic. Is this likely to increase my
     chances of developing eye complications later on?*

Short-sightedness makes not the slightest difference to
developing diabetic eye complications – it has been said that
those with severe short-sightedness may actually be less,
rather than more, prone to retinopathy. Vision may vary
with changes in diabetic control. Severe changes in blood
sugar can alter the shape of the lens in the eye and thus

alter its focusing capacity. It is therefore common for those diabetics with a high blood sugar (i.e. with poor control) to have difficulty with distant vision – a situation which changes completely when diabetes is controlled and blood sugar reduced. When this occurs, vision changes again, so that a person experiences difficulty with near vision and therefore with reading. This can be very frightening, at least until it is understood. After 2 or 3 weeks, vision always returns to the state it was in before diabetes developed.

11 *I have just been discovered to have diabetes and the glasses that I have had for several years seem no longer suitable, but my doctor tells me not to get them changed until my diabetes has been brought under control – is this right?*

Yes. When the sugar concentration in the body rises this affects the focusing ability of the eyes but it is only a temporary effect, and things go back to normal once the sugar has been brought under control. If you change your glasses now you will be able to see better but as soon as your diabetes is brought under control you will need to change them yet again, so it is better to wait until your diabetes has been controlled for at least a month before going to the optician again.

12 *As a diabetic how often should I have my eyes checked?*

If your diabetes is well controlled and your vision is normal and you have no diabetic changes then once a year is generally sufficient. It is important that you do have your eyes checked once a year as after many years diabetes can affect the back of the eye (the retina). The routine eye checks are aimed at picking this up at an early stage before it seriously affects your vision and at a stage where it can be effectively treated.

13 *Who is the best person to check my eyes once a year?*

This can be done by either the specialist in the diabetic clinic, the specialist in the eye clinic, your general practitioner if he feels that he is sufficiently well trained to do this, or your local ophthalmic optician if he feels able to do it. You need to undergo two examinations. The first is to test your visual acuity – which is basically the ability to read the letters on the chart down to the right line. The second is to have the back of your eyes looked at with an ophthalmoscope: this is the more difficult of the two examinations and can only be done by somebody with special training. These days some clinics offer a service to GPs which enables the patient to have the backs of the eyes photographed: the photographs are then looked at by an eye specialist, and the results are sent to the GP.

14 *Last time I was having my eyes checked from the chart, the nurse made me look through a small pinhole. Why was this?*

The pinhole acts as a universal correcting lens. If your vision was improved when looking through the hole it indicates that you may need spectacles for distant vision.

15 *Why do they put drops in my eyes at the clinic?*

These drops enlarge the pupil and make it easier for the doctor examining the back of your eye with an ophthalmoscope. It is sometimes not possible to examine the eye properly without dilating the pupil to get a clearer view. As these drops also paralyse the lens that allows your sight to focus properly, you should not drive immediately after leaving the clinic. The effect of the drops may last as long as 24 hours. It is often worthwhile taking sunglasses with you to the clinic if they are likely to put drops in your eyes, as otherwise the bright sunlight can be very uncomfortable until the drops have worn off.

16 *I have had diabetes for 20 years and seem to be quite well. When the doctor looked in my eyes at my last visit he said he could see some mild diabetic changes and referred me to a clinic called the Retinopathy Clinic. Am I about to go blind?*

There is no need for alarm. It would be surprising if after 20 years of diabetes it was not possible for him to find some changes in the eye. He probably considers it appropriate that you should be seen by an eye specialist and maybe

have some special photographs taken of the eyes in order
to examine them in more detail and to be of use for future
reference.

17   What is retinopathy?

Retinopathy is a condition affecting the back of the eye (the
retina) which may occur in long-standing diabetics, particularly those in whom control has not been very good. There
is a gradual development of abnormalities of the blood flow
to the back of the eye which can lead to deterioration of
vision as a result of either disturbance of the function of
the eye itself, or as a result of bleeding into the eye from
the abnormal blood vessels. Retinopathy is usually diagnosed
by examination of the eye with an ophthalmoscope, and it
can usually be picked up a long time before it leads to any
disturbance in vision. Treatment at this stage with a laser
usually arrests the process and slows or stops further
deterioration.

18   On a recent TV programme it was stated that diabetics over 40 years of age were likely to become blind. This has horrified me because my 9-year-old son is diabetic and unfortunately some of his school friends have told him about the programme. What can I say to reassure him?

Some damage to the eyes (retinopathy) occurs quite commonly
after more than 20 years of diabetes. Retinopathy is, however,
usually slight and does not affect vision. Only a very small
proportion of diabetics actually go blind, probably no more
than 7% of those who have had diabetes for 30 years. Because
of the tremendous advances that have occurred in diabetes
over the last 20 or 30 years, this proportion of diabetics
will be much less when your son has had diabetes for 30
years. The figure is likely to be smaller in well controlled
diabetics and larger in those who are always badly controlled.

19   Can I wear contact lenses and if so would you recommend hard or soft ones?

The fact that you are a diabetic should not interfere with
your use of contact lenses or influence the sort of lens you

are given. Of greater importance in the choice of type would
be local factors affecting your eyes and vision, and the correct
person to advise you would be an ophthalmologist or qualified
optician specializing in prescribing and fitting contact lenses.
It might be sensible to let him know that you are diabetic
and you must follow the advice you are given, particularly
to prevent infection; but this applies to diabetics and
non-diabetics alike.

*20   Are flashes of light and specks across one's vision
      symptoms of serious eye trouble with diabetic people?*

Although diabetics do get eye trouble, flashing lights and
specks are not usually symptoms of this particular problem.
You should discuss it with your own doctor who will want
to examine your eyes in case there is any problem.

21   Why does diabetes affect the eyes?

A simple question but difficult to answer. Current research
indicates strongly that it is the excess glucose in the
bloodstream that directly damages the eyes mainly through
affecting the lining of the small blood vessels that carry
blood to the retina. The damage to these vessels seems to
be directly proportional to how high the blood sugar is and
how long it has been increased. This is the reason why we
all believe that this can be avoided by bringing the blood
sugar down to normal.

22   What causes cataracts in diabetes?

Cataracts occur in non-diabetics as well as diabetics and as
such are not a specific complication of diabetes. There is a
very rare form of cataract that can occur in childhood with
very badly controlled diabetes; this is known as a 'snowstorm'
cataract from its characteristic appearance to the specialist.
The normal common variety of cataract which occurs in
diabetics is exactly the same as that occurring in
non-diabetics although it may occur at a slightly earlier age
in patients with diabetes. It is really due to the ageing
process affecting the substance that makes up the lens of
the eye. It begins to develop wrinkles and becomes less clear

than it was until eventually it becomes so opaque that it is not possible to see properly through it.

23 Please could you tell me what microaneurysms of the eye are?

Microaneurysms are little balloon-like dilations in the very small capillaries of the blood vessels supplying the retina at the back of the eye. They are one of the earliest signs that the high blood sugar has damaged the lining to these capillaries. They do not interfere as such with vision but give an early warning that retinopathy has begun to develop. There is some evidence to suggest that these can get better with the introduction of perfect control whereas at later stages of diabetic retinopathy reversal is not usually possible. Anyone who has microaneurysms must have regular eye checks so that any serious developments are detected at an early stage.

24 What is laser treatment?

Laser treatment is a form of treatment with a narrow beam of intense light used to cause very small burns on the back of the eye (retina). It is used in the treatment of many eye conditions including diabetic retinopathy. The laser burns are created in the parts of the retina not used for detailed vision, sparing the important areas required for reading, etc. This form of treatment has been shown to arrest or delay the progress of retinopathy, provided that it is given in adequate amounts at a sufficiently early stage before useful vision is lost. It is sometimes necessary to give small doses of laser treatment intermittently over many years; occasionally it can all be dealt with over a relatively short period. The eyes need continuous assessment thereafter, as it is possible that further treatment may be needed at any stage.

25 Can photocoagulation damage the eyes?

The strict answer to this is yes, but uncommonly. Occasionally the lesion produced by the photocoagulation treatment can spread and involve vital parts of the retina so that vision is affected. Normally treatment is confined to the parts of the retina which have no noticeable effect on vision other than perhaps to narrow the field of view slightly. Photocoagulation can also occasionally result in rupturing of a blood vessel and haemorrhage and after a great deal of photocoagulation there is a slight risk of damage to the lens causing a type of cataract.

26 Is glaucoma related to diabetes?

Yes. Although glaucoma can occur quite commonly in non-diabetics there is a slightly increased risk in diabetics. This is usually confined to those who have advanced diabetic eye problems (proliferative retinopathy).

Occasionally the eye drops that are put in your eyes to dilate the pupil to allow a proper view of the retina can precipitate an attack of glaucoma. The signs of this would be pain in the affected eye together with blurring of vision coming on some hours after the drops have been put in. Should this occur you should seek *urgent* medical advice either from your own doctor or from an accident and emergency department of your local hospital because this is reversible with rapid treatment but can cause serious damage if not treated.

27 Every time I receive my copy of Balance, the BDA newspaper, I have the impression that the print gets smaller. Is this true or is there something wrong with my eyes?

I am afraid that eyesight does tend to deteriorate with age whether one is diabetic or not. The first thing to do is to visit your optician and get your eyesight checked to see if it can be improved with glasses as this may be all that is required. For people who are unfortunate and suffer from retinopathy to the degree that reading becomes impossible there are things that can help. *Balance*, for example, is available to members of the British Diabetic Association as a cassette recording and this service is free of charge, although to satisfy Post Office regulations you have to have a certificate of blindness before the cassette can be sent to you. Books in large type can be obtained from most public libraries and most libraries also loan books on cassette. Some libraries now have Kurtzweil machines which can read to you, which are useful for letters.

The Royal National Institute for the Blind also has a talking book service which is excellent. It is planned that this book will be available as a talking book from the RNIB.

Feet, Chiropody and Footwear

28   I have just developed diabetes and have been warned that as a diabetic I am much more likely to get into trouble with my feet and need to take great care of them – what does this mean?

As long as you keep your diabetes well controlled and have no loss of sensation in your feet and good circulation to your feet then you are no more at risk than a non-diabetic. In the long-term there is a suggestion that diabetics are more prone to foot trouble and it pays to get into good habits – inspecting the feet daily, keeping the nails properly trimmed and avoiding ill-fitting shoes right from the outset. As a diabetic you usually have access to the local NHS chiropodist who will check your feet and advise you on any questions that you may have.

29   I have had diabetes for 10 years and as far as I can see it is quite under control and I am told that I am free from complications, but I cannot help worrying about the possibility of developing gangrene in the feet – can you tell me what it is and what causes it?

Gangrene is the death of tissues in any part of the body. It most commonly occurs in the toes and fingers. Gangrene also occurs in non-diabetics, and diabetics are prone to it only if they have serious impairment of blood supply to their feet or loss of sensation. If the major blood vessels get clogged up then this can lead to gangrene and the main cause of this is smoking; generally it occurs only in older people and is related to the progressive hardening of the arteries that is part of the ageing process. The other form of gangrene that can occur in diabetics is that due to the presence of infection which usually affects the feet in people who have lost sensation because of diabetic neuropathy. This can occur even in the presence of a good blood supply. Any ulcer or infection affecting the feet must be treated promptly and seriously, and if you see anything on your feet which you are worried about you should consult your doctor or chiropodist without delay.

30 As a diabetic do I have to take any special precautions when cutting my toenails?

It is important for everyone to cut their toenails straight across, following the shape of the end of the toe, and not cutting deep into the corners. The nails should not be cut too short, and you should not use any sharp instrument to clean down the side of the nail. These measures are to avoid the possibility of ingrowing toenails.

31 I have a thick callus on the top of one of my toes – can I use a corn plaster on this?

No. Do not use any corn remedies on your feet. Consult a State Registered chiropodist to have it treated.

32 My son has picked up athlete's foot. He is a diabetic treated with insulin – do I have to take any special precautions about using the powder and cream given to me by my doctor?

No. Athlete's foot is very common and is due to a fungal infection and should respond briskly to the treatment with the appropriate anti-fungal preparation, plus the usual precautions of keeping the feet clean and drying them carefully.

33 Does diabetes cause bunions?

No. Bunions are no more common in diabetics than non-diabetics.

34 I have had diabetes for 25 years and I have been warned that the sensation in my feet is not normal. I am troubled with an ingrowing toenail on my big toe which often gets red but does not hurt – what shall I do about it?

You should seek help and advice urgently. You are particularly vulnerable to the infection spreading without you being aware of the seriousness of it because it does not hurt as much as it would in someone with normal sensation.

35 I am 67 and have had diabetes for 15 years. As far as I can tell my feet are quite healthy but as my vision is not very good I find it difficult to inspect my feet properly – what can I do about it?

Do you have a friend or relative who can inspect your feet regularly and trim your nails? If this is not possible then the sensible thing to do would be to attend a chiropodist regularly.

36 Do I have to pay for chiropody?

Most hospital diabetic departments provide a chiropody service free of charge. Outside the hospital service chiropody under the NHS is limited to pensioners, pregnant women and school children. Although local rules do vary, most districts consider diabetics as a priority group and do offer free chiropody, but you should check locally before obtaining treatment. If seeing a chiropodist privately make sure that he or she is State Registered (SRCh after their name).

37 What are the signs that diabetes is affecting my feet?

There are two major dangers from diabetes which may affect the feet. The first is due to diminished blood supply from arterial thickening. This leads to poor circulation with cold feet even in warm weather and cramps in the calf on walking (intermittent claudication). This is not a specific complication of diabetes and does occur quite commonly in non-diabetics. The major problem here is arterial sclerosis and smoking is a more important cause of this than diabetes. In severe cases this can progress to gangrene. The other way that diabetes can affect the feet is through damage to the nerves (neuropathy) which results in diminished sensation. This can be quite difficult to detect unless the feet are examined by an expert. The danger is that any minor damage to the foot, be it from a cut or abrasion or ill-fitting shoe, will not cause the usual painful reaction so that damage can result from continued injury or infection spreading. It is important that you should know whether the sensation in your feet is normal or impaired. Make sure you ask your doctor this at your next clinic review.

38 My daughter is diabetic and often walks barefoot around the house. Shall I discourage her from doing this?

It is well known that diabetics are prone to problems with their feet which are, for the most part, due to carelessness and can be avoided. The reason these problems occur is probably because, with increasing duration of diabetes, sensation in the feet tends to be dulled. Most diabetics are unaware of this and this is the source of danger as, to the unwary, damage to the feet is the first indication of the problem. By then it may be too late!

The dangers to the feet of diabetic children, however, are really very slight and there is no reason to discourage your daughter from walking about barefoot at an early age.

39 What special care should I take of my feet during the winter?

In older diabetics the blood supply to the feet may not be as abundant as in non-diabetics and this will make the feet more vulnerable to damage by severe cold. As winter is cold and wet we tend to wear warmer thick clothing, and a pair of shoes which may be comfortable in the summer may be unpleasantly tight when worn with thick woolly socks or stockings. This may damage the feet and also make them more sensitive to the cold It could numb the sensation completely. All these effects will be accentuated if your feet become wet. Make sure your shoes are comfortable, fit well, and allow room for you to wear an adequately thick pair of socks, preferably made of wool or other absorbent material. Use weather-proof shoes, overshoes or boots if you are going to be out for any length of time in the rain or snow, and dry your feet carefully if they get wet. Do not put your cold – and slightly numb – feet straight onto a hot water bottle or near a hot fire because you may find that when the feeling comes back the heat was excessive, and chilblains are a likely result. Feet also need protection during the summer as wearing open sandals can cause problems from possible damage by sharp stones, etc.

40 How can one give continual protection to one's feet?

It is extremely difficult. If the sensation is normal then generally you have very little need to worry, but if there is even slight numbness of the feet you should be continually vigilant and seek the advice of another to inspect the parts that you find difficulty in seeing. If the circulation is poor go to great lengths to keep your feet warm and well protected.

41 I have suffered from foot ulcers for many years and would be grateful if you could suggest a cleaning fluid.

You should not attempt treatment of these yourself and should seek medical advice and expert chiropody. Foot ulcers in diabetics are most often associated with loss of sensation in the feet (neuropathy), and you need to have your feet examined by your specialist and find out whether you have loss of sensation. If this is the case then you need to attend for regular chiropody and to learn all the ways of avoiding trouble once sensation has become impaired. It may be necessary to have special shoes made by a shoe fitter (Orthotist).

42 Can you give me a simple list of rules for foot care?

The list of foot rules that follows is aimed specifically for those who have abnormalities of either blood supply or nerve damage (neuropathy). If you have any impairment of vision then you should get somebody else with good eyesight to help you in your regular inspection and care of your feet.

Foot care rules

Do Wash your feet daily with soap and warm water. Do not use hot water – check the temperature of the water with your elbow.

Do Dry feet well with a soft towel, especially between the toes.

Do Apply a gentle skin cream, such as E45, if your skin is rough and dry.

Do Change socks or stockings daily.

Do Wear well fitting shoes. Make sure they are wide enough, deep enough and long enough with a good fastening that you have to undo to get your foot in and out of the shoe. This will prevent the foot from slipping.

Do Run your hand around the inside of the shoes each day before putting them on to check that there is nothing that will rub your feet.

Do Wear new shoes for short periods of time and check your feet afterwards.

Do Cut toenails straight across following the shape of the end of the toe, not deep into the corners. This is easier after bathing.

Do Check your feet daily when bathing and see your chiropodist or doctor about any problems.

Do See a State Registered chiropodist if in any doubt about foot care.

Do not Put your feet on hot water bottles or sit too close to a fire or radiator, and avoid extremes of cold and heat.

Do not Use corn paints or plasters or attempt to cut your own corns with knives or razors under any circumstances.

Do not Wear tight garters. Wear a suspender belt or tights instead.

Do not Neglect even slight injuries.

Do not Walk barefoot.

Do not Let feet get dry and cracked. Use E45 or hand lotion to keep skin soft.

Do not Cut the toenails too short or dig down the sides of the nail.

Do not Wear socks with holes in them.

Do not Sit with your legs crossed.

Do not Smoke.

Seek advice immediately if you notice:
any colour change in your leg or foot,
any discharge from a break or crack in the skin, or from
a corn or from beneath a toenail,
any swelling or throbbing in any part of your foot.

First aid measures

Minor injuries can be treated at home provided professional
help is sought if the injury does not respond quickly to first
aid. Minor cuts and abrasions should be cleaned gently with
cotton wool or gauze and then a modern antiseptic, such as
Savlon or cetrimide cream, should be applied. Clean gauze
should be lightly bandaged in place. If blisters occur, do not
prick them. If they burst dress as minor cuts. Never use
strong medicaments such as iodine. Never place adhesive
strapping directly over a wound; always apply gauze first.

Kidneys

*43   Why does diabetes sometimes affect the kidneys and if
it does how is it revealed?*

There are several ways in which diabetes may affect the
kidneys. If there was a lot of sugar in the urine this
predisposes you to infection which can spread from the
bladder up to the kidneys (cystitis and pyelonephritis).
Occasionally chronic kidney infections can produce very little
in the way of symptoms and only be revealed by routine
tests. In long-standing and poorly controlled diabetics high
blood glucose can affect the small blood vessels supplying
the kidney in the same way as it may affect the small blood
vessels supplying the retina of the eye – this does not produce
any symptoms but will be picked up on a routine urine test
carried out at the diabetic clinic. Massive amounts of albumin
may be lost in the urine which may make the urine froth
and lead to accumulation of fluid in the body and the
development of swelling around the ankles (oedema). For
patients who have had long-standing kidney problems kidney

failure may eventually develop. This is usually picked up by blood tests and urine tests many years before the symptoms develop.

44 Are diabetics with kidney failure suitable for dialysis and transplantation?

Yes. The majority of diabetics who are unfortunate enough to end up with kidney failure are suitable for both forms of treatment.

Dialysis (or chronic renal replacement therapy) is of two major types. The older type is haemodialysis where the blood is washed in a special machine twice a week; the more recent is by a type of dialysis known as CAPD (chronic ambulatory peritoneal dialysis) where fluid is washed in and out of the abdomen on a daily basis. Diabetics seem to be rather good at this, it seems to be rather suitable for the patients with diabetes and is in many ways simpler and cheaper than haemodialysis. Eventual transplantation is the aim of most dialysis programmes but the supply of suitable kidneys is a limiting factor here. The source of kidneys is either from people dying accidentally who have donated their kidneys or from live related donors who have agreed to give one of their two normal kidneys, usually to a relative suffering from kidney failure. A normal person can manage perfectly well with one kidney without any shortening of life providing that kidney does not get damaged. The donor of course will have to have an operation and will be slightly more vulnerable as a result because he will have only one kidney to rely on instead of two.

45 I was found to have protein (albumin) in my urine when I last attended the diabetic clinic – what does this mean?

If it was only a trace of protein it may mean nothing but you should get your urine checked again to make sure it remains clear. If it is a consistent finding it may indicate that you have an infection in the bladder or kidney (cystitis or pyelonephritis) or it could indicate that you have developed a degree of diabetic kidney damage (nephropathy). There are innumerable other causes of protein (albumin) in the urine and it is not necessarily related to the fact that you are a diabetic. If it is a consistent finding it will usually need to be investigated and you should ask your doctor to keep you informed of the results of the investigation.

Nerves

46 I have been a diabetic on insulin for 3 years. Eighteen months ago I started to get pains in both legs and could barely walk. Despite treatment I am still suffering. Can you tell me what can be done to ease this pain?

There are many causes of leg pains, and only one is due specifically to diabetes. This is a particularly vicious form of neuritis – in other words, a form of nerve damage which causes singularly unpleasant pain, chiefly in the feet or thighs, or sometimes both. The pain sensation is either one of pins and needles, or constant burning, and is often worse at night causing lack of sleep. Contact from clothes or bedclothes is often acutely uncomfortable. Fortunately this form of neuritis is rather uncommon and always disappears, although it may take many months before doing so. Very good control of the diabetes is important and helps to alleviate the symptoms and speed their recovery. Relief is otherwise obtained by good pain-killers, as recommended by a doctor, and sometimes assisted by sleeping tablets. Vitamins may help. Remember that eventually recovery occurs – otherwise it is easy to get despondent. Also remember that the diagnosis must be made by a doctor who will consider all the various causes of leg pains before coming to a diagnosis of diabetic neuritis.

A new form of tablet treatment (aldose reductase inhibitors) has recently been introduced for this condition. This treatment is still very much in the experimental stage but the results so far look quite promising.

47 I have been a diabetic for many years but my general health is good and I am very stable. During the last year, however, I have developed an extreme soreness on the soles of my feet whenever pressure has been applied, e.g. when digging with a spade, standing on ladders,

*walking on hard ground or stones, even when applying
the accelerator in the car. If I thump an object with the
palm of my hand I suffer the same soreness. The pain
is extreme and sometimes lasts for a day or so. Could
you tell me if you have heard of this condition in other
diabetics and what is the reason for it?*

These symptoms may be due to diabetic neuropathy, a
condition which occasionally occurs in long-standing diabetes,
due to damage to the nerves. It affects the feet more often
than other parts of the body and often produces painful
tingling or burning sensations in the feet although numbness
is perhaps more common. Strict control of the diabetes is
important for the prevention and treatment of this
complication and it can be made worse by moderate or high
alcohol consumption.

*48   I am a diabetic controlled on diet alone. I suffer from
neuritis in my face. My GP says there is no apparent
reason for this but I wondered if it had anything to do
with my diabetes.*

There are a number of types of neuritis affecting the face
which have absolutely nothing to do with diabetes including
shingles (herpes zoster) and Bell's palsy although, of course,
both can occur in diabetics. The only forms of diabetic neuritis
affecting the face are those that occasionally affect the
muscles of the eye leading to double vision and the very
rare complication known as 'gustatory sweating' where
sweating breaks out across the head and scalp at the start
of a meal.

*49   I have recently been told that the tingling sensation in
my fingers is due to carpal tunnel syndrome and not
neuropathy as was first thought. Can you please explain
the difference?*

In carpal tunnel syndrome (which occurs almost as commonly
in non-diabetics as it does in diabetics) the nerves supplying
the skin over the fingers, the palm of the hand and some
of the muscles in the hand get compressed at the wrist.
Occasionally injections of hydrocortisone or related steroids

into the wrist will relieve it or it may require a small operation at the wrist to relieve the tension on the nerve. This usually brings about a dramatic relief of any pain associated with it and a recovery of sensation and muscle strength with time. Diabetic neuropathy more commonly affects the feet than the hands and is usually a painless loss of sensation starting with the tips of the toes or fingers and moving up the legs or arms. It is only very occasionally painful. This is due to some form of generalised damage to the nerves, not due to compression of any one nerve and is much more difficult to treat.

50 *I have been a diabetic for 27 years and have developed a complaint called bowel neuropathy. Please can you explain what this is and what the treatment is?*

Bowel neuropathy is one of the features of autonomic neuropathy which may occur in some long-standing diabetics where there is loss of function of the nerves supplying various organs in the body. In this case, the nerves that regulate the activity of the bowels have been affected. The symptoms include indigestion, occasionally vomiting and episodes of alternating constipation and diarrhoea. Occasionally episodes of diarrhoea are preceded by rumblings and gurglings in the stomach and not uncommonly this responds quite well to a short course of antibiotics. Otherwise eating a high fibre diet is encouraged to prevent constipation. Irritable bowel syndrome can cause symptoms not unlike this and this has nothing to do with diabetes although it not uncommonly occurs in diabetics. If there is ever passage of blood or mucus within the stool, medical advice should be sought without delay.

51 *The calf muscle in one leg seems to be shrinking. There is no ache and no pain. Is this anything to do with diabetes? I have been taking insulin for 30 years.*

You do not mention whether you have noticed any weakness in this leg. Occasionally diabetic neuropathy can affect the nerves which supply the muscles in such a way that the muscle becomes weak and shrinks in size without any accompanying pain or discomfort. It sounds as if this may be your problem.

52   *Please explain the condition called diabetic amyotrophy.*

Diabetic amyotrophy is a rare condition causing pain and weakness of the legs and is due to damage to certain nerves. It usually occurs when diabetic control is very poor, but occasionally affects people with only slight elevation of the blood sugar. Strict control of the diabetes leads to its improvement but it may take up to 2 years or so for it to settle. The nerves affected are those usually supplying the thigh muscles which often become wasted and get weaker.

Heart and blood vessel disease

53   *I have read that poor circulation in the feet is a problem for diabetics. Is there any way I can improve my circulation?*

Narrowing ('hardening') of the arteries is a normal part of growing older – and the arteries to the feet can be affected by this process, leading to poor circulation in the feet and legs. This occurs in diabetics and non-diabetics, but it is a little more common in diabetics. We do not understand the cause of arterial disease very well but we do know that smoking makes it worse. So if you are a diabetic and smoke, the risk of bad circulation really does increase. *Stop smoking* and keep active – these are the only known recipes for helping the circulation.

54   *Could you tell me if diabetes is likely to affect the heart of an elderly person? Is such a person likely to develop other ailments such as high blood pressure at this stage?*

Heart disease is only very slightly more common in diabetics than non-diabetics of the same age, but heart disease is, of course, not uncommon amongst both diabetics and non-diabetics in their seventies. High blood pressure may be more common amongst diabetics than non-diabetics.

55   *My husband died recently from a heart attack. He had been a diabetic for 12 years controlled on tablets, and*

*at about the same time that he developed diabetes he
started having angina attacks. I wondered whether these
were related and whether poor control had anything to
do with his fatal heart attack?*

It sounds very much as if your husband had trouble with
his coronary arteries before he developed diabetes. It is not
uncommon for people with arterial disease (arteriosclerosis)
to develop diabetes later in life and it does not sound to us
as if his heart attack had anything to do with poor diabetic
control.

56 *Is a couple of years of not very good control in a healthy
young diabetic likely to have much effect upon the arteries?*

No. It is unlikely to have much of an effect although any
period of poor control is not going to do any good either.
Our arteries get more rigid and more clogged up as we get
older and this process is aggravated by periods of poor diabetic
control and smoking.

57 *My left leg is amputated due to diabetic gangrene and
I get a lot of pain in my right foot and calf. Could too
much insulin be the cause of this pain?*

No. It sounds very much as if the blood supply to your legs
is insufficient and that the pain that you are getting in the
foot and calf is a reflection of the poor blood supply which
was the reason why you developed gangrene in your left
leg.

58 *My husband had a heart attack last year; 9 months
later he had part of his leg amputated. We have been
told that he could have further problems but have been
given no advice. Please give us some information on what
we should do to try and avoid this.*

It sounds as though your husband has generalised arterial
disease (arteriosclerosis) affecting his blood vessels to the
heart and to the leg. There are a number of things which
you and he can do which may be of help in preventing
further trouble. Firstly, if he smokes, stop smoking; secondly,
keep his diabetes as well controlled as is possible; thirdly,

keep his remaining foot and leg warm and make sure that he has expert foot care either by a chiropodist or by yourself under supervision of a chiropodist or district nurse. If you see any signs of damage to the foot or discolouration then seek medical advice at an early stage.

Blood pressure

59 Are diabetics more prone to high blood pressure and strokes?

No, not unless they develop diabetic kidney trouble when the blood pressure can rise as a complication of kidney failure. Strokes are definitely more common in people with high blood pressure.

60 I have been told that my blood pressure is raised as a result of diabetic kidney problems and, because of this, that it is very important that I take tablets to lower it – why is this?

There is good evidence to show that lowering the blood pressure to normal in patients such as yourself protects the kidneys from further damage and helps delay any further kidney problems.

The mind

61 Can diabetes cause memory loss?

Diabetes does not lead to a poor memory and it is really no excuse for that – except during a hypo!

62 My 68-year-old mother has been a diabetic for 44 years. In the past few years her mental state has deteriorated considerably and she is now difficult to manage. Is this common for someone who has been on insulin for so long?

No, this is not common for someone who has been on insulin for some time. You fail to mention whether your mother smokes or not. If she does we suspect that this is much more likely to be the reason why she has developed hardening of the arteries (cerebral arteriosclerosis) which may have contributed to the impairment of her mental functions. There are many other causes which could be important.

63 What illnesses or complications could occur in a diabetic man who had a brain haemorrhage 18 months ago?

Brain haemorrhages and strokes are no more common in diabetics than in non-diabetics and the management of somebody who has diabetes and a stroke is really no different from a non-diabetic with a stroke. The complications that one would be on the lookout for are primarily chest infections and pneumonia which need to be treated early, and secondarily injuries from accidents if the stroke sufferer had difficulty in getting about.

64 Are diabetics more prone to depression, suicide and other psychiatric illnesses?

There is some evidence to suggest that diabetics may be prone to depression and the suicide rate amongst diabetics is higher than in the non-diabetic population. Recent studies have found that the tendency to depression can be relieved in many cases by more involvement in their own management.

65 I have read that hypos can cause brain damage – is this true?

The strict answer is yes, but only very occasionally. It is only with hypos associated with long periods of unconsciousness that brain damage develops, and then it is extremely unusual. There is no evidence to suggest that the repeated hypos to which most insulin-treated diabetics are exposed, do any permanent damage to the brain at all.

9
Research and the future

Introduction

New developments and improvements in existing treatments can only occur through research. Research is therefore vital to every diabetic. In the United Kingdom the British Diabetic Association spends large sums each year (£1.92 million in 1989-90) on research into diabetes and similar large amounts of money are contributed by the Medical Research Council, the Wellcome Trust and other grant-giving bodies. The more money that is raised for diabetic research, the greater the benefits to the diabetic community. It costs about £25,000 to support a relatively junior research worker for a year. The discovery of insulin was made by a doctor and a medical student (Banting and Best) doing research together for just one summer (1921). There have been many important but

211

less dramatic discoveries since then, each in some way
contributing to our understanding of diabetes and many
improving the available treatment.

A cure?

1   Will diabetes ever be cured?

This question cannot be answered – yet. One must always
try to take an optimistic view, however, and if diabetes
cannot yet be cured it is not for want of research. Not only
does the British Diabetic Association have twice yearly
meetings to discuss research and progress but there is also
an annual European Association for the Study of Diabetes
meeting and an International Diabetes Federation congress
which meets every third year. In addition there are also a
great many national organisations which meet regularly.
More has been discovered during the last 15 years about
the cause of diabetes than ever before and during the same
period there have been important advances in treatment.
This is therefore a very exciting period in diabetic research
and we may continue to look forward to improvements in
our understanding of the disease even if, for the moment,
a cure is a little too much to hope for.

*2   I have a friend who has been treated with insulin for
     12 years who recently came off insulin altogether after
     having had an operation on his adrenal gland. He now
     tells me that his diabetes has been cured. I thought there
     was no cure for diabetes.*

It sounds as if your friend was one of the very few patients
in whom the diabetes was secondary to some other condition.
In his case, an adrenal tumour which when eventually
diagnosed and appropriately treated by operation resulted
in a cure for his diabetes. This has been recorded in two
forms of adrenal tumour. One is called a phaeochromocytoma,
where the tumour produces adrenaline and noradrenaline,
both of which inhibit insulin secretion by the pancreas. The
other adrenal tumour is one producing excess of adrenal
steroids and cortisone which again produces a form of diabetes

which is reversible on removal of the tumour. There are a number of other rare conditions often associated with disturbances of other hormone producing glands in the body. In these cases cure of diabetes is possible after appropriate therapy of the hormonal disturbance. Unfortunately, less than 5% of all patients with diabetes who have such a hormonal imbalance are suitable for surgery. Specialists are always on the lookout for these causes since the benefits from operation are so tremendous.

3   *Will it ever be possible to prevent diabetes with a vaccine?*

There is some evidence to suggest that certain virus infections can cause diabetes but we are not clear how often this happens; it is probably very infrequently. If a virus were isolated which caused diabetes, then it should be possible to produce a vaccine which could be given to children like polio vaccine, to prevent them from developing diabetes later on in life. At present this possibility seems rather remote.

4   *My son's diabetes has recently gone into remission following 3 months treatment with insulin. I have been told that this is the 'honeymoon period' and is likely to last only a few weeks or a few months. My question is, is there any way this honeymoon period can be extended and turned into a cure?*

That is a very good question and some research work has been done on it using anti-viral agents and drugs that interfere with body's immune responses. The results, so far, don't show any positive benefit from the anti-viral preparations but do suggest that the immunosuppressive therapy may prolong the honeymoon period in some patients. Unfortunately this form of therapy itself is not without risks and it certainly cannot be recommended.

5   *I gather that it is possible to identify people within a family who are at high risk of developing diabetes by looking at special blood tests. This sounds like an exciting development, as presumably children who have inherited a susceptibility to diabetes will be those most in need of vaccination should a vaccine become available.*

Yes, you are quite right. Studies of the so-called HLA tissue antigens in families where there appears to be a lot of diabetes indicates that certain patterns of inherited antigens carry with them the susceptibility to diabetes. Using these tissue markers it should be possible to identify the children who are likely to benefit most from a vaccine or an effective form of preventive treatment should one become available. It will be in these susceptible individuals that the first clinical trials will need to be done.

Transplantation

6   *I would like to volunteer to have a pancreas transplant. Is there someone I must apply to? How successful have these operations been?*

Pancreatic transplantation is still in the experimental stages and it will be difficult to find anyone who will accept you as a volunteer. Technically, pancreatic transplants are even more difficult than liver, kidney or heart transplants. The pancreas is very delicate and, as the seat of many digestive juices, has a tendency to digest itself if damaged even slightly. The duct or passageway through which these juices pass is narrow, and has to be joined up to the intestines in a very intricate way so that the enzymes do not leak. Even if everything goes well technically, the body will still react against transplant so several immunosuppressant drugs have to be given. Some of these (particularly steroids) given in high doses to suppress rejection of the transplant tend to cause diabetes or make existing diabetes worse! Some hospitals have carried out this operation successfully. At the moment, these centres in the UK do the operation only if another transplant (usually a kidney) is also necessary, as most doctors believe that the risks are too great to do on otherwise well people. In the USA, one hospital in particular has been transplanting half of a pancreas from a normal volunteer relative into well diabetics (not otherwise requiring a transplant); the results show that in the majority of patients operated upon the pancreas grafts do quite well and most patients can discontinue insulin injections and resume a normal diet, at least for a while. Although this is very important and exciting, there are a number of problems which make most of us agree that it is still too early to recommend this treatment in the UK. The problems include, in addition to the significant operative risks, the need to stay on immunosuppressive therapy for ever (see next question for further information on the problems of immunosuppression) and many of us have reservations about the ethical issues involved regarding the requirement of finding a suitable normal volunteer to undergo major surgery which is obviously not free from risk.

7   *Are there any hospitals which carry out transplants of the islets of Langerhans? Would I be able to donate my cells to my diabetic daughter?*

No, there are no hospitals carrying out such transplants yet, and it would not be possible for you to donate your pancreatic islet cells (islets of Langerhans) to your daughter. The question you raise, however, is an important one because experiments carried out in animals show that it is technically possible to isolate the islets of Langerhans of a non-diabetic animal and transplant them into a diabetic animal and cure the diabetes. There are two main steps to be overcome before this technique is available for humans. Firstly one has to find a way of culturing and growing the islet cells in a laboratory so that one can produce enough of them to transplant into a diabetic to produce enough insulin to cure the condition. Secondly, we have to get over the problems of transplantation of tissues from one individual to another: we have to prevent rejection of the transplant. Traditionally in kidney and other organ transplants this is done by giving large doses of steroids and immunosuppressive drugs. This form of treatment unfortunately has its own risks. These risks may be justifiable when the alternative is death through renal failure or heart failure. However, in the diabetic there is an effective form of treatment in the form of insulin injections which carries with it in the long-term much less hazard to health than the use of immunosuppressive therapy.

Research into 'microencapsulation' of these islets is making some progress which may one day offer a solution which will avoid lifelong immunosuppressive therapy. By enclosing the islets in a porous membrane and transplanting them into a diabetic animal it is possible to show that the insulin can get out of the 'bag of islets' and normalise the blood sugar at the same time as nutrients from the blood stream can get in to sustain the islets; while this is going on the membrane keeps at bay the cells responsible for tissue rejection. Unfortunately, after a while the membrane tends to get clogged with scar tissue and the islet graft stops working.

Until there has been a major breakthrough in transplantation of tissues from one individual to another, the hazards of long-term immunosuppressive therapy for a diabetic receiving either a pancreas transplant or an islet transplant are far greater than having diabetes treated with insulin. There are no tangible benefits yet for this form of therapy as a primary form of treatment for diabetes. This does not mean that the problems are insuperable but that much research remains to be done before the problems are overcome.

Insulin pumps and artificial pancreas

8   *I recently read about a device called a 'glucose sensor'*
     which can control the insulin administered to diabetic
     animals. Will this ever be used on humans and if so
     what can we expect from it?

The research into the development of a small electronic device which could be implanted under the skin and which could continuously monitor the level of glucose in the blood has been going on in the United States, the United Kingdom and several countries for many years. The technical problems of such a device are, however, considerable, and it seems unlikely to be of use in diabetics for at least some considerable time. Not only are there technical problems in achieving an accurate reflection of blood glucose level by such a subcutaneous implanted glucose sensor, but the further problem of 'hooking it up' to a supply of insulin to be released according to the demand is formidable. It may be that these problems may one day be resolved and one might then hope that very much better control of diabetes might be achieved than can be achieved by the current methods. There is, however, a very long way to go yet.

9   *I have heard about the artificial pancreas or 'Biostator'. Apparently this machine is capable of maintaining a diabetic's blood sugar at normal levels, irrespective of what they eat. Is this true? If so, why isn't it widely available?*

There are several versions of what you describe, namely an artificial pancreas, which measures the glucose concentration in the bloodstream continuously and infuses insulin in sufficient quantities to keep the blood glucose normal. Unfortunately these machines are technically very complex, bulky and extremely expensive. Their major value is for research purposes since they are quite unsuitable at present as devices for long-term control. Their use has however taught us a lot about the needs of such a device in the future, when it can be scaled down to something the same size as a cardiac pacemaker. There is a great deal of research going on amongst several bio-engineering groups to achieve this aim but it is still likely to be several years before the first machines become available for research studies, and it will be a long time before suitably reliable machines are available for daily treatment. Even when the technical problems have been resolved and it has been miniaturised to an acceptable size for implantation the costs are likely to be a limiting factor governing availability. The currently available, rather crude machines weigh in excess of 20 kg (44 lb) and cost thousands of pounds. There is a long way to go before this becomes a viable form of treatment.

10   *I hear that there are pumps available that can be transplanted like pacemakers – is this true? What are the likely developments with insulin pumps within the next 5 years?*

Yes, it is true that insulin pumps have been transplanted into diabetics as part of research studies. There has been some encouraging progress in this field. Although still experimental and with a long time to go before being a regular form of treatment, some pumps have been developed that are small enough to be transplanted into the muscles forming the wall of the abdomen and have been left there for over a year. These pumps do not have a sensor to detect glucose, they simply infuse insulin at a slow rate that can be regulated from the outside using a small radio transmitter. This can be used to command the pump to infuse more insulin just before a meal or to reduce the rate of infusion if the blood sugar readings are too low. The pumps have a reservoir of insulin that can be refilled with a syringe and needle, through the skin, without too much trouble but changing the batteries requires an operation! Although promising, the major disadvantages are cost and complexity. This is still very much a research procedure and cannot yet be recommended for routine treatment.

New insulin and oral insulins

11   What advances can we expect in the development of new insulin?

Over the last 15 years we have gone through a stage of producing purer and purer insulins with patterns of absorption varying from the very quick-acting to the very long-acting formulations. In recent times biosynthetic human insulins have replaced the animal insulins for most patients; these are manufactured by interfering with the genetic codes of bacteria and yeasts, inserting material that 'instructs' the organisms to produce insulin. By inserting the genetic material coding for human insulin scientists can get the organisms to produce human insulin; they can equally well get them to make any insulin with a known structure, indeed they can even get them to make 'new' insulins with 'invented' structures! We are now in the era of 'designer' insulins! There is virtually unlimited capability to modify the natural insulin and see if we can improve on this; by analogy to other areas we expect to be able to develop a whole new range of insulins with new properties that should be able to make therapy better.

We are already beginning to see the benefits from this remarkable advance in scientific manufacturing. Trials have shown that one of these insulins is absorbed much quicker than any of the existing fast-acting insulins, is very good for covering meals and can be given immediately before the meal rather that 15-30 minutes before.

We are also looking for variations in the structure of the insulin which will 'target' the insulin more directly on the liver, the major organ responsible for glucose production in the body. Normally insulin is produced by the pancreas and goes directly to the liver but, unfortunately, in insulin-treated patients the insulin which is injected only reaches the liver after it has been through all the other tissues in the body. It should be possible to modify the structure in such a way that it can be targeted at the liver and in that way perhaps turn out to be a more effective and easier way of controlling blood glucose level in diabetics.

12   *I have heard that it is possible to get away from insulin injections either from putting drops up the nose or by producing some form of insulin which is active when taken by mouth. Are these claims true and are we going to be able to get away from insulin injections in the future?*

There is no doubt that a small proportion of any insulin put up the nose is absorbed through the membranes into the bloodstream and can lower the blood sugar. Unfortunately only a small percentage of that which is put into the nose is ever absorbed and it is therefore an inefficient and expensive way of administering insulin. Because the absorption is erratic the blood glucose is not very stable. Experiments have been done with insulin suppositories showing that they too can lower the blood sugar without the need for injection but again the absorption is only incomplete and the response erratic. It is possible that new methods will be found for increasing the absorption from these sites and making this a possible alternative mode of insulin administration. Regarding oral insulins, it is possible to prevent the stomach digesting the insulin by incorporating it into a fat (lipid) droplet (liposome) which enables it to be absorbed from the gut without being broken down by the digestive juices. Unfortunately again, the absorption is erratic and the whole lipid droplet with the insulin is absorbed, the insulin remaining inactive until it is released from the droplet. So far technical problems with this have not been solved despite a great deal of research and at present it seems unlikely that effective oral insulins will be developed in the foreseeable future.

New technology

13 What benefits to diabetics are going to come from the computer and microelectronic revolution?

You will have already seen some of the benefits in the blood glucose monitoring devices, and all the modern insulin pumps rely heavily on microchips to control the rate of infusion. We are beginning to see microcomputer programmes which help store and analyse home blood glucose monitoring records. It should be possible soon to simulate the blood glucose response to different insulin injections and in this way produce means of exploring the effect of different types and doses of insulin and simulating the body's response. We are also going to use computers as a way of teaching people about diabetes and its management as well as a way of testing patients about their knowledge of diabetes. Microcomputers are being used to help record and analyse records from the diabetic clinic as well as to help to plan and organise monitoring of diabetic care. It is quite likely that this will lead to an improvement in the efficiency of the organisation of the diabetic clinics as it has done to the organising of airline tickets and flights. There are early experiments going on in the use of so-called 'expert systems' to transfer the expert knowledge and reasoning of specialists to general practitioners to facilitate their management of diabetic patients within general practice without the need for patients to attend hospital diabetic clinics so often. It is not unreasonable to expect that the microelectronic revolution will produce a lot of benefits to the diabetic over the next 10 years.

14   *I gather that by studying families who have several members with diabetes, it can help find a cure for the condition. Is this true?*

Family studies are very important for helping understand the inheritance of diabetes. In some families there is a clear association between a certain genetic background and the development of diabetes and some members not yet diabetic, may have 'markers' (results of blood tests) that indicate that they are at increased risk of developing the condition. When new forms of treatment aimed at preventing diabetes are tested for efficacy, then it will be important to see if they can prevent diabetes developing in those most at risk. So far the screening tests are rather crude and inaccurate but they are getting better as research continues and one day it should be possible to prevent diabetes developing in these high risk people.

15   *I gather there is evidence to suggest smoked meats could have something to do with the cause of diabetes.*

There have been at least two reports indicating that there may be a link between the eating of smoked meat and the development of diabetes. In one it was found that there was a suggestion that children in Iceland conceived around Christmas time had a higher risk of developing diabetes. It was suggested that there was evidence to indicate that this may result from the diet peculiar to that time of year which traditionally contains much smoked meat. The second report, also from Scandinavia, indicated that the families of children developing diabetes ate more smoked meat than other families. The common factor was a substance called nitrosamine which is formed during the meat-smoking process. There is some experimental evidence to show that nitrosamines can cause diabetes in experimental animals and there may well be something important in these observations. We await further research to clarify this but meanwhile perhaps we should cut down on smoked meat particularly, perhaps, if we are about to start a family.

16   *Our local diabetes unit has just run a successful Christmas Fair to raise a lot of money for a mass*

spectrometer. What good is this going to do for diabetes research?

A mass spectrometer is a very complicated machine which can be used to measure minute amounts of very similar substances present in the bloodstream or in other body constituents. It is often used to measure the amounts of naturally occurring stable isotopes which can be administered to people with diabetes to investigate their body's metabolism in great detail. In the past this type of study could only be done by injecting radioactive isotopes which could then be followed in the body as they were metabolised. Radioisotopes produce, as their name indicates, radiation which can have harmful effects on cells in the body. As we read in the papers, even the smallest amount of radiation is best avoided; mass spectrometry allows even more detailed research into metabolism than radioisotopes with none of the risk. Your local researchers are very lucky to have this facility.

10
Self-help groups

Introduction

This section is a description of various organizations that
have grown up to help their members. It is a straightforward
description of what is available and is not written in the
style of question and answer.

People react in different ways to the shock of diabetes:
some try to become recluses and hide, while others set out
to try to solve all the problems of mankind (including
diabetes) in a few weeks. Whatever your reaction, you should
make contact with your local Diabetic Association. You will
come across people who are *living* with diabetes and who
have learnt to cope with many of the daily problems. These
people should provide an extra dimension to the information

you have been given by doctors, nurses, dietitians and other
professionals.

The British Diabetic Association

This was founded in 1934 by two diabetics, H. G. Wells
the author and R. D. Lawrence, who was a doctor based at
the diabetic clinic of King's College Hospital, London. In a
letter to *The Times*, dated January 1933, they announced
their intention to set up an 'Association open to all diabetics,
rich or poor, for mutual aid and assistance, and to promote
the study, the diffusion of knowledge, and the proper
treatment of diabetes in this country'. They proposed that
diabetics, members of the general public interested in
diabetes, and doctors and nurses should be persuaded to
join the projected association. Nearly 60 years later the
British Diabetic Association is a credit to its founders. It
has more than 120,000 members, 70 permanent
administrative staff and an annual budget of £7 million. In
many countries there are separate organizations for patients
and for professionals but the BDA draws its strength from
the fact that both interest groups are united in the same
society.

The BDA is the biggest provider in the UK of funds for
diabetic research.

The BDA also provides help and advice on all aspects of
diabetes. Up to date information and news is published in
Balance, which appears every other month. The BDA also
produces a handbook, leaflets and videotapes for teaching
purposes and constantly lobbies for high standards of care
for those with diabetes.

A form for joining the BDA is printed in the back of this
book.

BDA camps

The first BDA holidays for children took place in 1935, and
the 'camps' have grown into a large enterprise. There are
now about 30 camps each year catering for up to 1,000

diabetic children aged 7-16 years. These educational holidays are organised by the Youth Department and they aim to give the children a good time, to teach them more about their diabetes and to provide a well-earned break for their parents. Equally important is the opportunity they give to children to meet other diabetics and to become more independent of their parents.

The Youth Department also organises weekends for parents of children with diabetes. These cater for about 250 families each year. The children, including brothers and sisters, are entertained by trained helpers while the parents have talks and discussions from specialist doctors, nurses, and dietitians. There are also talks from parents who have lived with diabetic children for many years and from young adults who have made a success of their lives, despite the problem of diabetes. These parent/child weekends are designed to encourage an informal atmosphere.

Local BDA branches

There are over 400 branches throughout the country. These are run entirely by volunteers and because of their commitment large sums of money are raised for diabetic research. The BDA branches also aim to increase public awareness of diabetes and arrange meetings for local diabetics and their families for support and information.

Parents' groups

Parents of young diabetic children often feel they have special needs – and that they can offer particular help to other parents in the same boat. Over 100 parents' groups exist throughout the UK and they have added a sense of urgency to the main aim of the BDA: the defeat of diabetes. In addition to self-help, the parents' groups also raise money for research.

Youth Diabetes (YD) project

The YD project was founded in 1983 under the inspiration of Professor Jim Farquhar of Edinburgh University. It aims to bring together young people with diabetes to share friendship, ideas, feelings and solutions to problems. There are YD groups all over the UK and they try to maintain close links with clinic teams. The project is strongly supported by the British Diabetic Association and receives a great deal of financial backing from Novo Nordisk. At a national level the YD project organises 3 separate events:

1 *YD Holiday Course* – since 1983 held at Firbush, a custom-built activity centre on the banks of Loch Tay. As well as canoeing, sailing, cycling and climbing the young people share their experiences of living with diabetes and examine some of the problems in a constructive way. For further information contact Dr Ray Newton, Ninewells Hospital, Dundee.

2 *YD Medical Workshop* – held at Firbush since 1986. Nurses, dietitians and doctors spend a few days discussing diabetes in adolescence and ways of improving services for the young diabetic. The professionals can learn for themselves that shared recreational activities help to break down formal barriers between groups.

3 *YD Conference* – annual weekend forum at Birmingham University since 1987. It provides a forum for views of young diabetics with plenty of recreation, socialising and breaking down of barriers. This is an opportunity to develop a consensus of young people's views with direct feedback to medical services, the BDA and manufacturers. If you want to attend contact the Youth Department of the BDA.

11
Emergencies

Introduction

This section of the book is for quick reference if things are going badly wrong. Firstly there is vital information for the diabetic himself and then some simple rules for relatives and friends. They are designed to be consulted in an emergency although it would be worth checking through them *before* you reach crisis point. It seems a pity to end this book in such a negative way by telling you what to do in a crisis. We hope that by keeping your diabetes well controlled you will avoid these serious situations.

What every diabetic on insulin must know

1 NEVER stop insulin if you feel ill or sick. Check your

blood sugar – you may need extra insulin even if you are not eating very much.

2 If you are being sick, try to keep up a good fluid intake (at least $2^1/_2$ litres (4 pints) a day). If you are vomiting and unable to keep down fluids, you probably need to go to hospital for an intravenous drip.

3 ALWAYS CARRY SUGAR on your person.

4 NEVER risk driving if your blood sugar could be low. Diabetics DO lose their driving licences if found at the wheel when hypo.

5 Physical exercise and alcohol are both likely to bring on a hypo.

What other people must know about diabetes

1 NEVER stop insulin in case of sickness (no apologies for repeating this).

2 Repeated vomiting, drowsiness and laboured breathing are bad signs in a diabetic. They suggest impending coma and can be treated ONLY in hospital.

3 A diabetic who is hypo may not be in full command of his senses and may take a lot of persuasion to have some sugar. Jam or a sugary drink (Lucozade) may be easier to get down than dextrose tablets.

4 NEVER let a diabetic drive if you suspect he is hypo. It could be fatal.

Foods to eat in an emergency or when feeling unwell

Each of the following contains *10 g* carbohydrate:

100 ml pure fruit juice
100 ml Coca-Cola (*Not* Diet Coke)
60 ml Lucozade
Small scoop ice-cream
2 sugar cubes or 2 teaspoons of sugar
1 ordinary jelly cube or 2 heaped tablespoons of made up jelly
$^1/_3$ pint (approx. 200 ml) of milk

Small bowl of thickened soup
2 cream crackers
1 natural yogurt
1 diet fruit yogurt
1 apple or pear or orange
1 small banana
3 Dextrosol tablets

If you are feeling unwell, eating solid foods may not be possible and you may need to rely on sweet fluids to provide the necessary carbohydrate. Liquids such as cold, defizzed Coca-Cola or Lucozade are useful if you feel sick. Do not worry about eating the exact amount of carbohydrate at the correct time but take small amounts often.

If you continue to vomit, SEEK MEDICAL ADVICE.

Signs and symptoms of hypoglycaemia and hyperglycaemia

Hypoglycaemia = LOW blood sugar. Also called a hypo, a reaction or an insulin reaction.

Fast onset.

Tingling of the lips and tongue
Weakness
Tiredness
Sleepiness
Trembling
Hunger
Blurred vision
Palpitation
Nausea
Headache
Sweating
Mental confusion
Pallor
Slurred speech
Bad temper
Change in behaviour

Lack of concentration
Unconsciousness (hypoglycaemic or insulin coma)

Hyperglycaemia = HIGH blood sugar.

Slow onset (usually more than 24 hours).

Thirst
Excess urine
Nausea
Abdominal pain
Vomiting
Drowsiness
Rapid breathing
Flushed, dry skin
Unconsciousness (hyperglycaemic or diabetic coma).

Appendix 1

Glossary of terms

Acesulfane-K A low-calorie intense sweetener.

Acetone One of the chemicals called ketones formed when the body uses up fat for energy. The presence of acetone in the urine usually means that more insulin is needed.

Adrenaline A hormone produced by the adrenal glands which prepares the body for action ('flight or fight') and also causes an increase in blood glucose level. Produced by the body when the blood glucose falls too low.

Albumin A protein present in most animal tissues. The presence of albumin in the urine may denote a kidney or bladder infection or early kidney damage.

Alpha cell The cell that produces glucagon – found in the islets of Langerhans in the pancreas.

Arteriosclerosis Hardening of the arteries. Loss of elasticity in the walls of the arteries due to thickening and calcification. Occurs with advancing years in those with or without diabetes. May affect the heart, causing thrombosis, or affect the circulation particularly legs and feet.

Aspartame A low-calorie intense sweetener. Brand name Nutra-Sweet.

Autonomic neuropathy Damage to the system of nerves which regulate many autonomic functions of the body such as stomach emptying, sexual function (potency) and blood pressure control.

Balanitis Inflammation of the end of the penis, usually caused by the presence of sugar in the urine.

Beta-blockers Drugs which block the effect of stress hormones on the cardiovascular system. Often used to treat angina and to lower blood pressure. Change the warning signs of hypoglycaemia.

Beta cell The cell which produces insulin – found in the islets of Langerhans in the pancreas.

Biguanides A group of anti-diabetes tablets which lower blood glucose levels. They work by increasing the uptake of glucose by muscle, by reducing the absorption of glucose by the intestine and by reducing the amount of glucose produced by the liver. The only used preparation is metformin.

Blood glucose monitoring System of measuring blood glucose levels at home using special reagent sticks or a special meter.

Bran Indigestible husk of the wheat grain.

Brittle diabetes Term used to refer to diabetes which is very unstable with swings from very low to very high blood glucose levels.

Calories Units in which energy or heat are measured. The energy value of food is measured in calories.

Carbohydrates A class of food which comprises starches and sugars and is most readily available by the body for energy. Found mainly in plant foods. Examples are rice, bread, potatoes, pasta, dried beans.

Cataract Opacity of the lens of the eye which obscures vision. It may be removed surgically.

Control Usually refers to blood glucose control. The aim of good control is to achieve normal blood glucose levels (3-7 mmol/l).

Cystitis Inflammation of the bladder causing frequency of passing urine and a burning sensation when passing urine.

Diabetic amyotrophy Rare condition causing pain and/or weakness of the legs due to the damage to certain nerves.

Diabetic coma Extreme form of hyperglycaemia, usually with ketoacidosis causing unconsciousness.

Diuretic An agent which increases the flow of urine, usually called water tablets.

Epidural Usually referring to the type of anaesthetic that is commonly used in obstetrics. Anaesthetic solution is injected through the spinal canal to numb the lower part of the body.

Exchanges Portions of carbohydrate foods in the diabetic diet which can be exchanged for one another. 1 exchange = 10 g carbohydrate.

Fibre Part of plant material which resists digestion and gives bulk to the diet. Also known as roughage.

Free foods Foods which contain so little carbohydrate (or fat) that diabetics may have liberal helpings without counting them in their diet. Examples include cabbage, rhubarb, lettuce, cauliflower, tea or coffee without milk.

Fructose Type of sugar found naturally in fruit and honey. Since it does not require insulin for its metabolism, it is often used as a sweetener in diabetic foods.

Fructosamine Measurement of diabetic control which reflects the average blood glucose level over the previous 2-3 weeks. Similar to haemoglobin A_1 which averages the blood glucose over the longer period of 2-3 months.

Gangrene Death of a part of the body due to a very poor blood supply. Combination of neuropathy and arteriosclerosis may result in infection of unrecognised injuries to the feet. If neglected this infection may spread, causing further destruction.

Glaucoma Disease of the eye causing increased pressure inside the eyeball.

Glucagon Hormone produced by the alpha cells in the pancreas which causes a rise in blood glucose by freeing glycogen from the liver. Available in injection form and can be used to treat a severe hypo.

Glucose Form of sugar made by digestion of carbohydrates. Absorbed into the bloodstream where it circulates and is used for energy.

Glucose tolerance test Test used in the diagnosis of diabetes mellitus. The glucose in the blood is measured at intervals before and after the person has drunk a large amount of glucose whilst fasting.

Glycogen The form in which carbohydrate is stored in the liver. It is often known as animal starch.

Glycosuria Presence of glucose in the urine.

Glycosylated haemoglobin see Haemoglobin A_1.

Guar A good source of dietary fibre obtainable from the cluster bean.

Haemoglobin A_1 The part of the haemoglobin or colouring matter of the red blood cell which has glucose attached to it. A test of diabetic control. The amount of haemoglobin A_1 in the blood depends on the average blood glucose level over the previous 2-3 months.

Honeymoon period Time when the dose of insulin drops shortly after starting insulin treatment. It is the result of partial recovery of insulin secretion by the pancreas. Usually the honeymoon period only lasts for a short time.

Hormone Substance generated in one gland or organ which is carried by the blood to another part of the body to stimulate another organ into activity.

Human insulin Insulin which has been manufactured to be identical to that produced in the human pancreas. Differs slightly from older insulins which were extracted from cows or pigs.

Hydramnios An excessive amount of amniotic fluid, i.e. the fluid surrounding the foetus.

Hyperglycaemia High blood glucose or blood sugar (above 10 mmol/l).

Hypoglycaemia Low blood glucose or blood sugar (below 3 mmol/l).

Insulin A hormone produced by the beta cells of the pancreas and responsible for the control of blood glucose. Insulin can only be given by injection because the digestive juices destroy its action if taken by mouth.

Insulin coma Extreme form of hypoglycaemia associated with unconsciousness and sometimes convulsions.

Insulin dependent diabetes (IDD) Type of diabetes which cannot be treated without insulin. Most common in younger people and is also called type I diabetes or juvenile-onset diabetes.

Insulin pen Device that resembles a large fountain pen that takes a cartridge of insulin. The injection of insulin is given after dialling the dose and pressing a button that releases the insulin.

Insulin reaction Another name for hypoglycaemia or a hypo. In America it is called an insulin shock or shock.

Intradermal Meaning 'into the skin'. Usually refers to an injection given into the most superficial layer of the skin. Insulin must not be given in this way as it is painful and will not be absorbed properly.

Intramuscular A deep injection into the muscle.

Islets of Langerhans Specialised cells within the pancreas that produce insulin and glucagon.

Isophane A form of intermediate-acting insulin which has protamine added to slow its absorption.

Joule Unit of work or energy used in the metric system. About 4.18 joules in each calorie. Some dietitians calculate food energy in joules.

Juvenile-onset diabetes Outdated name for insulin dependent diabetes so called because most patients receiving insulin develop diabetes under the age of 40. The term is no longer used because insulin dependent diabetes can occur at any age.

Ketoacidosis A serious condition due to lack of insulin which results in body fat being used up to form ketones and acids. Characterised by high blood glucose levels, ketones in the urine, vomiting, drowsiness, heavy laboured breathing and a smell of acetone on the breath.

Ketones Acid substances formed when body fat is used up to provide energy.

Ketonuria The presence of acetone and other ketones in the urine. Detected by testing with a special testing stick (Ketostix, Ketur Test) or tablet (Acetest). Presence of ketones in the urine is due to lack of insulin or periods of starvation.

Laser treatment Process in which laser beams are used to treat a damaged retina (back of the eye). (See photocoagulation).

Lente insulin A form of intermediate-acting insulin which has zinc added to slow its absorption.

Lipoatrophy Loss of fat from injection sites. It used to occur before the use of highly purified insulins.

Lipohypertrophy Fatty swelling usually caused by repeated injections of insulin into the same site.

Maturity onset diabetes Another term for non-insulin dependent diabetes most commonly occurring in people who are middle aged and overweight. Also called type II diabetes.

Metabolism Process by which the body turns food into energy.

Microaneurysms Small red dots on the retina at the back of the eye which are one of the earliest signs of diabetic retinopathy.

Represent areas of weakness of the very small blood vessels in the eye. Microaneurysms do not affect the eyesight in any way.

Micromole One thousandth ($^1/_{1000}$) of a millimole.

Millimoles Units for measuring the concentration of glucose and other substances in the blood. Blood glucose is measured in millimoles per litre (mmol/l). It has replaced milligrammes per decilitre (mg/dl mg%) as a unit of measurement although this is still used in some other countries. 1 mmol/l = 18 mg/dl.

Nephropathy Kidney damage. In the first instance this makes the kidney more leaky so that albumin appears in the urine. At a later stage it may affect the function of the kidney and in severe cases lead to kidney failure.

Neuropathy Damage to the nerves. This may be peripheral or autonomic (see peripheral neuropathy and autonomic neuropathy). It can occur with diabetes especially when poorly controlled, but also has other causes.

Non-insulin dependent diabetes (NIDD) Type of diabetes which occurs in older people who are often overweight. These people do not always need insulin treatment and usually can be successfully controlled with diet alone or diet and tablets. Also known as type II or maturity-onset diabetes.

Pancreas Gland lying behind the stomach which as well as secreting a digestive fluid (pancreatic juice) also produces the hormone insulin. Contains islets of Langerhans.

Peripheral neuropathy Damage to the nerves supplying the muscles and skin. This can result in diminished sensation, particularly in the feet and legs, and in muscle weakness.

Photocoagulation Process of treating diabetic retinopathy with light beams, either laser beams or xenon arc. This technique focuses a beam of light on a very tiny area of the retina. This beam is so intense that it causes a very small burn, which may close off a leaking blood vessel or destroy weak blood vessels which are likely to bleed.

Polydipsia Being excessively thirsty and drinking too much. Also a symptom of untreated diabetes.

Polyuria The passing of large quantities of urine due to excess glucose from the bloodstream. It is a symptom of untreated diabetes.

Protein One of the classes of food that is necessary for growth and repair of tissues. Found in fish, meat, eggs, milk and pulses (dried beans and peas). Can also refer to albumin when found in the urine.

Proteinuria Protein or albumin in the urine (see albumin).

Pruritus vulvae Irritation of the vulva. Caused by an infection that occurs because of an excess of sugar in the urine and is often an early sign of diabetes in the older diabetic. It clears up when the blood glucose levels return to normal and the sugar disappears from the urine.

Pyelonephritis Inflammation and infection of the kidney.

Renal threshold The level of glucose in the blood above which it will begin to spill into the urine. The usual renal threshold for glucose in the blood is about 10 mmol/l, i.e. when the blood glucose rises above 10 mmol/l, glucose appears in the urine.

Retina Light sensitive coat at the back of the eye.

Retinopathy Damage to the retina.

Saccharin A synthetic sweetener which is calorie free.

Sorbitol A chemical related to sugar and alcohol which is used as a sweetening agent. No significant effect upon the blood sugar level but has the same number of calories as ordinary sugar so should not be used by those who need to lose weight. Poorly absorbed and may have a laxative effect.

Subcutaneous injection An injection beneath the skin into the layer of fat which lies between the skin and muscle.

Sucrose A sugar (containing glucose and fructose in combination) derived from sugar-cane or sugar beet (i.e. ordinary table sugar). It has a high carbohydrate and calorie content.

Sulphonylureas Anti-diabetes tablets which lower the blood glucose by stimulating the pancreas to produce more insulin. Commonly used sulphonylureas are glibenclamide and chlorpropamide.

Thrombosis Clot forming in blood vessel.

Toxaemia Poisoning of the blood by the absorption of toxins. Usually refers to the toxaemia of pregnancy which is characterised by high blood pressure, proteinuria and ankle swelling.

Type I diabetes Another name for insulin dependent diabetes. Age of onset is usually below the age of 40 years.

Type II diabetes Another name for non-insulin dependent diabetes. Age of onset is usually above the age of 40 years.

U40 insulin The old weaker strength of insulin which is no longer available in the UK. It is still the standard insulin in most European countries.

U100 insulin The standard strength of insulin in the UK, USA, Canada, Australia, New Zealand, South Africa, the Middle and Far East.

Visual acuity Acuteness of vision. Measured by reading letters on a sight testing chart (Snellen chart).

Appendix 2

Useful Addresses

Bayer Diagnostics UK Ltd
Evans House
Hamilton Close
Basingstoke
Hants RG21 2YE
Tel: 0256 29181

Becton Dickinson (UK) Ltd
Between Towns Road
Cowley
Oxford OX4 3LY
Tel: 0865 748844

Boehringer Mannheim UK
Rapid Diagnostics Division
Bell Lane
Lewes
East Sussex BN7 1LG
Tel: 0273 480444

British Diabetic Association
10 Queen Anne Street
London W1M OBD
Tel: 071 323 1531

239

Diabetic Care Ltd
Upton Industrial Estate
Rectory Road
Upton on Severn
Worcestershire WR8 OXL
Tel: 06846 2262

Fisons PLC
Pharmaceutical Division
Coleorton Hall
Coleorton
Leicestershire LE6 4GP
Tel: 0509 634000

Hypoguard (UK) Ltd
Dock Lane
Melton
Woodbridge
Suffolk IP12 1PE
Tel: 03943 7333/4

Eli Lilly & Co. Ltd
Kingsclere Road
Basingstoke
Hants RG21 2XA
Tel: 025647 3241

LifeScan
Enterprise House
Station Road
High Wycombe
Bucks HP10 9UF
Tel: 0494 442211

Mariner Medical Ltd
Mariner House
116 Windmill Street
Gravesend
Kent DA12 1BL
Tel: 0474 323456

Medic-Alert Foundation
17 Bridge Wharf
156 Caledonian Road
London N1 9RD
Tel: 071 833 3034

MediSense Britain Ltd
PO Box 2159
Coleshill
Birmingham B46 1HZ
Tel: 0675 467044

Novo Nordisk
Pharmaceuticals Ltd
Novo Nordisk House
Broadfield Park
Brighton Road
Pease Pottage
Crawley
West Sussex RH11 9RT
Tel: 0293 613555

Owen Mumford Ltd
(Medical Shop)
Brook Hill
Woodstock
Oxford OX7 1TU
Tel: 0993 812021

The Royal National Institute
for the Blind
224 Great Portland Street
London W1N 6AA
Tel: 071 388 1266

SOS/Talisman
Golden Key Co Ltd
1 Hare Street
Sheerness
Kent ME12 1AH
Tel: Sheerness 663403

Terumo Corporation
PO Box 119
Tunbridge Wells
Kent TN2 5TY
Tel: 0892 26331

Viggo-Spectramed
Faraday Road
Dorcan
Swindon
Wiltshire SN3 5HQ
Tel: 0793 513111

Index

compiled by Susan Bosanko

Numbers in **bold type** refer to the colour plates in the centre of the book and give the plate number. All other numbers are page numbers; illustrated pages are given in *italics*.

▶ JOIN THE BDA TODAY ◀

The British Diabetic Association –

- ▶ **provides practical help and information on living with diabetes**
- ▶ **publishes a wide range of useful leaflets, books and videos**

  'Balance', the BDA magazine, is sent free to members or can be ordered from newsagents
- ▶ **has over 400 groups which hold regular meetings and which give support locally**
- ▶ **supports research to improve treatment and to find a prevention or cure for diabetes and its complications.**

ENROLMENT FORM

Please enrol me as an:

Annual Member: £10 a year. ☐

Reduced Rate Member *(pensioner, student on Government grant and those in receipt of DHSS benefits):* £2 a year. ☐

Life Member: £175 ☐

Family Member £12.50 a year ☐

OR £25 a year for 7 years under covenant. ☐
Forms available on request.

Overseas Annual Member: £20 a year. ☐

Overseas Life Member: £200 ☐

Are you joining on behalf of a child?
(Children in the UK under the age of 18 can join free for one year if they wish.) ☐

I would like my name forwarded to my local group. ☐

I enclose remittance for £ _____

Date _____

Signature _____

Full name, Mr/Mrs/Miss _____
(BLOCK CAPITALS PLEASE)

_____

Address _____

_____

Post Code _____

Date of Birth _____

Occupation _____

(This information will be treated as strictly confidential.)

FOR OFFICE USE ONLY

**THE BRITISH DIABETIC ASSOCIATION,
10 QUEEN ANNE STREET,
LONDON W1M 0BD
Tel No. 071 323 1531**

Charity Registered No. 215199